CEDAR GROVE CEMETERY

Cedar Grove

Essex County
New Jersey

Carol Personette Comfort

HERITAGE BOOKS
2019

HERITAGE BOOKS

AN IMPRINT OF HERITAGE BOOKS, INC.

Books, CDs, and more—Worldwide

For our listing of thousands of titles see our website
at
www.HeritageBooks.com

Published 2019 by
HERITAGE BOOKS, INC.
Publishing Division
5810 Ruatan Street
Berwyn Heights, Md. 20740

Heritage Books by the author:

Cedar Grove Cemetery, Cedar Grove, Essex County, New Jersey

*Early Cemetery Inscriptions and Early Pastors: Fairfield Reformed Church
(Gansegat Reformed Dutch Church) Fairfield, Essex County, New Jersey*

*Old Burying Ground, Cemetery of the First Presbyterian Church:
Orange, Essex County, New Jersey*

*St. Mark's Episcopal Cemetery, Orange, Essex County, New Jersey, (Near the Southwest
Corner of Main Street and Scotland Road, Adjacent to the First Presbyterian Church
of Orange). History of the Cemetery; Expanded List of Interments; and
Early History of St. Mark's Church, Revised Edition*

International Standard Book Numbers
Paperbound: 978-0-7884-3401-3
Clothbound: 978-0-7884-6920-6

CEDAR GROVE CEMETERY, CEDAR GROVE, ESSEX COUNTY, NEW JERSEY. Carol Personette Comfort. Every effort has been made to identify the persons interred in this ancient burial ground which contains stones dated as early as 1765. Burials include many of the early settlers of the Cedar Grove section of Caldwell Township as well as many inhabitants of the Little Falls area of Passaic County and veterans of the American Revolution and the Civil War. This work begins with a brief history of the Cedar Grove Cemetery. The names are listed alphabetically and are supplemented with facts found in documented sources (state archives, church records, funeral home records, etc.) including occupations, military service, marriage, children and extensive census information.

CONTENTS

HISTORY OF CEDAR GROVE CEMETERY

"Cedar Grove Cemetery sometimes called the Jacobus or Canfield (or Doremus) Burying Ground, is located behind the United Presbyterian Church on the (2.2 acre) lot bounded by the intersection of the Pompton Turnpike (Route 23) and Commerce Road in Cedar Grove Township. The burying ground long antedates the church; in fact, it was never affiliated with any specific religious denomination, although it is known that the Second Reformed Church of Little Falls sold plots in the cemetery in the late 19th century.

"In 1931, the oldest standing stone was dated 1765... With the opening of the Pompton Turnpike in the early 19th century (1806), and the great influx of German and other immigrants to the area in the mid-19th century, came a great change in the ethnic base of the area as can be seen in the surnames listed.

"Over the years, like many other ancient burying grounds ...Cedar Grove has suffered from neglect and vandalism." (*Cedar Grove Cemetery*, GMNJ, Vol. II, p.108)

- - - - -

"In ancient times here, as elsewhere, burial of the dead was generally made by each family on a dedicated part of its own farm. Later, some of Cedar Grove's decedents were interred in cemeteries in localities now named Montclair, Caldwell and Little Falls. About 1850, Isaac Sloat, a son-in-law of Peter Doremus, joined with two or three others in opening a cemetery in Cedar Grove. An acre (adj. to the Canfield

Cemetery) for this purpose was acquired from Benjamin Canfield, the first, on high ground east of the turnpike near or against the north boundary line of, and cut out of, the strip of farm of Barnabas Simonson. A great many of the deceased men, women and children of Cedar Grove have been buried in this local resting place. It is reported that some bodies have been buried above other bodies; so fully occupied is this consecrated acre of land." (Boardman, p.8)

- - - - -

"...the Cedar Grove/Canfield Cemetery, described in 1862 as 'on the sand hill nigh Benj. Canfield'. In use since c. 1765, it harbors the remains of a number of the valley's early prominent families, including the Vreelands, Doremuses, Jacobuses, and other pioneering families, many of whom made their living cutting timber. A composite survey shows the original one-acre plot dedicated for use as a cemetery on the farm formerly belonging to the estate of Thomas Doremus; also shown are additional areas to the east and west, with plots laid out in 1871 and 1882, respectively, being the additions made by John Canfield and making a total of approximately two acres. The nearest cemeteries in the 18th Century were those of the Presbyterian Church in Caldwell and the Fairfield Church in Fairfield. When John Canfield added this acreage to the cemetery, it was a simple business undertaking, for he sold the lots.

"Numerous headstones remain, the earliest being of red sandstone quarried locally in Little Falls and West Orange; others are of cast iron, and recent ones are of marble. It is reported that some early markers were of wood inscribed with painted lettering. A total of 352(?) burials has been documented by the Cedar Grove Historical Society.

"The cemetery is more than a burial site to the township, for it was created at the beginning of its settlement by one of the area's original large landowners and later enlarged by a family that farmed the area from c.1822 well into the 1900's, tapering off in mid century, and it remains resident in the community. Furthermore, it contributes to the history of the township through its continued use into the 20th Century." (*Cedar Grove Historical Society Newsletter*)

- - - - -

EXPANDED LIST OF INTERMENTS

— Capital letters indicate person is known to have been buried at the Cedar Grove Cemetery.

—* indicates that this person and his/her relationship was given in the inscription; but, **no** specific gravestone or record was found

--** indicates that this person **is probably** buried at Cedar Grove Cemetery.

--The records found do not include many persons who are almost certainly buried at Cedar Grove Cemetery; e.g. Canfield, Doremus, Jacobus, Personett, Supenor family members.

--Notes on persons are meant to be research clues and should be checked carefully; e.g. in many cases there may have been additional children which were not found for this report.

- - - - -

DOCUMENTED INTERMENTS

Key:

birth cert.	Obtained from the State of New Jersey
Eberhart:	*The Doremus Family in America*
gmnj:	*The Genealogical Magazine of New Jersey*
lfrc:	Little Falls Reformed Church
npfh:	Norman Parker Funeral Home, Little Falls, NJ
observation	Stone seen in December 2002
Ougheltree	Burials recorded during 1920-1922 by Mrs. George Ougheltree (no dates given)

- - - - -

ABEEL

Abeel, DAVID, Capt.   b. (April 27, 1705)
(gmnj)   d. October 20, 1776

"Merchant of New York"
"Aged 72 years"

wife, Maria* (Duyckink)   b. (October 4, 1704)
                          d.

Notes:
--David Abeel was baptised April 29, 1705, Albany, New York, son of Johannes Abeel and Catharine Schuyler.
--David m. at the Dutch Church, New York City, February 4, 1725/6, Maria Duyckink. She was b. October 4, 1704, daughter of Garret Duyckink and Mary Abeel of New York.
--"At an early age, after his father's death, he was sent to New York and apprenticed to Mr. Schuyler in the dry goods business, and soon after reaching his majority he engaged in the flour and provision business, which he carried on successfully for many years. He succeeded to his father's business when the firm name was changed in 1750 from Abeel & Kierstede & Co. to Abeel & Co. He held the position of Captain of the company of militia of foot of the city and county of New York for many years until 1772." (*Abeel and Related Families*, Henry Whittemore, New York, 1899)
--David's father was mayor of Albany 1694-5 and 1709-10. (*Genealogy of the First Settlers of Albany*, John Pearson)
--On June 8, 1729, David Abeel and Maria "Walters" were sponsors at the baptism of Petrus, son of Johannes

Stoutenburgh and HenrickDuy'ckenk at the Second River Dutch Church, New Jersey.

--CHILDREN of David Abeel and Maria Duyckink:

Johannes   b. January 10, 1728, New York City;
              m. (?) Maria Krouts

Gerardus   b. 1729, bapt. February 9, 1729, New York
              City,d. bef. 1733

David   b. 1730, bapt. September 30, 1730, New York
              City, d. January 30, 1731
              --Son, David, was also a patriot of the
              Revolution whose estate was in the Catskill
              Patent.

Cathalina   b. 1731, bapt. December 8, 1731, New York
              City,d. bef. 1736

Gerardus   b. 1733, bapt. February 23, 1733, New York
              City

Garret   b. May 2, 1734, bapt. May 5, 1734, New
              York City; m. Mary Byvanck
              --Son, Garret, in 1772, was appointed Captain
              of the company of militia of foot of New
              York, in place of his father. He was a member
              of the New York Provincial Congress 1776-7.
              He and wife,Maria Byvanck,baptised two
              sons (1778 and 1782) at the Acquackanonk
              Dutch Church. Later he was in the iron
              business in New York. Due to the British
              occupation of New York, he was obliged to
              leave and located at **Little Falls**, New
              Jersey.

Cathalina   b. 1736, bapt. January 13, 1736, New York
              City

Jacobus   b. 1738, bapt. May 17, 1738, New York City;
              m.(?)Abigail VanBuren
              --Son, James/Jacobus, was attached to the
              staff of General Washington as Deputy
              Quartermaster General, New Jersey

Continental Line during the winter the army was encamped at Morristown.

- - - - -

ACKERMAN

Ackerman, James J.*
(gmnj)
wife, Helen Storms*
daughter, Eliza Catherine
m. JACOB H. DEBAUN (q.v.)

- - - - -

ALESSIA

ALESSIA, CARMINIA   b.
(npfh)   d. May, 1916
    Buried May 14, 1916

Notes:
--(?)1910 Census, p.71b, Acquackanonk Twp, Passaic County: Joseph Alessi, age 65, widower, b. Italy
--(?)1910 Census, p.101A, 1st Ward, Passaic: Frank Alessi, age 27, m. 4 yrs, b. Italy; Guiseppe, wife, age 23, b. Italy, 3 born 2 living; Mauro, son,age 3; Consetta, age 1 yr and 1 month, b. Italy
--(?)1910 Census p.113B,, 1st Ward Passaic: Giacomo Alessi, age 42, m. 22 yr, b. Italy; Domenica, age 42, 4 born 4 living; Consetta, age 21; Anna, age 17; Rosario, son, age 11; Bartolo, age 3; Antonio Alessi, brother, age 50, m. 15 years, b. Italy, Carmela, sister-in-law, age 36, 1 born 1 living; Concetta, niece, age 14
--(?)1920 Census, p.143B, Little Falls: John Lanetta, age 45, b. Italy, labor at stone quarry; Mary A., age 35, wife, b. Italy;

Joseph Alessio, age 39, b. Italy, labor,road contractor; wife, Minnie, age 32, b. Italy; Jennie, age 12, b. NJ; Mildred age 10; Julia age 8; Patrick age 6; Caroline, age 3 yr 9 months; Gladis, age 4 months; Angeline Croak, sister, age 26, widow, b. Italy; Charles Croak, age 2, grandson, b. NJ
--(?)1920 Census, p.143B, Little Falls: Patrick Alessio,age 33, b. Italy, labor at stone quarry; Florence, age 27, b Italy; James, age 9, b. NJ; Carmen, age 6, dau; Louis?, son, age 5; Joseph, age 3 yr and 2 months; Larry?,son, age 6 months
--(?)1930 Census, p.291A, Minnie Alessio, age 43, widow; Mildred, age 10; Julia, age 17, shaker at launday; Patsy, son, age 15, folder at laundry; Carmine, dau., age 13; Gladys age 10; Josie, age 8; George, age 6

- - - - -

AMMERAAL

Ammeraal, BERTHA   b. (September 1831)
(npfh)   d. March, 1919
                          (bur. March 7, 1919)

Notes:
--1900 Census, p.89A, Little Falls, NJ: Bertha Amarall, b. September 1831, Holland, age 68, widow, 3 born 3 living; Peter, son, b. February 1875
--1910 Census, p.193b, Little Falls Twp: Peter Ammeral, b. Holland, age 35, m. 8 yrs, supt. at carpet mill; Bertha, age 30, wife, b. Holland, 4 born 4 living; Helen, dau.,age 7, b. NJ; Cornelius, age 5; Peter, age 3; Frederick age 11 months; Fred 'Rittermey', age 24, single, b. Holland, brother-in-law; Bertha Ammeral, mother, age 79, widow, b. Holland
--CHILDREN of ..... Ammeraal and Bertha .....:
Peter   b. February 1875; m. Bertha 'Rittermey'?

- - - - -

Ammeraal, Cornelius*   b. (1863)
                           d. (aft. 1920)
wife, Christina (DePater)   b. (April 1878)
                           d. (aft. 1920)
son, JACOB   b. (abt. 1902)
(npfh)   d. September, 1910
                           (bur. September 26, 1910)

Notes:

--Cornelius was son of Renne Ammeraal (q.v.)

--Christina was dau. of Jacob DePater and

--Cornelius, d. Totowa(?); m. October 22, 1898, Dutch Church, Paterson, Christina DePater, daughter of Jacob DePater and Tryntye Oudman. Christina was b. 1878 in Holland and d. in Totowa. *(World Family Tree,* Volume 19)

--Cornelius Ammeraal arrived at the Port of New York in 1888. Christina DePater arrived at the Port of New York in 1891.

--1900 Census, p. 89, Little Falls: Cornelius Amerall, labor at carpet mill, b. 1863,Holland, m. 1 yr; Christina, b. April 1878, Holland, 1 born 1 living; Ann, dau, b. 1899, NJ; Rene Amerall, November 1833 Holland, m. 45 years; Anna Amerall b. October 1843 Holland, 4 born 1 living

--1910 Census, p. 190B, Little Falls Twp: Cornelius Ameraal, age 41, m. 12 yrs; Christina, age 31, 5 born, 5 living; Annie, age 10; Jacob, age 8; Raymond, age 5; Cornelius Jr. age 3; Christina, age 3 months.

--1920 Census, p.173A, Totowa, Passaic Co: Cornelius Ameraal, age 52, b. Holland, labor rug mill; Christina, age 40, b. Holland; Raymond, age 15, b. NJ; Cornelius, age 12; Christina age 10; Joseph, age 7; William age 6; Henry age 1 yr and 6 mos.

--CHILDREN of Cornelius Ameraal and Christina DePater:

Ann   b. abt. 1899
Jacob   b. abt. 1902; d. September 1910
Raymond   b. abt. 1905
Cornelius Jr.   b. abt 1907

Christina	b. 1910
Joseph	b. abt. 1913
William	b. abt. 1914
Henry	b. abt. 1918

- - - - -

AMMERAAL, RENNE   b. November 1833
(npfh)   d. August, 1907
    (bur. August 19, 1907)
wife, Aaltye/Anna**(DeVries)
    b. (October 1843)
    d. (after 1900 Census)

Notes:
--Renne Ammeraal was b. in Holland (and d. at Totowa?)
--Renne Ammeraal m. Aaltye DeVries** who was b.
October 1843 in Holland (and d. at Totowa?)
--'Reine Ammeral' arrived in the United States via Germany
between 1875 and 1888.
--1900 Census, p. 89, Little Falls: Cornelius Amerall, labor at
carpet mill, b. 1863,Holland, m. 1 yr; Christina, b. April
1878, Holland, 1 born 1 living; Ann, dau, b. 1899, NJ; Rene
Amerall, November 1833 Holland, m. 45 years; Anna
Amerall b. October 1843 Holland, 4 born 1 living
--CHILDREN of Renne Ammeraal and Aaltye DeVries:
Cornelius(q.v.)b. 1866, Holland; m. Christina DePater
    --1900 Census, p. 89, Little Falls: Cornelius
    Amerall, labor at carpet mill, b.
    1863,Holland, m. 1 yr; Christina, b. April
    1878, Holland, 1 born 1 living; Ann, dau, b.
    1899, NJ; Rene Amerall, November 1833
    Holland, m. 45 years; Anna Amerall b.
    October 1843 Holland, 4 born 1 living
    --1910 Census, p. 190B, Little Falls Twp:
    Cornelius Ameraal, age 41, m. 12 yrs;
    Christina, age 31, 5 born, 5 living; Annie, age

10; Jacob, age 8; Raymond, age 5; Cornelius
Jr. age 3; Christina, age 3 months

- - - - -

BACH

Bach, Charles**   b. (September 1833)
(gmnj)   d. (aft. 1910)

wife, ELIZABETH(Wetter)
(gmnj)   b. January 1, 1829
                         d. August 9, 1895

Notes:
--(?)NJ Will #21190G, 1884
--1860 Census, p. 842, South Ward, Paterson: Charles Bach,
age 28, brass finisher, b. Germany; Elizabeth, age 29;
William, age 7; Louis, age 4
--1870 Census: #389, Caldwell Twp:Charles Bach, age 38, b.
Prussia, farmer; Eliza, age 40; Louis, age 14; Ralph, age 9;
George age 6; Emma, age 4 Adj. to Cornelius Stager
--1880 Census: p.418C,#342 Caldwell(Cedar Grove)NJ:
Charles Bach, age 48, b. Prussia, farmer; Elizabeth, wife, age
50, b. Prussia; George, son, age 17, b. NJ; Emma, daughter,
age 14, b. NJ
--1900 Census: p. 246A, Caldwell Twp: Charles Bach, b.
September 1833, b. Germany, farmer
--1910 Census: Sheet 2, ED216, N. Caldwell Boro: Charles
Bach, widower, b. September 1833, age 76, b. Germany, m.
35 years; Ralph, b. Sept. 1862, age 37, m. 8 yrs; Eliza, b.
Feb. 1866, age 34, b. NJ, father b. England, mother b. NJ, 4
born, 4 living; George W. b. May 1892; Allen R. b. May
1894; Haren M. dau., b. July 1896; Alice S., b. Dec. 1898
--CHILDREN of Charles Bach and Elizabeth Wetter:
William   b. abt. 1853
Louis   b. abt. 1856

Ralph C.　　　b. September 1862; m. Eliza Andrews
　　　　　　　--1900 Census, p.246A, Caldwell Twp: Ralph
　　　　　　　Bach, b. Sept. 1862, m. 8 yr, b. NJ, parents
　　　　　　　b. Germany; Eliza, b. Feb. 1866, 4 born, 4
　　　　　　　living, b. NJ, mother b. England, mother b.
　　　　　　　Germany; George W., b. May 1892; Allen R.
　　　　　　　b. May 1894; Hazel M. b. July 1896; Alice S.
　　　　　　　b. December 1898; Charles Bach, b.
　　　　　　　September 1833, Germany, farmer
　　　　　　　--1910 Census, p. 1A, North Caldwell Boro:
　　　　　　　Ralph C. Bach, age 47, m. 18 yr, b. NJ, car-
　　　　　　　penter, house builder; Eliza, age 44, 5 born
　　　　　　　5 living, b. NJ; George W., age 17; Allen R.
　　　　　　　age 15; Hazel M. age 13; Alice B. age 11;
　　　　　　　Robert C. age 6; Maria Andrews,
　　　　　　　mother-in-law, age 63, b. NJ; Charles Bach,
　　　　　　　father, age 76, b. Germany
George　　　　b. abt. 1863
Emma　　　　　b. abt. 1866

- - - - -

BAKER

Baker, CLARA　　　　b.
(npfh)　　　　　　　　d. October, 1916
　　　　　　　　　　　(bur. October 5, 1916)

Notes:
--(?)Clara Baker, b. February 11, 1888, Passaic City, Passaic
Co., NJ; daughter of Jacob Baker and Clara Heerschap.
--(?)1900 Census: Jacob Baker, b. April 1851, b. Holland, m.
27 yrs.,millhand; Clara, b. June 1851, b. Holland; Madie,
dau., b. Feb. 1889, New Jersey; Clara, b. Feb. 1889, b. New
Jersey; Lane?, son, b. May 1881 Holland; John, son, b. Jan.
1880, Holland

--(?)1910 Census #7, Cedar Grove: Eva W. Baker, age 36, widow, dressmaking; Edward W., son, age 9

- - - - -

BAKKER

Bakker, HESSEL	b. May 21, 1841
(gmnj)	d. January 11, 1892
(wooden marker)	
wife, JANTIE	b.
(gmnj)(wooden marker)	d.
son(?), SIMON	b. June 4, 1891
	d. September 19, 1893

Notes:
--(?)Hessel Bakker b. March 2, 1834, Urk, Noord Holland, Netherlands; son of Kobes Bakker and Marritjen Korf.
--(?)1910 Census: p.197A, Little Falls Twp: Meindert Baker, age 27, m. 3 yrs.; Mary, age 21, wife, 2 born 2 living; Hessel, age 2; Cornelius age 9/12

- - - - -

BELDING
(In many records this name is spelled Belden.)

Belding, AUGUSTUS	b. December 7, 1834
(gmnj)(Plot 12)	d. January 1, 1902
wife, MARGARET	b. October 30, 1835, Scotland
(gmnj)	d. June 6, 1914

"HIS WIFE"

son, CHARLES	b. (October 17, 1860)

(gmnj)   d. October 23, 1864

"Age 4 yrs. & 6 dys"

son, ELLSWORTH   b. (September 14, 1862)
(gmnj)   d. March 1, 1864

"Aged 1 year 5 mos. & 17 days"

daughter, JANE   b. (February 4, 1852)
(gmnj)   d. June 22, 1860

"Aged 3 (8) yrs, 4 mos. & 18 days"

Notes:
--Augustus' full name was George Augustus Belden.
--He was son of Barnabas Belden(q.v.)and Catharine Sindle.
--1860 Census: #559, Acquackanonk, Passaic County:
Augustus Belden, age 25, b. NJ, works fancy store; Margaret,
age 25, b. Scotland; William, age 2; Sarah, age 3. (Near John
Belden, age 34 and John Belden, age 54)
--1870 Census: #393, Caldwell Twp: Augustus Belden, age
35, b. NJ, farm labor, real estate $1500; personal $5500;
Margaret, age 34, b. Scotland; William age 11; Jean/Jane,
age 5; Charles age 2
--1880 Census: p.184C, Little Falls, Passaic Co., NJ:
Augustus Belding, age 45, b. NJ, US Mail carrier, father b.
MA, mother b. NJ; Margret, wife, age 44, b. Scotland;
William, son, age 21, teaching school; Jane, daughter, age
14; Charles, son, age 12; Irvin, age 7
--1900 Census, p.891, Little Falls: Augustus Belden,
capitalist, b. NJ, father b. MA, mother b. NJ, b. Dec. 1834,
m. 43 yrs; Margaret, wife, b. October 1835, Scotland
--1910 Census, p.201B, Little Falls: Margaret Belding, age
74 widow, b. Scotland, 9 born 4 living.
--CHILDREN of Augustus Belden and Margaret .....:
Jane   b. February 4,1852; d. June 22, 1860

Sarah	b. abt. 1857
William	b. July 1858; m. Ida R. .....

--1900 Census, p.77, Little Falls Twp:
William Belding, b. NJ, parents b. Scotland,
b. July 1858, m. 12 yrs; Ida R. b. Oct. 1857, 2
2 living, b. N, parents b. NJ; Lewis A., b. Jan.
1890; Allan C., b. Feb. 1895, b. NJ
--1910 Census, p.127A, 5Wd.Hoboken:
William Belding, age 52, retired merchant,m.
yr, b. NJ, father b. NJ, mother b. Scotland;
Inez, age 51, b. NJ, 2 born 2 living; Louis A.,
age 20, student

Henry(?)   b. abt. 1859
--1880 Census, #245, Caldwell: Henry
Belden, age 21, b. NJ, teamster at
Newark City Home.

Charles	b. October 17, 1860; d. October 23, 1864
Ellsworth	b. September 14, 1862; d. March 1, 1864
Jean	b. abt. 1865; m. ..... Clark (q.v.)
Charles	b. abt. 1868

--1910 Census, p.200B, Little Falls Twp;
Charles A. Belding, age 42, m. 20 yrs.,Supt. at
carpet factory, b. NJ; Caroline, age 37, wife, 4
born, 4 living; Oscar, age 20; Rhoda, age 18;
Willie, age 17
--1920 Census, p.117B, Little Falls: Charles
A. Belding, age 51, finisher at carpet mill;
Carrie A. age 50; Ruth D. age 21, teacher;
--1930 Census, p.263A, Little Falls: Charles
A. Belding, age 62, janitor at municipal bldg;
Carrie A., age 61; Oscar, age 40, single; Ruth,
granddaughter, age 13

Irving H.   b. abt. 1873; m. Julia C. .....
--1900 Census, p.84A, Little Falls: Irving
Belden, advertising manager, b. June 1872, m.
6 yrs; Julia C. b. Dec. 1872, 2 born 2 living;

Margaret L. b. September 1894; James A. b.
Feb. 1898
--1910 Census, p.198A, Little Falls Twp:
Erving H. Belding, age 37, m. 16 yrs; Julia
C.S., age 37, 5 born, 5 living; Margaret J. age
15; James A. age 12; Cardwell E., son, age 9;
Miriam, age 7; Irving Jr., age 2
--1920 Census, p.119A, Little Falls: Ervin H.
Belding, age 47, adv. agt. for magazine; Julia
C. age 47; James A. age 21; Cardwell E. age
19; Miriam C. age 16; Erwin, age 12; Jean,
age 8
--1930 Census, p.266B, Little Falls: Ervin
H. belding, age 57, b. NJ, adv. rep for
hardware; Julia, age 57; Miriam, age 27,
teacher; Ervin, age 22; Jean, age 18

- - - - -

Belding, BARNABAS b. 1804 (May 5, 1805)
(gmnj) d. 1882 (September 23, 1882)
wife, CATHARINE (Sindle) b. 1808
(gmnj) d. 1896

Notes:
--Barnabas Belden was b. Ashfield, Massachusetts, son of
Daniel Belden and Hannah Howes. (Hannah Howes was
daughter of Barnabas Howes and Hannah Sears.)
--Barnabas m. #1, ___ Unknown
--Barnabas m. #2, widow Catharine Sindle (Atkins).
   (Catharine m. #1, Thomas Atkins, September
   9, 1827, Caldwell)
--1840 Census: #238, Caldwell Twp.
--1850 Census: #93, Caldwell Twp.: Barnabas Belden, age
45, lawyer, b. Mass.; Catharine, age 42; Thomas, age 18,
spinner; George A.(Augustus), age 15, spinner; Sarah C. age

13; Ruth Ann, age 10; Abby Jane, age 6; John G. age 3;
Charles A. age 9 months.

--1860 Census: #392, Caldwell: Barney Belden, age 57,
lawyer, b. Mass: Catharine, age 52; Ruth, age 19; Sarah C.
age 23; Abby J. age 16; John, age 13; Josephine, age 6 (adj.
to Wm. Pfizenmayer)

--1870 Census: #392, Caldwell: Barney Belden, age 57,
lawyer, b. Mass.;Catherine, age 52; Ruth, age 19; Sarah C.
age 23; Abby J. age 16; John age 13; Josephine, age 6

--1880 Census:p.415A, #281 Caldwell(Cedar Grove) NJ:
(adj. to Wm. Pfizenmayer)Barnabas Belden, age 75, b. MA,
parents b. MA, no occupation; Catharine, wife, age 71, b. NJ

--CHILDREN of Barnabas Belden and Catharine Sindle:

Thomas b. July 1832
    --1860 Census, p.1030 Acquackanonk:
    Thomas Belden, age 28, carpenter; Ellen, age
    24; Isabella, age 5; Kate age 3
    --1870 Census: p. 246A, Little Falls: Thomas
    Belden, age 35, carpenter; Ellen, age 32;
    Kate, age 13; Ellen, age 10; George age 7;
    Isabel, age 5
    --1880 Census, p.181A, Little Falls, NJ;
    Thomas Belding, age 47, b. NJ, carpenter,
    father b. MA, mother b. NJ; Ellen, wife, age
    43, b. NJ, father b. Scotland, mother b. NJ;
    Ella, dau., age 19, b. NJ; parents b. NJ;
    George, son, age 17, b. NJ, works fancy
    store; Laura, dau.,age 8, b. NJ
    --1900 Census, p.83A, Little Falls: Thomas
    Belden, father-in-law b. July 1832, landlord;
    at res. of Charles and Ella Newman

George Augustus (q.v.) b. December 7, 1834

Sarah C. b. abt. 1837

Ruth Ann b. abt. 1840, m. January 12, 1862, Caldwell
    Twp., Thomas Cisco
    --1880 Census, p.185B, Newark, NJ: Thomas
    Sisco, age 37, b. NJ, carpenter; Ruth, wife

age 36, b. NJ, father b. MA, mother b. NJ; Abby Joan, dau., age 14; Peter A., son, age 11; Catherine, age 6

Abby Jane	b. abt. 1844
John G.	b. abt. 1847, m. Amanda _____

--1880 Census, p.160B, Paterson: John Belden, age 33, b. NJ, store clerk; Amanda, wife, age 28, b. NJ; Almah B., son, age 1, NJ

Charles A.	b. abt. 1849; d. bef. 1860
Josephine	b. abt. 1854

- - - - -

BONE

Bone, Catharine
(gmnj)
m. William M. Morrell (q.v.)

- - - - -

BORCHER

Borcher, LIZZIE   b.
(npfh)   d. August, 1907
                                  (bur. August 27, 1907)

Notes:
--(?)1860 Census, p.426, 7 Wd,Newark: Lewis Borchers, age 38, b. Hanover, occupation, 'daguerian'; Amanda, age 13, b. Hanover; Louis, age 10, b. 'on the ocean'; Caroline Friederhel, age 62, b. Hanover(mother-in-law??)
--(?)1870 Census, p. 5A, 7 Wd, Newark: Louis Borches, age 48, b. Hanover; photographer; Rosellia, age 39, b. Hanover(no children listed)

--(?)1880 Census, p.222A, South Orange, Essex Co., NJ:
Louis Borchers, age 58, b. Hanover,Germany, farmer;
Rosalie, wife,(?) age 50, b. Hanover.(no children listed)

- - - - -

BORGIA

Borgia, FRANK   b.
(npfh)   d. September, 1911
     (bur. September 16, 1911)

Notes:
--(?)1910 Census: p. 226A, Little Falls: Francisco 'Borch',
age 32, m. 8 yrs., b. Italy, laborer; Mary, age 28, b. Italy, 5
born 4 living; Jennie, age 7, b. Italy; Nicholas, age 4, b.
Italy; Antonio, age 4 months, b. NJ; Loretta, age 2, b. NJ

- - - - -

BRASH

Brash, James*   b.
     d.
wife, Margaret Muir*   b.
     d.
son, JAMES WALTER   b. October 23, 1871
(gmnj)   d. July 19, 1872

Notes:
--(?)1880 Census: p.362B, Paterson: William Muir, age 45,
b. Scotland, works in carpet factory; Margaret, wife, age 40,
b. Scotland; William Muir, son,single, age 24, plumber
--CHILDREN of James Brash and Margaret Muir:
James Walter b. October 23, 1871; d. July 19, 1872

- - - - -

BRITTAIN

Brittain, WILLIAM J. b. (abt. 1796)
(gmnj) d. July 26, 1851

"Native of England"
"Aged 54 yrs & 10 mos."

wife, Martha** b. (abt. 1800)
 d. (aft. 1850)

Notes:
--1850 Census: #64, Caldwell /Cedar Grove: William Brittain, age 52, military ornament mfr., b. England, real estate value $400; Martha, age 50, b. England; John, age 20, silversmith, b. England;Charles, age 17, military ornament mfr., b. England; Sarah, age 16, b. England.
--CHILDREN of William and Martha Brittain:
William A. b. abt. 1820, England;d. bef. 1870?
 m. 1850, Esther A. Jacobus,dau. of Richard Jacobus.
 --1850 Census: #76, Caldwell/Cedar Grove: William A. Brittain, age 30, lamp maker, b. England; Esther A. Brittain, age 23, b. NJ; At residence of Esther's father, Richard P. Jacobus, age 53, mason.
 --1860 Census, p.714, 11 Wd.Newark: William J. Britton, age 41, machinist, b. England; Esther, age 32, b. NJ; Richard, age 8, b, NY; William, age 6, b. NJ; Esther, age 4, b. NJ; Edward P., age 2, b. NJ; Sarah E. age 6 months b. NJ
 --1870 Census, p.438A, 11 Wd.Newark: Esther Brittain, age 42, works hat mfg; Richard, age 18, telegraph operator; William,

age 15; Edward, age 12; Sarah, age 10;
Charles, age 9; Nellie, age 7
--1880 Census, p.446B, Newark: Ester
Brittan, widow, age 52, b. NJ, keeping house;
Ester, dau., widow, age 24, b. NJ, hat binder;
Edward C. son, age 22, b. NJ,
machinist;Sarah E. dau., age 20, hat trimmer;
Charles H., son, age 19, b. NJ, button maker;
Nellie J., dau., age 17, b. NJ, button maker
--1910 Census, p.77A, 6Wd.Newark: Ester
A. Brittan, age 82, widow, b. NJ; 1 servant

John J.   b. abt. 1830, England, goldsmith, m.1850,
Araminta Jacobus, dau. of Richard Jacobus
--(?)1880 Census, p.359C, New York City:
John Britten, age 51, b. England, retired
merchant; Carrie, wife, age 31, b. NY, father
b. France, mother b. NJ; Marie, stepdaughter,
age 25, b. England; Edgar, son, age 7, b. NY,
father b. England, mother b. NY; Florence,
dau., age 5, b. NY, father b. England, mother
b. NY

Charles   b. abt. 1833, England
Sarah   b. abt. 1834, England

- - - - -

BROKAW

Brokaw, Cyrenius Thompson**
                    b.
                    d. (1833)
wife, RACHEL (Doremus)   b. September 11, 1802
(gmnj)   d. January 15, 1890

Notes:
--Rachel was daughter of Pieter Doremus,q.v. and Hannah
Norwood. She lived in Paterson after her marriage. A

Paterson newspaper article reported that "she remembered
seeing the Marquis deLaFayette as he passed through
Paterson while on a visit to this country."
--Rachel was baptised November 7, 1802, Ref. Dutch
Church, Stone House Plains, NJ
--Rachel m. June 14, 1828, Essex Co., Cyrenius Thompson
Brokaw, aka Cyrus T. Brokaw. The marriage record reads
"Serranas Tompson Brocor m. Rachel Doremas".
--1870 Census, p.541A&B, Haverstraw, Rockland Co., NY:
John C. Coe, age 45, merchant tailor; Catherine age 41; Ada,
age 21; Edward, age 15; Rachel Brokaw, age 60
--1880 Census, p.88A, Haverstraw, Rockland Co.,NY: John
C. Coe, age 54, b. NY, tailor; Catharine, wife, age 50, b. NJ;
Ada Cosgrove, dau., age 30, b. NY, married, at home;
Eugene S. Cosgrove, grandson, age 6, b. NY, father b. NY;
Rachel Brokaw, mother-in-law, widow, age 77, b. NJ
--CHILDREN of Cyrenius T. Brokaw and Rachel Doremus:

Theodore**   b. at Cedar Grove; d. in infancy

Edwin**   b. at Cedar Grove; d. in infancy

Catharine   b. August 23, 1829, d. December 30, 1891.
              m. January 6, 1848, John C. Coe of Paterson,
              Passaic Co., New Jersey
              --1860 Census, p. 33, Haverstraw, Rockland
              Co., NY: John C. Coe, age 33, clothier, b.
              NY; Catharine, age 30, b. NJ; Ada, age 11, b.
              NY; Edwin P., age 6, b. NY
              --1870 Census, p.541A&B, Haverstraw,
              Rockland Co., NY: John C. Coe, age 45,
              merchant tailor; Catherine age 41; Ada, age
              21; Edward, age 15; Rachel Brokaw, age 60
              --1880 Census, p.88A, Haverstraw, Rockland
              Co.,NY: John C. Coe, age 54, b. NY, tailor;
              Catharine, wife, age 50, b. NJ; Ada Cosgrove,
              dau., age 30, b. NY, married, at home;
              Eugene S. Cosgrove, grandson, age 6, b. NY,
              father b. NY; Rachel Brokaw, mother-in-law,
              widow, age 77, b. NJ

- - - - -

BROWER

Brower, Eleanor
(gmnj)
m. John J. Vreeland (q.v.)

- - - - -

BRUCE

Bruce, ALEXANDER   b.
(npfh)   d. June, 1908
                 (bur. June 10,1908)

Notes:
--(?)1870 Census: p.666a, 8th Ward, Paterson: Alexander
Bruce, age 31, b. Ireland, lithographic printer; Mary A. age
28, b. Ireland; Eliza J. age 8, b. Ireland; Robert, age 6, b.
Ireland; Alexander age 3, b. NJ; Thomas age 1, b. NJ; Eliza
J. Woods, age 58, b. Ireland
--(?)1880 Census: Alex M. Bruce, brother, single, age 31, b.
Scotland, silk worker, parents b. Scotland; Head: Donald
Bruce, age 30, b. Scotland, wife, Ann, age 42, b. Ireland;
Dau., Isabella, age 4, b. NJ; Peter Frazar, age 26, Scotland,
silk worker; James Bawn, age 21, silk worker, b. NY
--(?)1880 Census:p.441B, Paterson, NJ: Alexander Bruce,
age 40, b. Ireland, Lithographer; wife, Mary A. age 37, b.
Ireland; dau., Eliza, age 18, b. Ireland, works in flax mill;
Robert, son, age 16, b. Ireland, works in Flax mill; Thomas,
son, age 11, b. NJ, works in flax mill;Minnie, dau., age 9, b.
NJ; Wallace, son, age 7, b. NJ;Louisa, daugher, age 6, b.
NJ;Inez, daughter age 2 mos. b. NJ

- - - - -

BUBBS

Bubbs, CHARLES   b.
(lfrc)   d. July, 1918
                     Bur. July 2, 1918

Notes:
--(?)1880 Census: p.289B, Paterson, NJ: Conrad Bup, age 26,
b. Germany, baker; Barbara, wife, age 26, b. Germany;
Charles, son, age 4, b. NY; Kate, daughter, age 3 mos. b. NY

- - - - -

BUCKLEY

Buckley, BEN   b. (abt. 1839)
(gmnj)   d. May 29, 1882

"Aged 43 years"

wife, Julia* (Metcalf?)   b. (abt. 1845)
                     d.

son, ERNEST B.   b. (September 29, 1876)
(gmnj)   d. April 9, 1882

"His son"
"Aged 5 yrs. & 8 mos."

Notes:
--1870 Census, p.540A, 1Wd.Poughkeepsie, Dutchess Co.,
NY; Benjamin Buckley, age 30, b. England; Julia, age 25, b.
NY; Benjamin, age 2, b. Connecticut
--1880 Census:p.183A, Little Falls, Passaic Co., NJ: Ben
Buckley, age 41, b. England, works in felt factory;Julia,
wife, age 35, b. NY, parents b. England; Ben Buckley, son,
age 12, b. Connecticut; Helen, daughter, age 5, b. New

York;Ernest B. Buckley, son, age 3, b. NY;Mary A. Metcalf, married, age 68, b. England (mother-in-law?)
--CHILDREN of Benjamin Buckley and Julia (Metcalf?):

Benjamin	b. abt. 1868
Helen	b. abt. 1875
Ernest B.	b. Sept. 29, 1876;d.April 9,1882

- - - - -

CAMPBELL

CAMPBELL, Nicholas*	b. (1805)
	d. (aft. 1870)
1st wife, CHARITY	b. 1810
(gmnj)	d. 1857

"Aged 47 yrs. 10 mos. 7 days"

2nd wife, Catharine*	b. (abt. 1805)
	d. (aft. 1870)

Notes:
--(?)Nicholas Campbell, b. June 26, 1805, Bergen, NJ; son of Petrus Campbell and Maria Westervelt.
--1830 Census: p.374, Acquackanonk, Passaic County, NJ
--1840 Census: p.106, Acquackanonk, Passaic County, NJ
--1850 Census:p.355B, Acquackanonk, Passaic County, NJ:
Nicholas Campbell, age 44, shoemaker; Charity, age 40;
Ann, age 21; Lydia, age 19; Peter, age 15, shoemaker; Sarah, age 6
--1860 Census:p.1015 Acquackanonk: Peter Campbell, age 25, shoemaker, b. NJ; Hester, age 26; John, age 4; Sarah age 2; Nicholas, age 56
--1870 Census, p.403A, 4Wd.Paterson: Nick Campbell, age 65, shoemaker, b. NJ; Catharine, age 65, b. NJ
--CHILDREN of Nicholas Campbell and Charity _____ "
Cornelius(?)   b. abt. 1827(possible child); m.Caroline.....

	--1850 Census, p.355B, Acquackanonk: Cornelius Campbell, age 23, shoemaker; Caroline, age 21; Abraham, age 1; Ellen Garrison, age 9
Ann	b. abt. 1829
Lydia	b. abt. 1831
Peter	b. abt. 1835
	--1860 Census, p.1015, Acquackanonk Twp: Peter Campbell, age 25, b. NJ, shoemaker; Hester, age 26; Richard, age 6; John, age 4; Sarah, age 2; Nicholas, age 56 --1870 Census, p. 605A, 7Wd.Paterson: Peter Campbell, age 35, shoemaker; Hester, age 36; Richard, age 16, works on canal; John, age 14, works silk mill; Sarah, age 12 Sarah, age 12; Peter, age 9; Emanuel, age 3
Sarah	b. abt. 1844

- - - - -

CANFIELD

CANFIELD, **_____

Notes:
--There are probably many members of the Canfield families buried at the Cedar Grove Cemetery.
--See also: more than 25 Canfield persons buried at Prospect Hill Cemetery, Caldwell, NJ.

- - - - -

CHESNEY

CHESNEY, _____   b.
(ougheltree)   d. (abt. 1920-22)

Notes:

--(?)Robert Chesney, incorporator of the Cedar Grove Union Congregational Church.

--(?)Robert Chesney, Jr., florist, m. Susan, daughter of William Bortic, principal of the Cedar Grove School. They had one child, William B. Chesney, veteran of WW I.

--(?)1880 Census, p.415B, Caldwell: William Bortic, age 36, b. NJ, parents b. Ireland, school teacher; Eliza, wife, age 32, b. NJ; Susan, dau., age 8, b. NJ; 2 other daughters

--(?)Priscilla, daughter of Robert Chesney, Sr.,the florist, m. George E. Taylor. They had two sons, Earle A. and Robert I

--(?)1900 Census: #69, Verona: Robert A. Chesney, b. August 1873, NY, age 26, m. 2 yrs., florist; Susan, b. May 1873, age 27, b. NJ

.--(?)1900 Census: #70, Verona/Cedar Grove, NJ:Robert Chesney, b. March 1844, m. 29 yrs., b. Scotland, florist; Mary, b. February 1844, NY; Edward b. August 1877; Hugh M. b. March 1876; Mildred, dau-in-law; Harriet Clapp, nurse; 2 hired men

--(?)1910 Census: #61,Verona, Robert Chesney, age 68, b. Scotland; Mary, age 65, b. NY

--(?)1910 Census: #64, Verona,Robert A. Chesney, Jr., age 35, florist, b. NY, Susan (Bortic), age 35; William B., age 9

--(?)1920 Census #17, Cedar Grove: Robert A. Chesney, age 45; Susie, wife, age 46; William, son, age 19

--(?)1920 Census #223, Cedar Grove: George E. Taylor, age 47, dairy farmer; Mary Priscilla (Chesney) wife, age 46, b. NY, father b. Scotland, mother b. NY; Robert age 20; Mary A. Chesney, age 79, widow, mother-in-law

--(?)1930 Census Sheet 10B, Cedar Grove: Robert Chesney,age 53, b. NY, father b. Scotland, mother b. CT, florist; Susan, wife age 51, b. NJ;

- - - - -

CISCO
(Sisco?)

Cisco, Anthony*   b. (abt. 1848?)
                   d.

1st wife,RACHEL LUTECIA (Jacobus)
(gmnj)   b. (December 31, 1850)
               d. July 12, 1878

'Aged 27.6.12"

Notes:
--(?)Anthony P. Sisco (1806-1879) carpenter at Paterson, m. Sarah VanOrden. (parents of Anthony Cisco?)
--(?)1860 Census, p.879, South Ward, Paterson: Anthony Sisco, age 60, laborer; Sarah, age 49; Frances, age 20, laborer; Henry age 16; Thomas age 14; Catherine age 13; Phebe age 10; Joseph age 7
--(?)1870 Census, p.737A, Wayne Twp., Passaic Co.: Anthony Sisco, b. NY, age 22, farm laborer on farm of George R. Berdan
--(?)1870 Census, p. 739B, Wayne Twp, Passaic Co: James Jacobus, age 48, shoemaker, b. NJ; Martha, age 47; Rachel, age 19; Frank, age 14; Thomas age 11; John, age 8; Linus, age 4
--(?)1880 Census, p.501B, Paterson: Sarah Sisco, widow, age 71, b. NJ; Cathrine Claxon, dau., widow, age 34, b. NJ, works silk mill; Ellen Claxon, granddau., age 14, b. NJ, works silk mill.

- - - - -

CLARK

Clark, ...*	b.
	d.
wife, JEAN (Belding)	b. August 9, 1865
(gmnj)	d. April 9, 1914

Notes:
--on Augustus Belding monument
--Jean was dau. of Augustus and Margaret Belding(q.v.)
--(?)1900 Census, p.81, Little Falls: Jesse Clark b. February 1864, widower, Lizzie, dau b. July 1883; Mary b. April 1885; Isabell b. April 1891(same page as August Belden,q.v.)

- - - - -

COPELAND

Copeland, JOHN	b. (abt. 1839)
(npfh)	d. December, 1910
	(bur. December 8, 1910)
wife, Nancy*	b. (abt. 1843)
	d. (aft. 1880)

Notes:
--(?)1850 Census, #465, Acquackanonk NJ: Richard Copelton, age 45, carpet weaver, b. Ireland; Ann J., age 40, b. Ireland; James, age 19, b. Ireland, carpet weaver; John, age 15, b. Ireland, wool mill hand; Eliza, b. Ireland, age 13; William, age 11, b. Ireland; Samuel, age 7, b. Ireland; Robert, age 2, b. NJ; Richard, age 5 months, b. NJ
--(?)1860 Census, p.1028, Acquackanonk, Little Falls: Robt. Copelton,age 45, b. Ireland, laborer; Mary, age 48, b. Ireland: Ellen, age 20, weaver, b. Ireland; John, age 19, cotton spinner, b. Ireland; Robert, age 16, b. Ireland, laborer

--1870 Census, p.246A, Little Falls: John Copland, age 28, spinner at carpet factory, b. Ireland; Nancy, age 25, b. Ireland; William, age 6, b. NJ; John, age 4, b. NJ; James, age 1, b. NJ

--1880 Census, p.181A, Little Falls, NJ: John Copland, age 41, b. Ireland, works in carpet factory; Nancy, wife, age 37, b. Ireland; William, son, age 16, b. NJ, works in carpet factory; John, son, age 14, b. NJ, works in carpet factory; James, son, age 11; Albert, son, age 9; Emma, dau., age 7; Margret, dau., age 4; George, son, age 1

--1910 Census, p.195A, Little Falls Twp: John Copeland, age 71, widower, b. Ireland, labor at water company; Robert Copeland(q.v.), brother, age 69, single

--Children of John Copeland and Nancy .....:

William	b. abt. 1864
	--1900 Census, p.88A, Little Falls: William Copeland, b. 1864, NJ, father b. Ireland, mother b. 'Scotland',Inspector
	--1910 Census, p.181A, Union Twp, Union Co.; William Copleton, age 50(?), m. 3 yr, 0 born 0 living, farmer; Katherine, age 35, b. NY, parents b. NJ
John	b. abt. 1866
James	b. abt 1869
	--1900 Census, p.162, 2Wd Paterson;James Copleton, b. Feb. 1867, m. 6 yr, silk mill weaver, b. NJ, father b. Ireland, mother b. (?); Mary, b. Dec. 1870, b. Germany, 4 born 2 living; Mary, b. Dec. 1870; Willie b. Sept. 1897; Viola b. Feb. 1899
	--1910 Census, p.181B,2Wd.Paterson: James Copleton, weaver silk mill, age 43, m.x2; Emily, age 28, b. NJ, parents b. NJ
Albert	b. abt. 1871
Emma	b. abt. 1873
Margaret	b. abt. 1876
George	b. September 1879

--1900 Census, p.8, Acquackanonk Twp:
George Copeland, boarder, b. September
1879, age 20, bartender, b. NJ, father b.
Ireland, mother b. NJ
--1910 Census, p.245A, Hanover Twp:
George Copeland, barber, age 31, m. 12 yr, b.
NJ, father b. Ireland, mother b. NJ; Mable,
age 32, 3 born 3 living, b. California, father b.
Scotland, mother b. California; James, age 9;
George, age 8; Everitt, age 6 months

- - - - -

Copeland, ROBERT   b. (abt. February 1845)
(npfh)   d. September, 1917
                          (bur. September 28, 1917)

Notes:
--(?)1850 Census, #465, Acquackanonk NJ: Richard
Copelton, age 45, carpet weaver, b. Ireland; Ann J., age 40,
b. Ireland; James, age 19, b. Ireland, carpet weaver; John,
age 15, b. Ireland, wool mill hand; Eliza, b. Ireland, age 13;
William, age 11, b. Ireland; Samuel, age 7, b. Ireland;
Robert, age 2, b. NJ; Richard, age 5 months, b. NJ
--(?)1860 Census, p.1028, Acquackanonk, Little Falls: Robt.
Copelton, age 45, b. Ireland, laborer; Mary, age 48, b.
Ireland: Ellen, age 20, weaver, b. Ireland; John, age 19,
cotton spinner, b. Ireland; Robert, age 16, b. Ireland, laborer
--1880 Census, p.183A, Little Falls, NJ: Robert "Copleten"
age 70, b. Ireland, laborer; Mary, wife, age 79, b. Ireland,
father b. Ireland, mother b. Scotland; Robert, age 36, single,
b. Ireland, parents b. Ireland
--1900 Census, p.79, Little Falls: James Riker, b. Aug 1848,
restaurant proprietor; Robert Copeland, b. February 1843,
single, b. Ireland, 'huxter"

--1910 Census, p.195A, Little Falls Twp: John Copeland, age 71, widower, b. Ireland, labor at water company; Robert Copeland, brother, age 69, single

- - - - -

CORBY

Corby, CORNELIUS   b. (November 6, 1836)
"Old Section" (gmnj) d. May 4, 1903

"Co. E, 5th Regt. N.Y. Heavy Art."

1st wife , HARRIET L. (Riker)
         b. (abt. 1843)
(gmnj)(wife #1)   d. June 12, 1880

"Age 36 years"
"and 10 children by her side"

2nd wife, Mary*(Hamill) b. (abt. 1853?)
         d.

3rd wife, Johanna*(Louter) b. (abt.1845)
         d. (aft. 1880)

4th wife, Orazella*(Ash) b. (July 1869)
         d.

Notes:
--Cornelius was b. at Little Falls, Passaic County, NJ, son of Cornelius Corby and Ellen Riker. He d. at Paterson. He was a shoemaker in 1862.
--Cornelius m. #1, February 19, 1859, Little Falls, Harriet L. Riker. She was daughter of Abraham Riker and Sophia ...... She was b. Passaic County and d. at Little Falls.
--Cornelius m. #2, abt. 1882, Mary Hamill.

(?)1880 Census, p.358B,Paterson, NJ: Mary Hamil, widow, age 27, seamstress, b. NJ, parents b. Ireland.)

(?)1880 Census, p.96B, Paterson:Mary Hamil, widow, age 27, b. NJ, father b. Ireland, mother b. Scotland, servant; at res. of 'Alexandria' (and Marietta Smith)

--Cornelius m. #3, abt 1883, Johanna DeBlock. She was widow of ..... Blaker, b. Holland; she was b. April 2, 1844, Texel Island, North Sea, Holland; dau. of Daniel DeBlok and Johanna Moeland

(1880 Census, p.117B, Paterson: Johanna Blaker, widow, age 35, b. Holland, works in silk mill; Mary Blaker, dau., age 10, b. NJ, works in silk mill; Johanna Blaker, dau., age 5, b. NJ, works in silk mill; Johanna Block, mother widow, age 71, b. Holland; adj. to brother Jacob DeBlock)

--Cornelius m. #4, June 12, 1886, Orazella/Orzella) Ash. She was daughter of William Ash and Ellen Elizabeth Stouble.

(1870 Census, p.618B, 6 Wd Newark: William Ash, age 35, hatter, b. PA; Ellen E. age 28, b. NJ; Arazella, age 2)

(1880 Census, p.245A, Newark: William Ash, age 56, b. PA, parents b. Germany, gardener; Ellen E., wife, age 39, b. NJ,parents NJ; Grazella, dau., age 12, b. NJ, at service; 5 other Ash children.)

(1900 Census, p.263, 13 Wd. Newark: Orzella Corby, b. July 1879, age 31, widow, 4 born 4 living; Henry b. June 1884; Ida, b. Jan, 1890; Sarah b. June 1892; Malvina b. October 1894.)

--In June 1886 he lived at 16 Fulton Street, Paterson.

--In May 1898 he lived at 131 Belmont Avenue, Newark.

--"He served as private, Co. E, 5th Regiment, New York Heavy Artillery; enlisted January 20, 1862; discharged October 9, 1862. His right hand was wounded in service and amputated. Both marriage number two and three were bigamous. Affidavits from members of Orazella Ash's family state that they lived apart for five years before his death because 'he was addicted to the use of strong drink and was so ugly and abusive to his family that it was impossible for them to live in peace together'." (Corby family information compiled by George King Nichols, Decatur, Illinois)

--1850 Census, #265, Acquackanonk, NJ: Cornelius Corby, age 12, b. NJ; at farm of Hartman A. and Roberta Vreeland.

--(?)1860 Census, p.1029, Acquackanonk: Sophia Riker; John age 5; Charles age 2

--1880 Census: p.190D, Little Falls, Passaic Co., NJ: Cornelius Corby, age 44, widower, b. NJ, wood turner; Cornelius Corby, age 10, b. NJ;Jennie Corby, age 8, b. NJ; W. Corby, age 8, b. NJ;Gustus C. Corby, age 5, b. NJ

--CHILDREN of Cornelius Corby and Harriet Riker:

Mary E.	b. January 18, 1863
Ellen	b. December 19, 1864
	--(?)1880 Census, p. 190D,Little Falls: (adj. to Cornelius Corby) William Dorsen, age 32, b. NY, brick mason; Ella, age 17, b. NJ, keeping house; Lafena, age 13, b. NY; Peter E.age 12;William,age 9;Freddie, age 7
Cornelius	b. abt. 1870
Jennie	b. abt. 1872
Walsey(?)	b. abt. 1874
	--1910 Census, p.131B 1 Wd Bloomfield: Walsey E. Corby, age 36, m. 7 yr, b. NJ, plumber; Mary J., age 30, b. Ireland, 3 born 3 living; Harriet B. age 7; Florence J. age 6; George E. age 3
Infant	b. 1875, d. 1875
Augustus C.	b. abt. 1876
	--m. Emma G. Kruger,dau. of ...Kruger and Julia Hoffman
	--1910 Census, p.152B, 2Wd Montclair: Augustus C. Corby, age 48, m. 20 yr, bank cashier; Emma G. age 42, b. NJ, parents NY Edmond A. age 16; Julia H. Kruger, mother-in-law, age 63, widow

--CHILDREN of Cornelius Corby and Mary Hammill
??

--CHILDREN of Cornelius Corby and Orazella Ash:

Henry	b. June 1884(?)
Ida L.	b. January 16, 1890
Sarah Ann	b. February 26, 1891
Melvina	b. October 24, 1894

- - - - -

COURTER

Courter, B. (Benjamin?)	b.
(lfrc)	d.
wife, (Sarah C.Deeths?)*	b.
	d.

Notes:

--B. Courter purchased 1/2 of Lot #24 in 1871.(Perhaps he and his brother, Emmons,q.v.,purchased this lot for their parents?)

--(?)Benjamin Courter was b. February 6, 1847; son of Jacob Courter, and Alice Freeman; brother of Henry Emmons Marcus Courter (q.v.)

--(?)Benjamin Courter m. Sarah C. Deeths; she was born July 1843.

--(?)1880 Census, p.190D, Little Falls, NJ: Benjamin Courter, age 33, b. NJ, laborer; Sarah, age 36, b. NJ; Ada,(Julia) age 5; John, age 1

--(?)1880 Census, p.183A, Little Falls, NJ: Benjamin Courter, age 33, b. NJ, laborer; Sarah, age 34, b. NJ; no children listed

--(?)1900 Census, p.82, Little Falls: Sarah Courter, b. July 1843; Ada, b. May 1875; John, b. March 1879

--CHILDREN of Benjamin Courter and Sarah C. Deeths:

Ada	b. May 1875
John	b. March 1879

- - - - -

Courter, Emmons*   b.
(lfrc)   d.
wife, Rachel Ann*(Paxton)   b.
                              d.

Notes:
--He purchased 1/2 of Lot #24 in 1871.(See B. Courter who also purchased 1/2 of this lot.)
--(?)Henry Emmons Marcus Courter, b. March 9, 1845, son of Jacob Courter and Ellen Alice Helen Freeman.
--(?)Henry Emmons Marcus Courter m. August 5, 1865, Caldwell, Rachel Ann Paxton; she was b. abt. 1848, dau. of Isaac Paxton.
--(?)1860 Census: #215, Caldwell: Emmons Courter, age 15; at residence of Daniel Pilling,(q.v.) age 66, farmer, b. England; and his wife, Alice (Johnson), age 67.
--(?)1880 Census: p.16D, Montclair, NJ: Henry E. Courter, age 40, b. NJ, driver;Rachel, wife, age 32, b. NJ, father b. NJ mother b. NY;Charles B., son, age 13, b. NJ;Frank N. Courter, son, age 5, b. NJ;Simeon W. Courter, son, age 1, b. NJ;William Paxton, age 18, b. NJ, plumber.
--CHILDREN of
Henry Emmons Marcus Courter and Rachel Ann Paxton:
Charles B.   b. March 1867; d. July 3, 1906
           --1900 Census, p.68A, 2Wd.Montclair:
           Charles Courter, b. Mar 1867, m. 10 yrs; coachman; Ellen, b. September 1874, 1 born 1 living; William, b. July 188; Frank Courter, brother, plumber, b. February 1875, single; Simeon Courter, brother, b. Jan. 1881, age 19, plumber
           --1910 Census, p.46A, 1Wd.Newark:
           Ella Courter, age 35, widow, 1 born 1 living; William, son, age 21, butcher; Frank, age 32, single, brother-in-law, plumber
Frank B.   b. February 1875; d. August 10, 1924

--1900 Census, p.68A, 2Wd.Montclair:
Charles Courter, b. Mar 1867, m. 10 yrs;
coachman; Ellen, b. September 1874, 1 born
1 living; William, b. July 188; Frank Courter,
brother, plumber, b. February 1875, single;
Simeon Courter, brother, b. Jan. 1881, age 19,
plumber
--1910 Census, p.46A, 1Wd.Newark: Ella
Courter, age 35, widow, 1 born 1 living;
William, son, age 21, butcher; Frank,
brother-in-law, age 32, single, plumber

Simeon W.   b. June 1879; d. December 26, 1901
--1900 Census, p.68A, 2Wd.Montclair:
Charles Courter, b. Mar 1867, m. 10 yrs;
coachman; Ellen, b. September 1874, 1 born
1 living; William, b. July 188; Frank Courter,
brother, plumber, b. February 1875, single;
Simeon Courter, brother, b. Jan. 1881, age 19,
plumber

- - - - -

Courter, JOHN   b. (October 9, 1838?)
(ougheltree)   d. (aft. 1911)
COURTER, MARY (Supenor?)
(ougheltree)   b. (February 14, 1830?)
                  d. (aft. 1911)

Notes:
It is not certain that these notes are relevant to the above
individuals.
--(?)John Henry Courter was b. October 9, 1838 and d. after
1911.
--(?)John Henry Courter m. Mary Supenor, daughter of
Abraham Supenor and Catherine VanNess. Mary d. after
1911.

--(?)1870 Census: #542 Caldwell/Cedar Grove: John Courter, age 35, works brush factory; Mary, age 40; Henry, age 12; Also, Abraham Supenor, age 64, carpenter

--(?)1880 Census: #325 Caldwell: John Courter, age 40, works in brush factory; Mary, wife age 49; adj. to Cornelius Supenor(q.v.)

--(?)1885 State Census: p.41, Caldwell Twp.

--(?)1900 Census: #123 Verona/Cedar Grove: John Courter, b. September 1840; Mary b. February 1830

--(?)1905 State Census: #142 Verona: John Courter, works corset factory

--(?)1910 Census: #130, Cedar Grove: John Courter, age 71, brushmaker; Mary, age 80

--(?)1911: John Courter, lives in Caldwell. John and Mary had a son, James Henry Courter, b. abt. 1856;he d. unm.

- - - - -

CRANE

Crane, LINUS   b. (abt. 1819)
(gmnj)   d. May 7, 1855

"Aged 36 years"

wife, MARGARET (Yorks)   b. (abt 1815)
(gmnj)   d. September 19, 1878

"Wife of Linus Crane"
"Aged 63 years"

son, CHARLES VANNESS   b. (March 4, 1849)
(gmnj)(Lot #34)   d. September 15, 1851

Son of Linus & Margaret Crane
Aged 2 Y'rs 6 mo's 11 d'ys

son?, WARREN S.   b. (abt 1842)
(gmnj)   d. May 28, 1876

"Aged 34 yrs."
"San Francisco"

Notes:

--This family is on the monument of Linus Crane and (Reuben?) Daniel.

--Linus Crane was son of Jeremiah Crane and Elizabeth Corby;Linus was brother of Israel Crane.

--Linus Crane m. December 31, 1840, West Bloomfield, Margaret Yorks, daughter of Garret Yorks(q.v.) and Elsje Doremus.

--Linus' sister, Hannah, m. Thomas Stanley; Linus' sister, Julia m. Henry Stanley

--1850 Census, #370, Acquackanonk, NJ: Linus Crane, age 32, constable; Margaret, age 32; (Warren S.?), male, age 9; Leah E., age 4; Charles age 1; adj. to Cornelius Yorks, father-in-law

--1860 Census, p. 1021, Acquackanonk: Margaret Crane, age 39; (Leah) Elizabeth, age 13; near Cornelius Yorks

--1870 Census, p.236, Little Falls Twp: Margaret Crane, age 52, keeping house; Reuben Daniel age 30, blacksmith; Eliza Daniel age 23; Melvin S. Daniel age 6; Evelyn Daniel age 4

--1870 Census, p.236A, Little Falls: Margaret Crane, age 52; Reuben Daniel, age 30, b. NY, blacksmith; Eliza Daniel, age 23, b. NJ; Melvin S. Daniel, age 6, b. NJ; Evelyn Daniel, age 4, b. NJ

--CHILDREN of Linus Crane and Margaret Yorks:

Warren S.   b. abt 1841; d. May 28, 1876

            --1860 Census, p. 1060 9 Wd, New York City: Warren Crane, age 18, b. NJ, boarder;apprentice to carpenter

Leah Elizabeth b. abt 1846; m. Reuben Daniel (q.v.)

Charles   b. March 4, 1849; d. September 15, 1851

- - - - -

Crane, Francis H.*   b. (abt. 1834)
         d. (aft 1880)
wife, Anna Maria*(Post) b. (abt. 1837)
         d. (aft. 1880)

CRANE, WILBUR   b. 1862 (November 10, 1862)
(gmnj)   d. 1881

Notes:
--1860 Census, p.118A, Caldwell Twp: Francis H. Crane, age 26, carpenter; Anna M. age 23; Alice, age 3
--1870 Census, p.118A, 7 Wd., Newark: Francis Crane, age 38, carpenter; Ann M. age 33; Alice, age 13; Alonzo, age 9; Wilbur, age 7
--1880 Census: p.418A, Newark, NJ: Francis F. Crane, age 47, b. NY, carpenter, parents b. NJ; Annie M. wife, age 42, b. NJ; Alonzo, son, age 19, b. NJ, bookkeeper; Wilbur, son, age 17, b. NJ, clerk in store; Leah, daughter age 9, b. NJ.;
Notes:
--CHILDREN of Francis H. Crane and Anna Maria Post:
Alice, b. abt. 1857
Alonzo, b. abt. 1861
Wilbur, b. November 10, 1862; d. 1881
Leah, b. abt. 1871

- - - - -

DANIEL

DANIEL, (Reuben), monument
(Includes Linus Crane family, q.v.)

Daniel, Reuben**   b. (January 1839)
         d. (aft. 1920)
wife, Leah Elizabeth**(Crane)

b. (August 1846)
d. (aft. 1920)

Notes:
--Reuben was son of Samuel Daniel and Mary (or Elizabeth) Isherwood.
--Leah Elizabeth was dau. of Linus Crane (q.v.) and Elizabeth Yorks.
--(?)1860 Census, p.693, Marshall, Oneida Co., NY: Elijah Conger, age 61, farmer; Sarah, age 54; Reuben Daniel, age 20, farm labor
--1870 Census, p.236, Little Falls Twp: Margaret Crane, age 52, keeping house; Reuben Daniel, age 30, blacksmith, b. NY; Eliza Daniel age 23; Melvin S. Daniel age 6; Evelyn Daniel age 4
--1880 Census, p.187A, Little Falls: 'Reuben Daniels' age 41, b. NY, parents b. England; Elizabeth, age 33, b. NJ; Melvin, age 15; Eveline, age 13; Libbie, age 9; Warren, age 1; 2 boarders
--1900 Census, p.103A, Little Falls: Ruben Daniels, b. January 1839, m. 37 yr, b. NY, parents b. England, road contractor; Elizabeth b. August 1846, 4 born 4 living; Warren C., b. December 1878, road contractor
--1910 Census, p.224A, Little Falls Twp: Reuben Daniel, b. NY, parents b. England; age 71, road inspector, m. 46 years; Lea E., wife, age 63, b. NJ, parents b. NJ; 4 born, 4 living
--1920 Census, p.138B, Little Falls: Reuben Daniels, age 80, blacksmith, b. NY, parents b. England; Elizabeth L., age 73, b. NJ;
--CHILDREN of Reuben Daniel and Leah Elizabeth Crane:
Melvin S.   b. August 1864; m. Mary .....
          --1900 Census, p. 101A, Little Falls: Melvin Daniels, b. August 1864,NJ; blacksmith; Mary, b. Mary 1866, NJ; m. 13 yr. 6 born 6 living; Arthur, b. May 1887; Reuben, b. December 1888; Harold, b. November 18891;

Melvin, b. December 1893; Lynus, b. May 1896; Cecelia b. Dec. 1898
--1910 Census, p.200A, Little Falls: Melvin S. Daniels, age 45, m.24 yr; Marie E. age 43, 6 born 6 living; Cecelia, age 11; Reuben age 21; Harold age 17; Melvin age 16; Lynus, age 13
--1920 Census, p.114A&B, Little Falls: Melvin S. Daniel, age 55, blacksmith; Mary E. age 53; Melvin Jr. age 24; Cecelia, age 21

Evelyn   b. abt 1866
Elizabeth "Libbie" b. abt. 1871
Warren C.,   b. abt 1879
--1930 Census, p.272A, Little Falls: Warren C. Daniel, age 51; real estate dealer, b. NJ; Sylvia L., wife, age 48, Kansas; Dwight C., age 20, b. NJ

- - - - -

DAVIS

DAVIS, ROZIL (Roswell?)   b. (abt. 1764)
                            d. September 10, 1804

"in 40th year"

wife, Mehetabel** (Cobb)   b.(abt. 1769?)
                            d. (December 26, 1813?)
son, BENJAMIN   b. (March 9, 1793)
(gmnj)   d. April 21, 1794

"Aged 1. 1. 12"

Notes:
--NJ Estate Inventory, #10402G, 1806
--Rozil Davis m. May 9, 1790, Fairfield, Mehetabel Cobb.

--?Mehetable m. #2 (Jacob VanNess?)
--?"David Roset and Trintje Spyr bapt. son, Abraham, August 11, 1728" Second River Ref. Church, Belleville, NJ
--?"Davidt Roset and Tryntie Spier bapt. Davidt, April 1734, Second River Ch."
--CHILDREN of Rozil Davis and Mehetable Cobb:
Benjamin   b. March 9, 1793; d. April 21, 1794

- - - - -

DE BAUN

DEBAUN, ABRAM   b. February 8, 1856
(gmnj)   d. August 21, 1922
wife, Mary Elizabeth**(Peer) b. (abt. April 1859)
                                 d. (after 1930)

Notes:
--Abraham was son of Jacob H. DeBaun(q.v.) and Elizabeth Catharine Ackerman.
--Abraham m. February 12, 1881, Mary Elizabeth Peer, daughter of Jacob B. (q.v.)and Mary C. Peer of Cedar Grove.
--1870 Census, p.226A, Franklin Twp., Bergen Co.: Jacob DeBaun, age 45, farmer; Catherine, age 44; Jacob H., age 16; Abraham, age 14; Charles, age 8
--1880 Census:p.205A, Manchester, Passaic Co., NJ: Jacob H. DeBaun, age 26, b. NJ, carpenter; Rachel, wife, age 25, b. NJ; Walter, son, age 4, NJ; Abraham, brother, single, age 24, b. NJ, carpenter
--1900 Census: #87, Verona/Cedar Grove: Abram DeBaun, age 44, m. 18 yrs., gardener; Lizzie, b. April 1859, age 41;Charles A., son,age 16;Bertie C., son, age 15; Ernest, son age 8
--1910 Census: #10, p. 15A, Cedar Grove: Abraham DeBaun, age 54, farmer; M. Elizabeth, age 51; Charles A., age 26, labor, farmer; Ernest, age 18, labor, farmer;Adj. to son, Albert

--1920 Census, p.163A, Cedar Grove: Abram DeBaun, age 63, farmer; Mary L. age 60; Charles A. age 36; Ernest age 25
--1930 Census, Sheet 11B, Cedar Grove: Mary E. DeBaun, age 71, widow; Charles A., son, age 46, mgr, truck driver at farm; Ernest, son,age 38, assistant manager at farm
--CHILDREN of Abraham DeBaun and Elizabeth Ackerman:
Charles A.   b. November 10, 1883
Albert C.   b. February 14, 1885 (q.v.)
Ernest   b. February 6, 1892
    --1930 Census, Sheet 11B, Cedar Grove:
    Mary E. DeBaun,age 71,widow;
    Charles A. son, age 46, mgr, truck driver at
    farm; Ernest, son,age 39, assistant manager
    at farm.

- - - - -

DEBAUN, ALBERT   b. February 14, 1885
(gmnj)   d. March 6, 1934
wife, WINNIE (Barnett)   b. (abt. 1885)
   d. (aft. 1930)

Notes:
--Albert C. was son of Abraham DeBaun (q.v.) and Mary Elizabeth Peer.
--Albert m. June 12, 1907, Winnie Barnett of Brooklyn, New York
--1920 Census:p.163A, #11, Cedar Grove: Albert J. DeBaun, age 35, caretaker, county hospital; Minnie, age 35, b. New York; Albert, age 11;Adj. to father, Abraham DeBaun, q.v.
--1930 Census Sheet 12A, Cedar Grove: Albert DeBaun, age 45, operator of .... plant at county hospital; Minnie, age 46, b. NY; Albert, son, age 21, clerk at insurance office
--CHILD of Albert DeBaun and Winnie Barnett:
--Albert C.,Jr. b. June 3, 1908

- - - - -

Debaun, CHARLES   b. (November 10, 1883)
(ougheltree)   d. (Aft. 1930)

Notes:

--Charles A. Debaun, b. November 10, 1883, son of Abraham DeBaun(q.v.) and Mary Elizabeth Peer.

--1900 Census: #87, Verona/Cedar Grove: Abram DeBaun, age 44, m. 18 yrs., gardener; Lizzie, b. April 1859, age 41;Charles A., son,age 16;Bertie C., son, age 15; Ernest, son age 8

--1910 Census: #10, p. 15A, Cedar Grove: Abraham DeBaun, age 54, farmer; M. Elizabeth, age 51; Charles A., age 26, labor, farmer; Ernest, age 18, labor, farmer;Adj. to son, Albert

--1920 Census, p.163A, Cedar Grove: Abram DeBaun, age 63, farmer; Mary L. age 60; Charles A. age 36; Ernest age 25

--1930 Census, Sheet 11B, Cedar Grove: Mary E. DeBaun, age 71, widow; Charles A., son, age 46, mgr, truck driver at farm; Ernest, son,age 38, assistant manager at farm

--1930 Census, Sheet 11B, Cedar Grove: Mary E. DeBaun, age 71, widow; Charles A., son,age 46, mgr. truck driver at farm; Ernest, son, age 38, assistant manager at farm

- - - - -

DEBAUN, JACOB H. b. (February 11, 1822)
(gmnj)   d. July 11, 1893

"Aged 71 yrs. & 5 mos."

wife, ELIZA CATHARINE (Ackerman)
(gmnj)   b. (November 23, 1823)
     d. July 13, 1889

"Aged 65.7.19"

Notes:

--Jacob (J.)was son of Johannes P. DeBaun and Maria Storms.

--Jacob m. January 22, 1843, Wyckoff, Bergen Co., NJ, Elizabeth Catharine Ackerman, daughter of James J. Ackerman and Helen Storms of Franklin Twp.Bergen Co. The marriage record listed him "of Saddle River".

--1870 Census, p.226A, Franklin Twp.,Bergen Co:Jacob DeBaun, age 45, farmer; Catherine age 44; Jacob H. age 16; Abraham, age 14; Charles, age 8; Adj. to Henry J. Storms, age 27, farmer

--1880 Census:, 431B, Dist. 2, Caldwell, NJ: Jacob DeBaun, age 55, b. NJ, general mason; Eliza Catharine, wife, age 54, b. NJ; Charles, son, age 18, b. NJ, works on farm

--CHILDREN of Jacob H.DeBaun and Elizabeth Ackerman:

John J.	b. 1843; d. February 1918; m. Mary Jane Peterson
	--1880 Census, p.275A, Franklin, Bergen Co; John J. DeBaun, age 36, b. NJ, carpenter; Mary J., wife, age 34, b. NJ; Elizabeth J., dau., age 3, b. NJ
	--1900 Census, p.118, Hohokus, Bergen Co.: John J. DeBaun, b. June 1843, farmer; mary J. b. September 1844, m.37 yrs, 6 born 6 living; Fred b. March 1880, farm labor
	--1910 Census, p. 120B, Hohokus, Bergen Co.: John DeBaun, age 66, farmer, m. 46 yrs; Mary J., age 64, 2 born 2 living; Fred, age 25, labor
Ellen Jane	b. May 21, 1845; m. #1, Daniel VanZile; m. #2, Cornelius VanNess m. #3, John Henry Duryea
Cornelius D.	b.
James	b. Oct. 4, 1849; d. September 8, 1917; m. Rachel Catharine Vanderbeck

--?1910 Census, p.234A, 5Wd.Paterson, James DeBaun, age 64, widower, carpenter; Ida Doughty, dau., age 35, widow; James Doughty, grandson,a ge 16

Gerritt F. b. 1849, d. March 9, 1860

Jacob H. b. 1854; d. 1891; m. Rachel Bertholf

--1870 Census, p.226A, Franklin Twp.,Bergen Co:Jacob DeBaun, age 45, farmer; Catherine age 44; Jacob H. age 16; Abraham, age 14; Charles, age 8; Adj. to Henry J. Storms, age 27, farmer

--1880 Census, p.205A, Manchester,Passaic Co., NJ: Jacob H. DeBaun, age 26, b. NJ; carpenter; Rachel, wife, age 25, b. NJ; Walter, son, age 4, b. NJ; Abraham(q.v.), brother, age 24, b. NJ, carpenter

Abraham(qv) b. February 8, 1856; d. August 21, 1922 m. Mary Elizabeth Peer

--1870 Census, p.226A, Franklin Twp.,Bergen Co:Jacob DeBaun, age 45, farmer; Catherine age 44; Jacob H. age 16; Abraham, age 14; Charles, age 8; Adj. to Henry J. Storms, age 27, farmer

--1880 Census, p.205 A, Manchester, Passaic Co., NJ; Abraham DeBaun, age 24, b. NJ, carpenter; at res. of his brother, Jacob H. Debaun (q.v.)

--1910 Census, p.15A,Cedar Grove: Abraham DeBaun, age 54, farmer; M. Elizabeth, age 51; Charles A., age 26, labor, farmer; Ernest, age 18, labor, farmer.

Charles b. February 1, 1862,d. November 18, 1933; m. #1 Estella Husk; m. #2, Mrs. Rita Alexander

--1900 Census, p.225, Caldwell Twp: Charles DeBaun, b. Feb.1862, farmer, 2 born 2 living;

Estella, b. September 1863, m. 17yr.; Frank,
b. Dec. 1887; William W. b. August 1892
--1910 Census,p.287A, Caldwell Twp:
CharlesDeBaun, age 48, m. 27 yrs; Frank, age
21,and Ruth F. age 17, dau in law, m. 1 yr;
William W., age 17
--1920 Census, p.126A, Little Falls, Charles
DeBaun, age 57; Estella, age 56

- - - - -

DEGRAW

DEGRAW, CHARLES   b.
(gmnj)   d. October 28, 1888

Co. B,3rd Regt. N.J. CAV

Notes:
--He served in the Civil War as a private in Co. B., 3rd
Regiment, NJ Calvary; enlisted December 25, 1863;
discharged August 8, 1865.
--See: Sons of Union Veterans of the Civil War.

- - - - -

DEGRAW, EDWARD   b.
(npfh)   d. November, 1928
                  (bur. November 5, 1928)

Notes:
--(?)1910 Census, p.199A, Little Falls Twp: Rachel A.
DeGraw, age 63, widow; Frank, son, age 32; Edward, son,
age 24; Margaret, dau., age 22; Irving, son, age 20;
Elizabeth, dau., age 16
--(?)1920 Census, p.115A, Little Falls: Rachel DeGraw, age
71, widow, Elizabeth (Wayne?), dau., age 26; Arie

(Wayne?), son in law, age 26, b. Argentina, parents b. Holland, chief clerk RR; Elizabeth (Wayne?), granddaughter, age 1 yr and 9 months;Edward DeGraw, son, age 32, single, machinist. (adj. to Frank DeGraw, machinist, age 43; Anna M. age 26, b. NJ; Frank Jr. age 5; Margaret E. age 1 yr and 3 months.)
--(?)1930 Census, p.264B, Little Falls: Rachel A. DeGraw, age 81, widow; Orris M. Meyne, age 36, son-in-law, rr clerk, b. South America; Elizabeth R., dau., age 36, b. NJ; Elizabeth L. granddaughter, age 12; Margaret Brandan, age 41, widow, daughter

- - - - -

DEGRAW, ELIZABETH   b.
(npfh)   d. July, 1913
                     (bur. July 30, 1913)

Notes:
--(?)1880 Census, p.188C, Little Falls, NJ: John Degraw, age 39, b. NJ,farmer; Elizabeth, wife, age 39, b. NJ; William, son, age 15, b. NJ; Alonzo, son, age 11, b. NJ, works in carpet factory; Charles, son, age 9, b. NJ
--(?)1880 Census, p.188D, Little Falls, NJ: Mary DeGraw, age 6; John DeGraw, age 5; Annie DeGraw, age 3; Elizabeth DeGraw, age 6 months; at res. of John and Annie Cook.(next page to John and Elizabeth DeGraw.)
--(?)1910 Census, p.212A,Little Falls Twp: Elizabeth DeGraw, age 63,b. NJ, widow, 10 born 9 living; Joseph, son, age 23,mason; Clara dau., age 30
--1910 Census, p.199A, Little Falls Twp: Rachel A. DeGraw, age 63, widow; Frank, son, age 32; Edward, son, age 24; Margaret, dau., age 22; Irving, son, age 20; Elizabeth, dau., age 16

- - - - -

DEGRAW, JOSEPH   b.
(npfh)   d. April, 1908
     (bur. April 21, 1908)

Notes:
--(?)1910 Census, p.212A,Little Falls Twp: Elizabeth
DeGraw, age 63,b. NJ, widow, 10 born 9 living; Joseph, son,
age 23,mason; Clara dau., age 30

- - - - -

DEGRAW, MYRTLE   b.
(npfh)   d. July, 1910
     (bur. July 12, 1910)

Notes:
--(?)1910 Census, p.213B. Hanover Twp, Morris Co: John H.
Conkling, age 38, m. 10 yr, b. NJ; Adelia, age 27, 1 born 0
living; Myrtle DeGraw, age 6, b. NJ, sister-in-law

- - - - -

DEGRAW, RAYMOND   b.
(npfh)   d. October, 1911
     (bur. October 19, 1911)

Notes:

- - - - -

DELANY

DELANY, Charles*   b.
(gmnj)   d.
wife, JANE   b. (May 8, 1803)
(gmnj)   d. December 2, 1829

"Aged 26.6.25"

daughter, MARGARET CAROLINE
(gmnj)   b. (October 6, 1823)
                               d. March 27, 1829

"Aged 5.5.21"

daughter, SARAH JANE   b. (April 26, 1828)
(gmnj)   d. September 26, 1829

"Aged 1 year & 5 mos."

Notes:
--(?)1859 Paterson City Directory:Edward Delany, laborer,
res. 22 Ward; James Delany, blacksmith, 52 Market St.;
Patrick Delany, laborer, 399 Main Street
--(?)1860 Census: #76, Manchester, Passaic Co.,NJ: John
Delany, age 60, laborer, b. Ireland.

- - - - -

DEL FOSSE

Del Fosse, Ernest*   b. (abt. 1882)
                             d. (bef. 1930)
wife, Hedwig*(Stackelberg)   b. (abt. 1885)
                             d. (aft. 1930)
son, FRANK   b. (July 27, 1907?)
                             d. (November 1974?)

"Memorial Garden"

Notes:
--This stone was observed in December, 2002
--Frank Del Fosse, b. July 27 1907; d. November 1974
(Social Security Death Index)

--(?)1880 Census, p.402C, Sioux City, Woodbury Co. Iowa: E. C. Delfosse, age 58, b. France, professor of languages; H., wife, age 33, b. CT, school teacher; Edward, son, age 8, b. CT

--1920 Census, #178, Cedar Grove: Ernest DelFosse, age 38, salesman, b. Maine, father b. France, mother b. Scotland; Hedwig, age 36, b. NY, parents b. Sweden; Frank, age 12; Oscar Stackelberg, father-in-law, age 82, b. Sweden; Heda Stackelberg, mother-in-law, age 75, b. Sweden; Tura Stackelberg, age 38, sister-in-law,

--1930 Census, Sheet 9B, Cedar Grove: Hedwig DelFosse, age 45, widow, real estate $10,000, b. NY, parents b. Sweden; Frank E. son, age 22, b. NY, parents b. NY, assistant cashier at bank

--CHILDREN of Ernest DelFosse and Hedwig Stackelberg:
Frank E.   b. July 27, 1907? d. November 1974?

- - - - -

DENT

DENT, John*   b. (abt. 1815)
(gmnj)   d. (aft. 1880)
wife,RUTH ANN(Mitchell)
                   b. (November 28, 1822)
(gmnj)   d. March 29, 1872. Age 49.4.1

"Age 49.4.1"

Notes:
--Ruth Ann was married first to Halvor Poulsson, q.v.
--John Dent m. March 11, 1859, Newark, Anna Poulsson.
--1860 Census: p.63D, 1st Ward, Newark; John Dent, age 40, barber, b. England; Anna, age 36, b. NY; Ingeborg, age 13, b. NY; Laura, age 8, b. NY; Anna 6, b. NJ(daughters of Halvor Poulsson?); Cornelius Jacobus, age 17, apprentice barber

--1870 Census, p.167A, 8 Wd.Newark: John Dent, age 56, barber, b. England; Anna, age 48; John, age 9

--1880 Census: p.8D, Newark, NJ: John Dent, widower, age 64, b. England, boarder, no occupation listed.(at boarding house of Michael Loeser)

--CHILDREN of John Dent and Anna Poulsson:

John   b. abt. 1861

- - - - -

DOREMUS

Doremus, Ann
(gmnj)
m. Isaac Stor (q.v.)

- - - - -

DOREMUS, BENJAMIN R. b. December 13, 1822
(gmnj)   d. May 3, 1891

Notes:

--Benjamin Roome Doremus was son of Thomas Doremus and Elisabeth Wilkison of Pompton, Morris County, NJ.

--1860 Census, p.1036, Acquackanonk Twp: Peter A. Sisco, age 42, hotel keeper; Mary, age 36; Thomas age 18; Horace age 10; Benjamin age 7; William age 4; Loretta age 4 months

--1870 Census:p.203A, 8 Wd, Newark, NJ: Peter A. Sisco, age 51, b. NJ, 'keeps Clifton House'; Elizabeth age 47; William age 14; Lauretta, age 10; Benjamin Doremus, age 44, laborer

--1880 Census: p.157A, Newark, NJ: Peter A. Sisco, age 60, b. NJ, health inspector; Elizabeth N., wife, age 56, b. NJ; Benjamin A., son, son, age 27, brick mason; William A., son, age 24, machinist; Laura, daughter, age 20; Benjamin

Doremus, brother-in-law, single, age 54, b. NJ, policeman; Frank Mandeville, other, single, age 24, news agent.

- - - - -

Doremus, Catherine
m. Isaac Sloat (q.v.)

- - - - -

DOREMUS, Cornelius E.**   b. (June 6, 1791)
                             d. (abt. October 1841)
wife, Leah (Jacobus)**   b. (abt. 1797)
                             d. (aft. 1860)
son, Garret**   b. July 18,1817
                             d. (abt. 1829)
son, James**   b. December 9, 1827
                             d. (abt. 1892)

Notes:

--Cornelius E. Doremus was son of Egbert Doremus and Geesje Jacobus. By his father's 1817 will, he inherited "the dwelling house, barn, cattle, etc., and the homestead at Cedar Grove, 55 acres."

--Cornelius E. Doremus m. Leah/Letty/Aaltje Jacobus

--1841 Will of Cornelius E. Doremus: ...whole estate to his wife during widowhood; his son James "to be brought up in habits of industry and sobriety." and to have the estate after his mother's death.

--1850 Census: #117, Caldwell: Letty Doremus, age 53, real estate $1000; James Doremus, age 23, farmer

--1860 Census, #420, Caldwell: James Doremus, age 30, farmer; Letty, age 63

--CHILDREN of Cornelius E. Doremus and Leah Jacobus:

Garret   b. July 18, 1817, bapt. August 31,1817
                d. abt. age 12 years
James   b. December 9, 1827; d. abt. 1892
                bapt. May 4, 1828, Ref. Dutch Church,

Stone House Plains, Bloomfield, NJ
"He is said to have been a young man of
exemplary character, but having formed an
attachment which was unreciprocated; after
the marriage of the young lady he was very
much depressed and became feeble-minded.
He boarded with his relative, Cornelius
Supenor,(q.v.) at Cedar Grove, Essex Co.,
N.J."(Eberhart, p.96) (Cornelius Supenor
was m. to Mary Post, dau. of Francis R. Post
and Elenor Doremus,aunt of James Doremus)
--1870 Census: #500 Caldwell/Cedar Grove:
James Doremus, age 40, no occupation; at
res. of Cornelius Supenor(q.v.)
--1880 Census:p.417A, #324, Caldwell/
Cedar Grove: James Doremus, single, age
52, no occupation; at res. of Cornelius
Supenor(q.v.)

- - - - -

Doremus, Elsy
m. Garret Yorks (q.v.)

- - - - -

Doremus, Jane
m. John Moon (q.v.)

- - - - -

Doremus, Leah
m. Francis R. Post (q.v.)

- - - - -

DOREMUS, PETER C.   b. ((March 30, 1768)
(gmnj)   d. August 31, 1820

"Aged 52.5.1"

wife, HANNAH (Norwood) b. (November 29, 1770)
(gmnj)   d. February 19, 1856

"Aged 85.2.20"

son, CORNELIS (P.)   b. (April 12, 1799)
(gmnj)   d. August 8, 1862
(same stone as Peter C. Doremus)

"Aged 63.3.26"

daughter, ELIZABETH   b. November 12, 1794
(gmnj)   d. August 28, 1876
(same stone as Peter C. Doremus)

Notes:
--NJ Estate Inventoryof Peter Doremus #11251G,1820
--Peter/Pieter was son of Cornelis Doremus and Elsje
Egbertse. "He occupied the house which had been his
father's at Cedar Grove, but as it had fallen into decay, he
tore it down and built a new one, his wife assisting in
carrying the materials from the old to the new, in a
wheelbarrow. The product of their joint labors was a house
of stone and wood, a story and a half high, with a one-story
extension, with the ceiling beams standing out prominently,
the workmanship rough, but so substantial that after a
century the building seems good for another hundred years
(as of 1897). It stands (at 32 Peckmantown Road) near the
crossing of the Caldwell Railroad and the main road, at
Cedar Grove Centre station." (*The Doremus Family in
America*, E. W. Eberhart). The house was inherited by

Emma Sloat through her mother Catharine Doremus Sloat.
The house was sold August 13, 1906 to Frank Farron.
--Peter m. December 28,1793, Caldwell Presbyterian
Church, Hannah Norwood.(NJ Estate Inventory, 14991G,
1857(
--"Hannah Norwood Doremus recalled seeing George
Washington and his staff pass the country school where she
was a pupil."
--CHILDREN of Pieter C. Doremus and Hannah Norwood:
Elizabeth "Batty"**

> b. November 12, 1794, d. aft. 1870;unm.
> --Elizabeth, "Batty" died unmarried
> and was only about four feet high." (*The
> Doremus Family ofAmerica*, E. W. Eberhart)
> One report says Elizabeth died of a snake
> bite.
> --1870 Census, p.136B, Caldwell: Isaac Sloat,
> age 56, farmer; Catherine, age 61; Emma, age
> 23, seamstress; Theodore, age 21, farmer;
> Lavinia, age 18; Elizabeth Doremus, age 75

Elsje**   b. abt. 1797, m. George Personett (q.v.)

Cornelius P.   b. April 12 1799, d. August 8, 1862, unm.

> --Cause of death "palsy"
> --1860 Census: p.112A, Caldwell/Cedar
> Grove: Cornelius P. Doremus, age 61, farmer;
> Rachel, age 55,sister; Elizabeth,sister age 67
> --Cornelius, "died unmarried at Caldwell
> Twp. The Will of Cornelius P. Doremus, of
> Caldwell Township, dated July 30, 1862,
> witnessed by Patrick Marley and Aaron
> McCloud, of Cedar Grove, was proved
> October 21, 1862. He directed his executors
> to sell his whole estate, pay $300 to his sister
> Rachel Benjamin; invest the residue and pay
> the interest to his sister Elizabeth during her
> lifetime and after her death to divide the same
> among his three sisters--Rachel Benjamin,

Elcy Personett and Catharine Sloat. Executors
David H. Doremus of Paterson, and Stephen
Personett of Verona"(NJ Will #15613G,
1862) (*The Doremus Family of America*, E.
W. Eberhart)

Rachel   b. Sept. 11,1802;m.Cyrus T. Brokaw(q.v.)

Catharine   b. October 29, 1808, m. Isaac Sloat (q.v.)

- - - - -

Doremus, Sarah
m. John R. Neafie (q.v.)

- - - - -

DOREMUS, THOMAS   b. (bapt. April 1687)
(Eberhart, p.69-70)   d.

"Age 52.5.0"

wife, ANNEKE(Ackerman)   b. (bapt. December 27, 1691)
                                   d.

Notes:
--Thomas was son of Cornelis Doremus and Jannetje Joris.
--Thomas Doremus m. Anneke Abramse Ackerman, October
4,1712, Hackensack, NJ; daughter of Abraham Ackerman
and Aeltie VanLaer.
--"Thomas settled near Cedar Grove, at the headwaters of the
Peckamin River on the portion of the Garret Mountain tract
given to him by his father's will. It included at least part, of
the Cedar Grove mill sites." (*The Doremus Family in
America*, pp.69,70)
--"I can remember seeing the Doremus plot there (Cedar
Grove Cemetery) with brownstone markers and a fence
around it." (statement by Helen T. Carpenter, *Early Cedar
Grove*, p.34)

--CHILDREN of Thomas Doremus and Anneke Ackerman:

Cornelis	b. April 16, 1714, d. March 8, 1803,m. Antje Yong
Abraham	b. August 31, 1716, m. Helena VanHouten
Johannes	b. March 29, 1719, m. Franscyntje Mouritzen
Golijn	b. March 20, 1722, m. Elisabeth Yong
Aeltje	b. December 14, 1725, m. John Fransisco
Thomas(q.v.)	b. May 9, 1730

- - - - -

DOREMUS, THOMAS   b. May 9, 1730
(Eberhart, pp.69-70)   d. October 7, 1801
wife, #1,Sarah** (Sanford)   b.
   d.
wife, #2, Margrietje** (Vanderhoof)
   b.
   d. (December 31, 1829)

wife #3, Margrietje**(Riker) b. (Abt. 1759)
(widow of Simeon VanNess) d. (December 31, 1829)

Notes:
--He was son of Thomas Doremus and Anneke Abramse Ackerman.
--Thomas Doremus m. #1, Sarah Sanford
--Thomas Doremus m. #2, Margrietje VanDerhoof
--Thomas Doremus m. #3, Margrietje Ryker, widow of Simeon VanNess
--He served in the Militia from Essex County during the Revolution. He was later a captain and then, a major.
--"He owned the southwesterly corner of the Acquackanonk Mountain land, a rectangular tract of about 220 acres on the Peckamin River."
--CHILDREN of Thomas Doremus and Sarah Sanford:

Goline	b. October 14, 1754, m. Catherine Farver
Anneke	b. May 17, 1756, m. Uldrick VanRypen

Aeltje	b. October 15, 1759, m. John Hopkins
Thomas	b. April 21, 1760, m.Elizabeth VanHouten
Pieter	b. September 11, 1764, m. Catherine Doremus

--1850 Census #123 Caldwell: Peter T. Doremus, age 86, farmer; real estate $1000; Catherine, age 71; Caroline Farver, age 13, b. New York

Marytje	b. March 2, 1767, m. Henry VanNess
Cornelius	b. July 17, 1769, m. Jane VanOrden
Jennetje	b. January 14, 1772, m. Merselis VanGiesen
Elisabeth	b. May 13, 1774, m. Simon VanNess
Lena	b. July 17, 1776
William	b. June 7, 1778;
	m. #1, Gertrude VanHouten;
	m. #2, Mrs. Elizabeth Lash
Abraham	b. June 22, 1781/June 19, 1779, m. Elsje Bush

--CHILD of Thomas Doremus and Margrietje VanDerhoof:

Dirck	b. April 14, 1789

- - - - -

DOREMUS, THOMAS   b. April 21, 1760
(Eberhart)   d. (abt. December 15, 1799)
wife, Elizabeth*(VanHouten) b. (March 14, 1764
                d. (May 8, 1846)

Notes:
--"He is interred in the ancient burying ground at Cedar Grove beside his father and grandfather." (*The Doremus Family in America*, pp.69,70) He was killed by his gun going off accidentally.
--Thomas is son of Capt. Thomas Doremus (q.v.)and Sarah Sandford; grandson of Thomas Doremus (q.v.) and Anneken Abramse Ackerman

--Thomas m. Elizabeth VanHouten, b. March 14, 1764, d. May 8, 1846, daughter of Cornelius VanHouten and Marretje VanGiesen. She m. #2, Barent Simonson.

--CHILDREN of Thomas Doremus and Eliz. VanHouten:

Marretye	b. December 10,1788;d. June 12, 1869; m. Jeptha Crane, b. July 17,1780,d. August 23, 1815; son of Aaron Crane and Tabitha Baldwin; his will mentions daughter, Jane, "under 21".
Cornelius	b. July 20, 1791;d. Nov. 8, 1875; bur. Rosedale Cemetery, Orange, NJ m. Sarah Harrison; children: Joseph, b. 1817; Ann Elizabeth b. abt. 1819; Thomas, b. December 20, 1821; Horace, b. April 23, 1824; Hannah Charlotte, b. abt August 1826; Mary, b. June 1833; Elizabeth
Daniel	b. August 30, 1794, d. War of 1812, United States Navy
Sarah	b. June 15, 1797; d. October 15, 1869; m. John R. Neafie (q.v.)
Elisabeth	b. November 26, 1799;d. January 29, 1875; m. Aaron Baldwin, b. July 12, 1798; children: Stephen, Joseph; Emeline --1860 Census, p.720, 9 Wd Newark: Aaron Baldwin, age 61, b. NJ, grocer; Elizabeth, age 60,b.NJ; Sarah, age 17, b. NY --1870 Census, p.299A, 9Wd Newark: Aaron Baldwin, age 72; Elizabeth, age 70 --(?)1880 Census, p.117A, Orange: Anna B. Francisco, widow, age 59, b. NJ; Aaron Baldwin, uncle, age 81

- - - - -

DOUGHERTY

DOUGHERTY, Charles A.*
1st wife, ADA E. (Jacobus)   b. March 30, 1870
(gmnj)   d. December 5, 1899

*"Daughter of William G & Sarah
A. Jacobus
wife of
Chas. A. Doughtery"*

Notes:
--Ada E. Jacobus was daughter of William Jacobus and
Sarah Ann Courter.
--Charles A. Dougherty was b. June 24, 1858, Pennsylvania;
d. March 5, 1933; buried Hillside Cemetery, Fairfield,NJ
--Charles Dougherty m. #1, Ada E. Jacobus; dau. of William
Jacobus and Sarah Ann Courter
--Charles Dougherty m. #2, Bertha O. Courter. She was b.
January 15, 1869 and d. May 2, 1892, bur. Hillside
Cemetery, Fairfield,NJ; dau. of Charles Courter and Mary
Elizabeth Pierce.
--Charles Dougherty m. #3, Loretta Cole. She was b. March
8, 1860 and d. March 12, 1933, bur. Hillside Cemetery,
Fairfield; dau. of John R. Cole and Hannah M. .....
--1880 Census:p.413B, #250 Caldwell, NJ: William B.
Allen, age 66, b. NJ, father b. CT, mother b. NJ, farmer;
Margaret, wife, age 60, b. NJ; Charles H. Jacobus,
son-in-law, age 34, b. NJ, farmer; Sarah S. Jacobus,
daughter, age 36, b. NJ; Charles A. Dougherty, other, single,
age 21, b. PA, laborer on farm, parents b. Ireland
--1880 Census: p.586D, Westfield, Union Co., NJ: Bertha
Courter, daughter age 12, b. NJ; res. with her parents
Charles, age 37, farmer, b. NJ and Mary E. wife, age 35, b.
NJ

--1880 Census: p.421A, Dist. 2, Caldwell, NJ: Lauretta Cole, daughter, single, age 20, b. NJ; at res. of her parents, John R. Cole, age 44, b. NJ, farmer and Hannah M. age 41, b. NJ

--(?)1880 Census, p.183A, Little Falls, NJ. Sarah Doherety, single, age 20, b. PA, father b. Ireland, mother b. PA; servant; at res of Benjamin J. and Sarah M. Crane.(?Sister of Charles Dougherty)

--1900 Census #292 Caldwell Twp: Charles A. Dougherty, b. June 1858, age 41, widower, farmer, b. PA, parents b. Ireland; Ethel dau., b. November 1894; Sarah A. Jacobus, b. December 1841, m. 37 yrs. 4 born 3 living,mother-in-law

--1910 Census: West Caldwell: Charles Dougherty, age 51, widower; Ethel M., age 15; Sarah A. (Courter) Jacobus, mother-in-law, age 67

--CHILD of Charles A. Dougherty and Ada E. Jacobus: Ethel Marie   b. November 2, 1895

- - - - -

DUCHER

DUCHER, WILLIAM b. (abt. 1795) Scotland
(gmnj)   d. July 29, 1861

"Aged 66 yrs."

wife, ELIZABETH   b. (abt. 1795) Scotland
(gmnj)   d. June 22, 1867

"Aged 72 years:
"Natives of Scotland"

Notes:
--(?)1850 Census #91 Caldwell: William Duker, age 51, carpet weaver, b. Scotland
--(?)1860 Census #442, Caldwell: William Duker, age 63, farmer, b. Scotland; Elizabeth, age 63, b. Scotland

- - - - -

DUMMGO

DUMMGO, JOSE   b.
(npfh)   d. (no dates)

Notes:
--(?)1860 Census: #141, Acquackanonk, Passaic Co., NJ:
Jacob Dumge, age 18, farm labor, b. Germany; (on farm of
Henry Hillman)

- - - - -

DURK

DURK, LUDWIG   b. (June 1855)
(npfh)   d. October, 1906
                       (bur. October 14, 1906)
wife,Innis*   b. (October 1864)
                       d. (aft. 1900)

Notes:
--1900 Census, p.79, Little Falls: Ludwig Duirk, b. Germany
June 1855, m. 8 yrs, labor at carpet mill; Innis, wife, b. Oct.
1864, Germany; Martha b. June 1896, Pennsylvania
--(?)1900 Census, p.79 Little Falls: William Duirk, b. April
1873, Germany; Artilla, b. November 1865 Germany;
Harman, nephew, b. June 1884, Germany
--(?)1900 Census, p.79A, Little Falls: Charles Duirk, b.
October 1863, Holland, dyer at carpet mill; Augusta, b.
November 1864; Otto b. January 1896; Rose, b. August 1898
--(?)1920 Census, p.126B, Little Falls: Charles Dirk, age 56,
b. Prussia, labor at carpet mill; Augusta, age 55, b. Prussia;
Otto son, age 24, b. NJ; Rosa, dau., age 21, b. NJ; Charles,

age 16, b. NJ; Michael Schimonski(q.v.), father-in-law, age 88, widower, b. Prussia
--(?)1930 Census, p.253A, Singac,Little Falls Twp: Charles Dirk, age 66, b. Germany, carpet mill foreman; Augusta, age 65, b. Germany; Rose M. age 31, b. NJ; Charles F. age 26, b. NJ, accountant at electric company
--CHILDREN of Ludwig Durk and Innis .....:
Martha b. June 1896

- - - - -

DUTCH

DUTCH, PETER   b.
(npfh)   d. February, 1910
     (bur. February 17, 1910)

Notes:
--(?)1930 Census, p.251A, Singac, Little Falls: Peter Dutko, age 38, b. Poland, carpet mill; Mary, age 37, b. Poland; Anna, age 16, b. NJ; Nicholas, age 14; John, age 12; Eva, age 10; Cornelius, age 9; Olga, age 8
--(?)1930 Census, p.256A, Singac, Little Falls: John Dutko (Dutkiewiz?), age 43, b. Austria; Fannie, age 37, b. Austria; William W., age 18, b. Massachusetts; Stephen, age 16, b. NJ; Peter, age 12, b. NJ; Mary, age 11; Paul, age 8; Michael, age 1

- - - - -

EGBERTSON

EGBERTSON, JOHN   b. (abt. 1823)
(gmnj)   d. March 5, 1852

"In 29th year"

wife, Leah*	b.
(gmnj)	d.
daughter, LOUISA MATILDA	
(gmnj)	b. (October 4, 1848)
	d. February 21, 1852

"Aged 3.4.17"

Notes:

--(?)Leah Egbertson, NJ Will #19059G, 1877

--(?)1910 Census, p.60A, 1Wd Paterson: John Egberts, age 41; Katie, age 41, 10 born 6 living; Annie age 17; Walter age 16; Jennie age 15; Ida, age 15; John, age 12; Matilda, age 9 (adj. to Frank S. Hemingway,q.v,)

--CHILDREN of John Egbertson and Leah .....:

Louise Matilda b. October 4, 1848; d. February 21, 1852

- - - - -

Egbertson, RACHEL
(gmnj)
m. William I. Jacobus (q.v.)

- - - - -

ELVER

ELVER, CHARLES	b.
(npfh)	d. March, 1914
	(bur. March 14, 1914)

Notes:

--(?)1900 Census, p.1A, 5Wd,Paterson: Charles 'Elvin', b. April 1855; b. Scotland, silk finisher; Delia b. May 1860 NJ, parents b. Ireland; Andrew b. June 1881, machinist; Katerhine, b. August 1889; Leo b. July 1894; Mary McMann, sister-in-law, b. February 1859, single, silk weaver

--(?)1910 Census, p.280A, 3Wd Paterson: Emil Elver, age 31, b. Germany; Frida, age 24, b. Germany, 0 born 0 living

- - - - -

ETTENBOROUGH

ETTENBOROUGH, THOMAS
(gmnj)   b. (Abt. April 22, 1786)
                                          d. July 22, 1875

"Aged 89 yrs & 3 mos"

wife, Mary**   b. (abt. 1803) England
(Will #21989G,1886)   d. (abt. 1886)

Notes:
--The surrogate division of the estate of David C. Dobbins mentions lands "along Corby Lane, adjoining Thomas Ettenborough's Mill Dam."
--Mary Ettenborough, NJ Will #21989G, 1886
--1840 Census: #240, Caldwell Twp:
--1850 Census: #37 Caldwell Twp: Thomas Ettenborough, age 56, miller, b. England, Real estate value $8,000; Mary, age 46, b. England; William, age 26, miller, b. England; Sarah Ann, age 16, b. NJ; George, age 14, b. NJ; Joseph, age 12, b. NJ; Frances H. age 9, b. NJ; James, age 7, b. NJ; Louis N.(Napoleon) B.(Bonaparte), age 1
--1860 Census: p.109B, Caldwell: Thomas Ettenborough, age 68, miller, b. England; Mary, age 57, b. England; Sarah, age 23; Joseph age 21; Francis, age 17; James, age 15; Lewis, age 10
--1870 Census: p.128A, Caldwell/Cedar Grove: Thomas Ettenborough, age 78, miller, b. England; Mary, age 67, b. England; Louis, age 21

--1880 Census: p.407A, Caldwell, NJ: Mary Ettenborough, mother-in-law, widow, age 77, b. England; res. with dau., Sarah Brooks and her husband, David Brooks.

--CHILDREN of Thomas and Mary Ettenborough:

William   b. abt 1824

--1860 Census, p.90, Dinwiddie P.O.,Dinwiddie Co., VA: Benjamin P. King, age 58, farmer, b. NJ; Sarah age 57; Wm. Ettenbouraugh, age 36, farmer, b. England; Eliza J. age 29, b. NJ; Virginia A., age 3, b. NJ

--1880 Census, p.217C, Rowanty, Dinwiddie Co., VA; William Ettenborough, age 55, general merchant; Eliza, age 50; Isabel, dau., age 20; Frances, dau., age 17

John   b. abt 1828, England; m. 1845,Susan Ann Baldwin, b. NJ.

--1850 Census: #35, Caldwell Twp: John Ettenborough, age 22, shoemaker, b. England; Real estate value $300; Susan Ann, age 24.

--1860 Census p.118B, Caldwell: John Ettenborough, age 33, carpenter, $1000, b. England; Susan Ann, age 31, b. NJ; Alice, age 8; Charles, age 3, two boarders

--1870 Census, p.39A, Belleville: John Ettenborough, age 46, b. England, real estate agent; Ann F. age 41, b. NJ

--1880 Census, p.68C, Newark: Ann Ettenborough, widow, age 53, b. NJ, father b. Ireland, mother b. England; Alice Hanner, dau-in-law, widow, age 28, b. NJ, father b. England, mother b. NJ; Charles Hanner, grandson, age 11, b. NJ; Mary F. Hanner, granddau., age 9, b. NY

Sarah A.   b. abt. 1834, m. David Brooks

--1850 Census #65 Caldwell: David Brooks, age 11, b. England, son; at res. of his parents,

William and Ellen Brooks

--1860 Census, p.116A, Caldwel: William Brooks, age 84, farmer; Catherine Thompkins, age 57; Abraham Brooks, age 50, farmer; David, age 19, carpenter; Mary E. age 25; Rachel A. age 16

--1870 Census p.136A, Caldwell: David Brooks age 29, carpenter; Sarah M. age 30; Ellsworth, age 9; Annie, age 6; Thomas E., age 5; Francis, age 2

--1880 Census, p.407A, Caldwell: David Brooks, age 37, b. NJ, parents b. NJ; carpenter; Sarah A., wife, age 36, b. NJ, Elmer E., son, age 19, b. NJ, clerk in store; Anna E., dau., age 16; Thomas E., son, age 14; Frannie M., dau., age 12, b. NJ; Mary Ettenborough, mother-in-law, age 77, b. England

--1910 Census, p.148A, Verona Twp: David Brooks, age 70, m.48 yr, carpenter; Sarah A., age 71, b. NJ, 4 born 4 living; Anna E., dau., age 40, single, teacher

George   b. abt. 1836

Joseph   b. abt. 1838

Frances H.   b. June 1841, m. 1861,Henry V.N. Jacobus,son of Isaac J. Jacobus

--1870 Census, #521, Caldwell: Henry V.N. Jacobus, age 30, carpenter; Frances, age 26; Alonzo, age 8; Raymond, age 6; Mary A., age 4; adj. to Isaac I. Jacobus

--1880 Census, p.416D, Caldwell, NJ: Henry V.N. Jacobus, age 42, b. NJ, carpenter; Frances A. wife, age 37, b. NJ; Alonzo H., son, age 17, b. NJ; Raymond, son, age 15, b. NJ; Mary E. dau., age 13, b. NJ

--1900 Census p.253, Verona: Henry Jacobus, b. April 1834; Frances b. June 1841;

Alonzo H. b. December 1861, widower;
Phebe A., granddau., b. June 1895
--1910 Census, #41, Cedar Grove: Henry F.
V.N. Jacobus, father, age 72; at res. of
Raymond V.N. Jacobus

James   b. July 1844; m. Alice Voght,dau. of Peter
Voght of Pennsylvania
--1880 Census, p.477D, 7th Ward, Easton,PA:
James Ettenborough, age 37, b. NJ, parents
b. England, machinist; Alice, wife, age 35,
b. PA, parents b. PA; Mary E., dau, age 8,
b. PA; Peter Voght, father-in-law, widower;
age 65, b. PA, laborer
--1900 Census, p.167, 6Wd,Easton,PA: James
Ettenborough, b. July 1844, NJ; Alice, b.
Jan.1845, PA; Mary Clark, dau., b. Oct. 1871;
James S. Clark, grandson b. November 1892;
Elizabeth granddau., b. Feb. 1895
--1910 Census, p.137B, 6Wd.Easton,PA:
James Ettenbourgh, age 65, b. Nj, machinist;
Alice, age 65, b. PA; Sarah Kuns, boarder,
age 65, single, b. PA

Louis N.B.   b. May 6, 1849,d.November 2, 1921,
Wilbur, Washington; m. 1879,Illinois,
Adeline Ann Dodd. He had 8 children b. in
Nebraska and Washington. He owned the first
hotel in Wilbur, Washington. His full name
was Louis Napoleon Bonaparte Ettenborough.
--1910 Census, p.86B, N.Wilbur Pct.,Lincoln
Co., Washington: Louis N. Ettenborough, age
60, b. NJ; hotel keeper; Adaline A., age 54, b.
Illinois; Uriah J., age 22, b. Nebraska, labor at
butcher shop; V.A., dau., age 18, b. WA; Levi
C. age 15, b. WA; Max M. age 12 b. MA

- - - - -

FAIRCHILD

Fairchild, John Jr.	b. (abt. 1797)
(gmnj)	d. (April 1871)
wife, EMILY (Roebuck?)	b. (abt. 1801)
(gmnj)	d. August 29, 1855

"Aged 53 yrs & 9 mos."

son, CLIFFORD	b. (abt. 1834)
(gmnj)	d. January 10, 1844

"age 10"

Notes:
-- John Fairchild, Jr. (or 3rd) was b. abt. 1797 Connecticut and d. April 1871, Connecticut, son of John Fairchild, Jr. and Betty Frasier. He was buried May 2, 1871 at St. Paul's Church Cemetery, Woodbury, Connecticut.
-- After the death of Emily, John m. #2, April 8, 1858, Cornelia Betts. She d. March 10, 1900 and is buried at St. Paul's Church Cemetery, Woodbury, Connecticut
--"At the time of his second marriage he was of East Townsend, Huron County, Ohio. St. Paul's Church Records show John as being of New Jersey at the time of his burial. One Ohio census shows John and Cornelia residing in Huron County, Ohio. (*Early Fairchilds*, Jean Fairchild Gilmore, Gateway Press, 1991)
--1830 Census: #380 Acquackanonk, New Jersey
--1840 Census p.102A, Acquackanonk; John Fairchild Jr.
--1850 Census: Acquackanonk, Passaic Co.: John Fairchild, age 53, b. CT, shoemaker, real estate $3000; Emily, age 48, b. Conn.; Lyman Wilcox, age 19, shoemaker, b. NY; John Masters, age 19, shoemaker, b. England; John Foster, age 17, shoemaker, b. NY
--1860 Census, p.258A, Townsend Twp.,Huron Co., OH:John J. Fairchild, b. CT, age 62, farmer; Cornelia, age

47, b. CT; (adj. to Curtiss Fairchild, age 50, b. CT; Abigail, age 43, b. NY; Cornelia, age 19; Sarah, age 14)
--1870 Census, p.81B, Chatham Twp, Morris Co., NJ: John Fairchild, age 71, farmer, b. CT; Cornelia, age 56, b. CT
--(?)1880 Census, p.350A, New Haven, Conn: Cornelia Fairchild, other, widow, age 66, b. CT, parents b. CT; at res. of William C. Bristol and Mary A. Bristol.
--CHILDREN of John Fairchild and Emily (Roebuck?):

Amanda	b. 1821, New York
Julia Ann	b. 1824, New York
John	b. (? abt. 1835, NY; m. Phebe Jane Carpenter

John   b. (? abt. 1835, NY; m. Phebe Jane Carpenter
--(?)1870 Census, p.384A, Oyster Bay, NY: John Fairchild, age 32, machinist, Phebe, age 25; Harry, age 6; Lizzie, age 2
--(?)1880 Census, p.415B, Oyster Bay, NY: John R. Fairchild, age 45, b. NY, machinist; parents b. CT; Phebe, wife, age 37, b. NY; Harry, son,a ge 16, b. NY; Susan, dau., age 9 b. NY; George, son, age 6, b. NY; Jennie, age 2, daughter, b. NY; Henrietta Fairchild, niece, age 25, b. NY, seamstress

William L.   b. 1833, Ulster Co., New York;m.Susan Tears
d. May 3, 1863, Chancellorsville, Virginia (Civil War);bur. Valley Cemetery, Walkill, Ulster Co., New York
--1860 Census, p.1157, Montgomery, Orange Co., NY: William L. Fairchild, age 27, b. NY, factory operator; Susan, age 28; Charles E. age 5; Carrie, age 3; Frances age 1; Anna M. Tears, age 80, b. NY
--1870 Census, p.124, Montgomery, Orange Co., NY: Susan Fairchild, age 39; Curtis, age 14, works knife factory; Carrie, age 13, works wool mill; Frances, age 10
--1880 Census, p.441A, Dist. 2, Walden, Montgomery, Orange Co., NY: Susan

Fairchild, widow, age48, b. NY; Frances,
dau., age 20, b. NY, works in knife shop
--1900 Census, p.31A, Montgomery, NY:
Susan Fairchild, b. Feb.1831, widow; 3 born
3 living, b. NY, parents b. NY

Clifford   b. abt. 1834 d. January 10, 1844, Age 10 years

Mary Eliza   b. 1835, New York, m. Sylvester J. Homan
--1870 Census, p.275 & 275A, 19 Wd.
Cleveland, Cuyahoga Co., Ohio:
Sylvester Homan, b. April 1837 NY, Sup't at
Rescue Mission; Mary E. wife, matron, b.
Feb.1835 NY, parents b. CT; 2 inmates'
--1880 Census, p.148A, Cleveland, Ohio:
Selvester Homan, age 43, b. NY, carpenter;
Mary, age 44, b. NY; Electa, dau., age 19, b.
NY; Minnie, dau., age 13, b. NY; William,
son, age 9, b. NY

- - - - -

FERGUSON

Ferguson, Joseph*   b. (abt. 1844?)
(gmnj)   d. (before 1900)
wife, LAVINIA (Sloat)   b. 1851
(npfh)   d. August, 1917
     (bur. August 25, 1917)

Notes:
--Lavinia was daughter of Isaac Sloat,q.v. and Catharine
Doremus.
--1870 Census, p.136B, Caldwell: Isaac Sloat, age 56,
farmer; Catherine, age 61; Emma, age 23, seamstress;
Theodore, age 21, farmer; Lavinia, age 18; Elizabeth
Doremus, age 75

--(?)1870 Census, p.505A, 6th Ward, Newark: Joseph Ferguson, age 26, b. NY, works stair rail mfg; Lizzie R. age 22, b. NJ, keeps house; Anna Roll age 67, at home

--1880 Census: #311, p.416D, Caldwell/Cedar Grove: Theodore Sloat, age 32, b. NJ, farmer; Hester A., wife, age 38, b. NJ; Emma Sloat, sister, age 34, b. NJ; Lavinia Sloat, sister, age 30, b. NJ.

--1900 Census, p.90A, Little Falls Twp: Lavinia Ferguson, b. June 1851 NJ, m. 8 years, 1 born 1 living; Emma, daughter, b. April 1875

--1910 Census, p.193b, Little Falls Twp: Lavinia Ferguson, widow, age 59, m. 19 yrs., 1 born 1 living, b. NJ, parents b. NJ; Emma M., dau., age 17, b. NJ, father b. NY, mother b. NJ; Emma Sloat, sister, age 60, single, b. NJ, parents b. NJ

--"She sold much of the Peter Doremus-Isaac Sloat strip as lay east of Fairview Avenue to the turnpike to Phineas Augustus Matthews who laid out Myrtle Avenue." (Boardman, p.12)

--CHILDREN of Joseph Ferguson and Lavinia Sloat: Emma b. April 1875

- - - - -

FIJLSTRA

Fijlstra, KLAAS K.	b. November 9, 1832
(gmnj)	d. February 3, 1899
wife, SIEBRIGJE (Stapert)	b. October 9, 1830
(gmnj)	d. January 2, 1891

Notes:
--(?)1910 Census: p.198A, Little Falls Twp:(son?) Nicholas Fylstra, age 44, m. 23 yr., b. Holland; Annie, wife, age 46, 6 born 5 living, b. Holland; Henry, age 21; Gary(Garrett?), age 19; Julia, age 13; Theodore, age 8; Frances Vliner?, niece, age 20

--1920 Census, p. 114B, Little Falls:Nicholas Fylstra, age 53, wet wash, b. Holland; Anna, age 55; Theodore, age 17, silversmith at Tiffany & Co; Julia Gedney, dau., age 23, stenographer; Ray Gedney, son in law, age 24, electrical engineer
--1930 Census, p.275B, Little Falls: Anna B. Fylstra, age 66, widow, b. Holland; at res. of Henry Joustra, age 33 and Julia, age 34

- - - - -

FORREST

Forrest, ANDREW   b. (abt. 1859)
(gmnj)   d. February 21, 1894
"A native of Scotland"
" In his 35th yr"

wife, Jennie*   b.
(gmnj)   d.

son, ROBERT A.   b. (September 1892)
(gmnj)   d. October 10, 1892

"Aged 1 mo."

Notes:
--(?)Andrew Forrest, b. April 10, 1858, Carluke, Lanark, Scotland (IGI)
--(?)1880 Census, p.378A, Farmington, LaCrosse Co., WI: Andrew Forest, son, age 23, b. Scotland, parents b. Scotland; at farm of his parents, Alexander and Jenette Forest
--CHILDREN of Andrew Forrest and Jennie .....:
Robert A.   b. September 1892; d. October 10, 1892

- - - - -

FRASER

Fraser, COLIN S.   b. August 26, 1862
(gmnj)   d. September 11, 1863

Notes:
--(?)Colin Shaw Fraser was son of John Frazer (sic) and
Jenette ___.
--(?)1880 Census, p.190C, Little Falls, Passaic Co., NJ: John
Frazer, age 62, b. Scotland, designer; Harriet?, wife?, age 38,
b. PA, parents b. PA; Hatty M. dau., age 15, b. NY;
Theodore, son, age 22, b. NJ, laborer

- - - - -

FRIEL

Friel, Michael*   b.(July 1850)
                            d. (bef. 1930)
wife, Emily F.* (Jacobus)   b. (July 1851)
                            d. (aft. 1930)
son, OSCAR M.   b. (abt. 1895)
(oughletree)   d. (abt. 1920-22)

Notes:
--Oscar M. Friel was son of Michael Friel and Emily F.
Jacobus.
--Michael Friel m. Emily F. Jacobus after 1880.
--Emily F. Jacobus was b. abt. 1845, daughter of Garret I.
Jacobus and his wife, Cordelia Williams; granddaughter of
Isaac I. Jacobus. She inherited the old homestead house and
yard at the south end of the property of Garret Jacobus.
--Michael Friel "used to boast of having been with Gen.
Custer in his last fight,1864, with the Indians." (Boardman,
p.15)
--"Michael Friel had an adopted son (Oscar?) who as a youth
died from being struck on the temple with a billiard cue by

an annoyed pool room keeper in the place where the boys were playing."(Boardman, p.15)

--1850 Census: p.115, Garret I. Jacobus, age 30, mason; Cordelia, age 28; Emily F., age 6

--1860 Census, p.115B, Caldwell: Garret Jacobus, age 40, mason; Cordelia, age 39; Emily F. age 16; Anna age 8; Amelia age 6; Frederick age 4; (adj. to Isaac I. Jacobus)

--1870 Census, p.137A, Caldwell: Garret Jacobus, age 69, brick mason; Cordelia, age 48; Emily, age 23, seamstress; Annie A., age 19; Freddie, age 13

--1880 Census,p.414C, Caldwell: Garret I. Jacobus, age 59, stone mason; Cordelia, wife, age 59; Emily F. dau., age 25, tailoress; Frederick, son, age 23, stone mason

--1900 Census: #66,p.251,Verona: Michael Friel, b.July 1851 Ireland, farmer; Emily F. (Jacobus), b. July 1850, NJ, age 57; Oscar M., age 15; Garret I. Jacobus, father-in-law, b. July 1820, widower, retired

--1910 Census, #77,p.16A, Cedar Grove: Michael Freil, age 60, b. Ireland, general labor; Emily F. age 57; Oscar M. age 15

--1920 Census:p. 164B, #29, Cedar Grove: Michael Friel, age 69, b. Ireland; to US 1860, naturalized 1902, county labor; Emily age 68, b. NJ

--1930 Census #187, Cedar Grove: Emily Friel, age 80, widow, b. NJ

--CHILDREN of Michael Friel and Emily Jacobus:
Oscar M.   b. abt. 1895 (adopted)

- - - - -

GARRISON

Garrison, WILLIAM   b. (November 17, 1740)
(gmnj)   d. April 17, 1765

"Aged 24 yrs. & 5 mos.

wife, Abigail* (Fortner)   b. (1740)
                                 d.

Notes:

--William Garrison was born in Montgomery Twp., Somerset County, New Jersey.

--William Garrison m. Abigail Fortner, daughter of Benjamin Fortner and Isabella Douglas. She was b. 1740 in Morris County. She married #2, Peter Anderson who d. 1828, Fredericton, New Brunswick, Canada. She and Peter named their first child William and lived at one time in Nova Scotia. (*World Family Tree*, Volume 4)

--The second husband of Abigail Fortner, Peter Anderson lived in Knowlton Twp., Sussex Co., NJ in 1773. He was a loyalist and on December 15, 1776, joined the 5th Battalion, New Jersey Volunteers commanded by Lt. Col. Joseph Barton. In 1778 he was transferred to the 1st Battalion of the Kings Rangers, commanded by Lt. Col. Robert Rogers. In October 1782 he was sent to Nova Scotia. The King's Rangers were disbanded June 12, 1784 and the roster shows Ens. Peter Anderson as having a wife and five children. In May 1798, Peter Anderson and his family went to Ontario, settling at Niagara Falls. (*Loyalists in Ontario*,1973, Hunterdon House Publ.) Children of Abigail Fortner Garrison and her second husband, Peter Anderson: William, Martin, Elizabeth, Charles, Mary, Andrew

--An interesting story about the parents of Abigail Fortner: "Lady Douglas, the daughter of the Earl of Douglas, fell in love with a young man whom the Earl forbade her to marry. The couple sailed for America in separate ships and Lady Douglas arrived safely in New York, but never heard of her lover again, his ship is supposed to have foundered. Lady Douglas found herself destitute except for her jewels which she decided not to sell. She found employment as a servant in the household of a wealthy New York merchant named Fortner. The Fortners realized that she was occupying a position subordinate to her birth, and made of her an equal.

She was persuaded to marry the merchant's son. A large family was born to this couple." (*Biographical Sketches of Welland County, Ontario*", p. 559, 1887)

--CHILDREN of William Garrison and Abigail Fortner:

William   b. bef. 1765

- - - - -

GEDNEY

Gedney, Jacob M.R.**	b. (abt. 1848)
	d. (bef. 1900)
wife, GEORGIA (Kinsted)	b. (May 1847)
(npfh)	d. December, 1914
	bur. December 10, 1914

Notes:

--Jacob was son of Edward Gedney and Sophronia (Ryerson?)

--Georgia was dau. of Christopher Kinsted and Sarah .....

--1860 Census, p.1033 Acquackanonk: Jacob Ryerson, age 73, farmer, b. NJ; Harriet, age 71; Ann age 41; Sophronia Gedney, age 38, b. NJ; Edward Gedney, age 45, b. NY; Harriet Gedney, age 15, b. NJ; Jacob Gedney, age 12, b. NJ; Edward Gedney, age 11, b. NJ; Harry Smith, age 9; John Munson, age 45, farm labor

--1870 Census, p.335, 20 Wd, New York City: Christopher Kinsted, b. NY, age 49, doctor; Sarah, age 44; Georgine age 23; 6 younger children

--1870 Census, p. 335, 20 Wd, New York City: Jacob Gedney, age 23, doctor, b. NJ; Georgine, age 23; Charles age 3 (adj. to Christopher Kinsted)

--1880 Census, p.181A, Little Falls: Jacob M.R.Gedney, age 32, b. NY, doctor, father b. NY, mother b. NJ; (Georgia) Leiza,wife, age 33, b. NY; Charles son, age 12; Edna, dau age 3; Mary F. Riker, age 19, servant; Samuel Jackson, age 21, servant

--1880 Census, p.184D, Little Falls: Sophronia Gedney, widow, age 64, b. NJ; and, (sister?) Annie Ryersen, single, age 66, b. NJ; both at res. of Frances W. and Harriet VanNess.

--1900 Census, p.82A, Little Falls, NJ: Charles Gedney, b. Nov.(7th) 1867, m. 6 yrs, bank clerk, b. NY, parents b. NY; Anna L. b. September 1872, 2 born 2 living, b. NY, parents b. NJ; Ray V.D. b. July 1895; J. Dudley b. Sept. 1998; Georgia L., mother, b. May 1847, New York, parents b. NY, widow, 2 born 2 living

--1900 Census, p.82A, Little Falls: Sophronia Gedney, mother-in-law, b. October 1815, NJ, father b. NJ, mother b. CT, age 84 widow; at res. of Frank and Harriet (Gedney) VanNess

--1910 Census, p.200B, Little Falls Twp: Charles Gedney, age 41, bank clerk, b. NY, parents b. NY, m. 15 yr; Anna, wife, age 37, b. NJ, parents b. NJ, Roy, son, age 14; Dudley son, age 11; Marion M. dau., age 5; Georgia, mother, age 62, widow, 3 born, 1 living

--CHILDREN of Jacob M.R.Gedney and Georgine Kinsted:

Charles K. b. November 1867; m. Anna .....

 --1900 Census, p.82A, Little Falls, NJ: Charles Gedney, b. Nov.(7th) 1867, m. 6 yrs, bank clerk, b. NY, parents b. NY; Anna L. b. September 1872, 2 born 2 living, b. NY, parents b. NJ; Ray V.D. b. July 1895; J. Dudley b. Sept. 1998; Georgia L., mother, b. May 1847, New York, parents b. NY, widow, 2 born 2 living

 --1910 Census, p.200B, Little Falls Twp: Charles Gedney, age 41, bank clerk, b. NY, parents b. NY, m. 15 yr; Anna, wife, age 37, b. NJ, parents b. NJ, Roy, son, age 14; Dudley son, age 11; Marion M. dau., age 5; Georgia, mother, age 62, widow, 3 born, 1 living

 --1920 Census, p.114B, Little Falls: Charles Gedney, age 52, bank clerk, b. NY, father b.

NJ, mother b. NY; Anna, age 47; Marion,
dau., age 15

--1930 Census, p.262A, Little Falls: Charles
K. Gedney, age 62, b. NY, bank clerk; Anna
L., age 57; Marion M. age 24; (adj. to Ray
V.D.Gedney, age 34; Jewell, age 33; Donald
R. age 8)

Edna   b. abt. 1873

- - - - -

HAGER

Hager, CORNELIUS P.   b. July 6, 1872
(gmnj)   d. December 3, 1891
Hager, JANTJE (Sapes)   b.
(gmnj)(no dates)   d.

Born in Friesland,Nederland

Notes:

--On the same marker with Harman Vander Meij,q.v.

--(son?) Cornelius Hager, b. January 22, 1892, Paterson; d.
May 14, 1897, Paterson.

--(?)1900 Census, p.86, Little Falls: (mother?)Annie Hager,
b. July 1836, widow; George b. September 1873; Ella, b.
Feb.1881(adj. to Michael Vandermay/Vandermeij?,q.v.)

--(?)1900 Census, p.152, Manchester Twp., Passaic Co:
Cornelius Hager, m. 41 years, b. March 1840 Holland; Dora,
wife, b. January 1835 Holland; Dora, dau. b. April 1881
Holland

- - - - -

HARDEN

Harden, JOSEPH   b.
(npfh)   d. September, 1910
     (bur. September 6, 1910)

Notes:
--(?)1900 Census, p.165A, 2Wd Paterson: Aaron Prall, b.
Dec. 1861, NJ, foreman of street labor; Mary, b. April 1865
NJ; 5 children; Mary Harden, b. NY, mother-in-law, b. May
1828, age 72, widow
--(?)1900 Census, p.92, 2Wd,Paterson: John Harden, b.
October 1852, RI, carriage painter; Elizabeth b. Nobember
1858, b. CT; Lilly b. October 1881, Rhode Island

- - - - -

HAWTHORNE

Hawthorne, David**   b. (October 1835)
(gmnj)   d. (aft. 1900)
wife, Margaret .....   b. (February 1838)
     d. (bef 1900)

Notes;
--He purchased Lot #33 in 1882.
--David was son of Robert Hawthorne (q.v.)
--1870 Census, p.244, Little Falls: David Hawthorne, age 34,
carpet weaver, b. CT; Margaret, age 31; Emma J. age 9;
Thomas W. age 6; Mary, age 4; David age 3
--1880 Census, p.184D, Little Falls, NJ: David Harthorn, age
44, b. CT, parents b. Ireland, carpet weaver; Margret, wife,
age 38, b. Ireland; Thomas, son, age 17; clerk in store; Mary,
dau.,age 15, b. NJ; David, son, age 13, b. NJ; Robert, son,
age 8 months, b. NJ; 5 boarders

--1900 Census, p.81A, Little Falls: David Hawthorne, b. October 1835, NY, parents b. Ireland, m. 40 yrs; Margaret b. Feb. 1838, Ireland; 7 born 6 living; Thomas W. b. October 1862, NJ: Robert b. September 1879, NJ; Sadie b. August 1883, NJ

--CHILDREN of David Hawthorne and Margaret .....:

Emma	b. abt. 1861; m. Eugene Gardner

        --1880 Census, p.182C, Little Falls, NJ: Emma Harthorn, single, age 19, b. NJ, father b. CT, mother b. Ireland; at res. of David and Mary Stewart.

        --1910 Census, p.202B, Little Falls: Eugene Gardner, age 54, b. France, printer at silk mill; Emma J. age 49, m.20 yr, 2 born 2 living, b. NJ, father b. NY, mother b. Ireland; Marion A., age 18; Margaret S., age 10; Sarah Stewart, aunt, age 61, b. Ireland; Robert Hawthorne, brother-in-law, age 30, b. NJ, rate clerk at railroad

        --1920 Census, p.114A,Little Falls: Eugene Gardner, b. France, age 62, widower, rug mill printer; Marion H. Ferguson, dau.,a ge 27; Thomas Ferguson, age 35, son-in-law; Margaret S. Gardner, dau.,age 19(adj. to David Hawthorne, age 51)

Thomas W.	b. October 1862

        --1910 Census, p. 196A, 3wd Orange: Thomas Hawthorne, age 47, m. 8 yr;woolen goods salesman; Anne, age 47, b. NY 1 born 1 living; Dorothy, age 5, b. NJ; Effie Ives, siser-in-law, age 43 single

        --1920 Census, p.221A, Clifton, Acquackanonk Twp., Passaic Co., NJ: Thomas W. Hawthorne, age 57, lunch room manager; Annie, age 56, b. NY; Dorothy E., age 15; Jennie Ives, sister-in-law, age 40, single

Mary	b. abt. 1866
David	b. abt. 1867

--1900 Census, p.62A, Pequannock Twp., Morris Co,NJ: Abram Ryerson, b. Nov. 1838, farmer, widower; Spencer, son, b. 1864, single, farmer; David Hawthorn Jr., RR brakeman, son-in-law,b. 1867, m. 7 yrs; Mary Hawthorn dau. b. Feb. 1869, 2 born 1 living; Spencer Hawthorne, grandson, b. Nov. 1898
--1910 Census, p.201B, Little Falls: David Hawthorne, age 42, m. 17 yr, b. NJ, father b. NY, mother b. Ireland, bookkeeper; Mary A. age 40, 2 born 2 living, b. NJ, parents b. NJ; Spencer? A., age 11; Lizzie VanHouten, aunt, age 53, single
--1920 Census, p.114A,Little Falls: David Hawthorne, age 51, b. NJ, father b. NY, mother b. Ireland, railroad conductor; Mary A., age 49; Spencer, age 21; Mabel C. age 23 dau-in-law
--1930 Census, p.273B, Little Falls: David Hawthorne, age 63, widower, RR conductor; Spencer, age 31; Mabel, age 33, dau.-in-law; Anite E. granddau., age 10; Audrey A., granddau., age 5

Robert   b. September 1879

--1910 Census, p.202B, Little Falls: Eugene Gardner, age 54, b. France, printer at silk mill; Emma J. age 49, m.20 yr, 2 born 2 living, b. NJ, father b. NY, mother b. Ireland; Marion A., age 18; Margaret S., age 10; Sarah Stewart, aunt, age 61, b. Ireland; Robert Hawthorne, brother-in-law, age 30, b. NJ, rate clerk at railroad

Sadie   b. August 1883

- - - - -

Hawthorne, ROBERT   b. (abt. 1805) Ireland
(gmnj)   d. 1862

"In his 66th year"

wife, MARY   b. (abt. 1800) Ireland
(gmnj)   d. 1861

"Aged 61 yrs. & 1 day"

Notes:
--(?)Robert Hawthorne, b. March 13, 1804, Annaghmore,
Nagherafelt, Londonderry, Ireland. Son of James Hawthorne
and Margaret ......
--1860 Census: p.111A, Caldwell/Cedar Grove: Robert
Hawthorne, age 54, b. Ireland; Mary, age 60, b. Ireland;
James R. age 27, carpenter; David, age 23, weaver, b. Conn.;
Thomas, age 21, b. NY; Samuel, age 17, b. NY. Also,
Charles ....., age 57, b. France. Also, Ella Personett, age 66
(may be, Elcey, widow of George Personett).
--(?)1870 Census, p.241A, Little Falls: Robert Hawthorne,
age 61, carpet weaver, b. Ireland; Elizabeth age 48, b. NJ;
Washington, age 12; Lucretia Vreeland, age 74
--CHILDREN of Robert Hawthorne and Mary ____:
James Robert bapt. April 6, 1834, Enfield, Hartford,
              Connecticut; m. Rebecca Jacobus,
              daughter of Willliam G. Jacobus (q.v.)
              --(?)1860 Census, p.324A, 1 Wd. Orange:
              James Hawthorne, no age listed, carpenter, b.
              NJ; at res. of John Calhoun, hatter
              --1870 Census: #409 Caldwell: James R.
              Hawthorne, age 36, carpenter; Rebecca, age
              32; Joseph, age 10; Cornelius, age 7; Charles
              age 2;
              --1880 Census: #193 Caldwell: James R.
              Hawthorne, age 45, carpenter, b. Connecticut;

Rebecca, age 40; Cornelius H. age 16;
Charles H. age 12
--1900 Census: p.264, Verona; James R.
Hawthorne, b. October 1834, carpenter;
Rebecca, b. May 1838, 4 born 3 living, b. NJ;
Cornelius H b. May 1863; Charles M. b. 1867

David   bapt. June 25, 1837, Enfield, Hartford,
Conn.; m. Margret _____
--1880 Census, p.184D, Little Falls, NJ: David
Harthorn, age 44, b. CT, carpet weaver,
parents b. Ireland; Margret, wife, age 38, b.
Ireland; Thomas, son, age 17, b. NJ; Mary,
dau., age 15, b. NJ; David, son, age 13, b. NJ
Robert, son, age 8 months, b. NJ; 5 boarders

Thomas   b. abt. 1839
Samuel   b. abt 1843

- - - - -

HEMINGWAY

Hemingway, Francis* b. (abt. 1805) England
(gmnj)   d. (aft. 1860)

1st wife, ELIZABETH (Croft)b. (abt. 1806) England
(gmnj)   d. May 12, 1849

"Aged 43 yrs."

Notes:
--Francis Hemingway was baptised September 22, 1805,
Dewsbury, Yorkshire, England; son of Benjamin
Hemingway (1783-1856) and Mary Lockwood;grandson of
Thomas Hemingway (1751-1822) and Mercy Senior. His
grandfather, Thomas, was a blanket manufacturer at
Earlsheaton, Dewsbury. Thomas died March 14, 1822 at
Dewsbury. (The complete 4-page Last Will & Testament of

Thomas Hemingway is available at
www.hemingway.uk.com.)
--Francis was brother of Titus Hemingway (q.v.)
--Francis Hemingway, clothier, m. September 20, 1831,
Elizabeth Croft, at Dewsbury, Yorkshire, England
--Francis and Elizabeth Hemingway, in 1831, lived in
Soothill, England.They had two sons, Milton, b. October 5,
1831, Dewsbury; and Isaac, b. August 1, 1833 in Soothill,
Yorkshire.
--Francis Hemingway m. #2, after May 1849, Mary ....
--1860 Census, p.600,Newburgh,Orange Co., NY: Isaac
Hemingway, age 27, b. England, master weaver; Mary, age
18, b. NY; Francis, age 55, master weaver, b. England;
Sarah, age 60, b. England; Edward Graham, age 12, b. NJ
--CHILDREN of Francis Hemingway and Elizabeth ....

Milton   --b. October 5, 1831, Dewsbury, England
            m. Mary Hinchcliffe, May 27, 1854, Paterson
            --1870 Census, p.369B, 2 Wd.Newburgh,NY
            Milton Hemingway, age 38,weaver, b.
            England; Mary, age 35, b. England; Frank,
            age 16, laborer, b. NJ; Thomas, age 13, b. NJ;
            Ann, age 10, b. NJ; Milton, age 3, b. NY;
            Hattie, age 1, b NY
            --1880 Census, p.104D, Dist. 2,Newburgh,
            Orange Co., NY: Milton Hemingway, age
            48, b. England, carpent manufact.; Mary,
            wife, age 45, b. England; Thomas, son, age
            23, b. NJ, works in woolen mill; Milton, son,
            age 12, b. NY; Hattie Ann, dau., age 11, b.
            NY; Joseph W., son, age 6, b. NY
            --1900 Census, p.37, 6Wd.Newburgh, NY;
            Milton Hemingway, b. October 1831, works
            carpet mill; Mary, b. June 1834; Joseph, b.
            Oct. 1874, compositor
            --1910 Census, p.316B, 6 Wd. Newburgh,
            NY: William Ditrich(Aldrich?) age 45,
            foreman elevator, b. NY, parents b. England;

	Hattie Ann, age 41, b. NY; William, age 18, grocery sales; Edna, age 13; Mary Hemingway, age 76, widow, mother-in-law
Isaac	b. August 1, 1833, Soothill, Yorkshire, Eng.

Isaac   b. August 1, 1833, Soothill, Yorkshire, Eng.
--1860 Census, p.600,Newburgh,Orange Co., NY: Isaac Hemingway, age 27, b. England, master weaver; Mary, age 18, b. NY; Francis, age 55, master weaver, b. England; Sarah, age 60, b. England; Edward Graham, age 12, b. NJ
--(?)1880 Census, p.184D, Derby, New Haven Co., CT: Isaac Hemingway, age 47, b. England, works at brass mill; Mary, wife, age 39, b. NY; Frank, son, age 19, b. NY; William, son, age 16, b. NY; Robert, son,age 14, b. NY; Mary, dau., age 7, b. Wisconsin; Isaac, son, age 6, b. CT; Albert I., son, age 3, b. CT

--CHILDREN of Francis Hemingway and Mary ....
Francis   b. August 3, 1852, Manchester Twp, Passaic Co., NJ; m. Mary ......
--1880 Census, p.386B, Paterson: Frank Hemmingway, age 27, b. NJ, parents b. England, ribbon weaver; Mary, wife, age 24, b. NJ; Frank W. son, age 5, b. NJ; Walter, son, age 3, b. NJ
--1900 Census, p.267 1Wd.Paterson: S. Frank Hemingway, loom fixer, b. August 1856, NJ, parents England; Mary E. b. October 1862; George b. June 1882 silk weaver; Fred b. October 1885
--1910 Census, p.60A, 1Wd Paterson: Frank S. Hemingway, age 55, m.32yr.,b. NJ, parents b. England; Mary E., age 43, 4 born 3 living, b. NJ, parents b. New York

--Note: Some information on the Hemingway families was provided by Satima Flavell Neist of Perth, Australia.

- - - - -

Hemingway, Titus*	b. (abt. 1820)
(gmnj)	d. (aft. 1860)
wife, Hannah* (Jackson)	b. (abt. 1820)
(gmnj)	d. (after 1880?)
son, GEORGE	b. (abt. 1844)
(gmnj)(twin of Isaac)	d. October 17, 1845

"Age 18 months"

son, ISAAC	b. (abt. 1844)
(gmnj)(twin of George)	d. September 13, 1846

"Age 2 years"

Notes:

--Titus Hemingway, bapt. December 2, 1820, Dewsbury, Yorkshire, England; son of Benjamin Hemingway and Mary Lockwood; grandson of Thomas Hemingway.

--Titus Hemingway was brother of Francis Hemingway (q.v.)

--Titus Hemingway, m. September 9, 1839, Dewsbury, Hannah Jackson: "Titus Hemingway, Minor, Bachelor & Clothier, b. Earlsheaton; son of Benjamin, clothier m. Hannah Jackson, Minor, Spinster, b. Dewsbury; daughter of James, clothier. Witnesses: Thomas Lee and Joseph Whitworth.

--Titus was a blanketmaker in 1841 when he and Hannah were living at Common Side, Soothill, Yorkshire.

--1860 Census, p.40, 1 Wd Poughkeepsie, NY: Titus Hemingway, age 40, b. England, beer making; Hannah, age 40, b. England; Francis age 18, b. England; Mary H., age 14, b. NY; Sarah, age 12; Harriet E. age 10; Esther A., age 9; Eliza, age 7; Julietta, age 6; Ellen, age 2

--1870 Census, p.549A, 1 Wd. Poughkeepsie, NY: Titus Hemmingway, age 58, brewer, b. England; Anna, age 58, b.

England; Eliza, age 16, b. NY; Julia, age 17, b. NY; Mary
Ellen, age 12, b. NY
--CHILDREN of Titus Hemingway and Hannah Jackson:

Francis	b. abt. 1842,England
	--1870 Census, p.555A, 1 Wd Poughkeepsie, NY: Frank Hemmingway, age 28, brewer, b. England; Isabelle, age 21, b. NY; Titus, age 3, NY; Charles, age 1, b. NY
	--1910 Census, p.156B, Harrison, Westchester Co., NY: Frank Hemingway, age 67, proprietor, b. England, m. twice; Natasha, age 51, m. twice; 0 born 0 living, b. Canada
	--1920 Census, p.145A, Poughkeepsie, Dutchess Co., NY: Harriet Joy, age 70, widow, b. NY; Frank Hemingway, brother, age 78, b. England; Julietta Decker, age 65, widow, sister, b. NY
George,twin	b. abt. 1844; d. October 17, 1845
Isaac,twin	b. abt. 1844; d. September 13, 1846
Mary H.	b. abt. 1846, England
Sarah	b. abt. 1848, New York
Harriet E.	b. abt. 1850,New York; m. ..... Joy
	--1920 Census, p.145A, Poughkeepsie, Dutchess Co., NY: Harriet Joy, age 70, widow, b. NY; Frank Hemingway, brother, age 78, b. England; Julietta Decker, age 65, widow, sister, b. NY
Esther A.	b. abt. 1851, New York
Eliza	b. abt. 1853
Julietta	b. abt. 1854; m. ..... Decker
	--1920 Census, p.145A, Poughkeepsie, Dutchess Co., NY: Harriet Joy, age 70, widow, b. NY; Frank Hemingway, brother, age 78, b. England; Julietta Decker, age 65, widow, sister, b. NY
Mary Ellen	b. abt. 1858

- - - - -

HENRY

Henry, DANIEL   b. December 29, 1837
(gmnj)   d. March 1, 1898

Notes:
--(?) 1871-1872 City Directory, Paterson:Henry Daniel,
farmer at Paterson
--(?)Annie C. Henry, Excr.; David Henry; Hannah Henry;
Margaret Henry - all were plot owners at Cedar Lawn
Cemetery, Paterson, New Jersey as of 1917.
--(?)1900 Census, p.311, 8Wd Paterson: Eliza Henry, b. April
1835, widow, b. Ireland, mother-in-law; at res. of John and
Catherine Finley
--(?)1910 Census, p. 149A, 11 Wd Paterson: Anne C. Henry,
age 50, widow, b. NJ, parents b Ireland; Jane?, dau., age 20?,
single, b. NJ, stenographer; Maul Mah..., nephew, age 11

- - - - -

HOLTZ

Holtz, JULIUS   b.
(npfh)   d. September, 1909
                       (bur. September 27, 1909)

Notes:
--1900 Census, p.1A, Acquackanonk: Julius Hultz, b. May
1857 Germany, m. 20 yrs, farm labor; Mary, b. May 1860
NJ, parents b. Ireland, 4 born 4 living; Susie, b. Sept. 1887;
Nellie b. September 1883

- - - - -

HUTTER

Hutter, DANIEL   b.
(npfh)   d. September 1908
                (bur. September 10, 1908)

Notes:

--See: George F. Hutter, veteran of the Spanish American War of 1898. He bought part of the Marley land. (Boardman, p.18)

--(?)1900 Census, p.254 Verona: George F. Hutter, b. September 1873, single, b. NY, parents b. Germany, carpenter; boarder

--(?)1900 Census, p. 124 3Wd Passaic: John Hutter, b. September 1858, b. Germany; Lizzie, b. Feb. 1864, 1 born 1 living; Barbara, b. 1883, b. NY

--(?)1920 Census: #140 Cedar Grove; George F. Hutter, age 41, widower, carpenter at Essex Co. Hospital, b. NY, father b. NY, mother b. Germany; George H., son, age 4 yr and 6 months, b. NJ, parents b. NY

--(?)1930 Census #199, Cedar Grove: George F. Hutter, real estate $12,000, b. NY, father b. NY, mother b. Germany, house carpenter; Jane E., age 39, b. NY, parents b. North Ireland; George H., son, age 14, b. NY, parents b. NY; M. Elizabeth, age 8; Thomas J. Graham, bro-in-law, age 41, b. NY, father b. NY, mother b. NJ; wholesale salesman of powder explosives; Robert C. Graham, nephew, age 13, b. NY, parents b. NY; Margaret Lemmon, mother-in-law, age 66, b. North Ireland, parents b. Ireland

- - - - -

JACOBUS

Jacobus, CHARLES   b.
(lfrc)   d.
--Charles Jacobus purchased Lot #19 in 1871.
--(?)Charles G. Jacobus (q.v.)
Notes:

- - - - -

Jacobus, CHARLES   b.
(oughletree)   d. (abt. 1920-22)

Notes:

- - - - -

Jacobus, CHARLES G.   b. April 17, 1842
(gmnj)   d. December 23, 1911
wife, Sarah E.**(Graham)   b. (abt. 1854)
                     d. (bef. 1880)
Notes:
--Charles G. Jacobus was son of Cornelius H. Jacobus,
farmer, and Eliza Low
--Charles G. Jacobus m. November 25, 1864, Sarah Graham,
dau. of John and Maria Graham.
--1850 Census: Caldwell Twp., #82: Cornelius H. Jacobus,
age 49, farmer; Eliza age 31; Caroline age 9; Charles G. age
8; Sarah, age 6;Ellen age 1
--1850 Census #83, Caldwell: Maria Graham, age 40, real
estate $1000; Eliza Bull,(m.Oct. 1851,. James M. Jacobus)
age 18; Ellen Bull, b. NY; Sarah Graham, age 6; adj. to
Cornelius H. and Eliza Jacobus
--1860 Census: #472, Caldwell: Cornelius H. Jacobus, age
59, farmer, real estate $10,000; Eliza, age 41; Carrie, age 19;

Charles age 18; Sarah, age 16; Ellen, age 11; William, age 7; Ellen Low, age 68; 2 boarders

--1870 Census:#396, Caldwell: Charles G. Jacobus, age 28, spoke mfg., real estate $8000; Sarah E., age 25; Herbert, age 4; Maria Graham, age 64

--1880 Census: p.406D, Caldwell, NJ: Cornelius H. Jacobus, age 79, b. NJ, no occupation; Eliza, wife, age 60, b.NJ; Charles G. son, widower, age 38, b. NJ, works in tobacco factory; William H., son, single, age 26, ice dealer; Herbert H., grandson, age 14

--1900 Census, p.253 Verona: Herbert H. Jacobus, b. April 1866, artist; Carrie E. b. Feb. 1862; Ethel M. b. July 1889; Roy H., b. July 1891; Mildred, b. May 1895; Charles G. Jacobus, father, widower, b. April 1842, carpenter; Charles G. Jacobus, artist, single, brother, b. April 1874

--1910 Census, p.13A, Cedar Grove: Herbert H. Jacobus, age 44, m. 22 yr; artist,photo engraving; Carrie E. age 48, 3 born 3 living; Ethel M. age 20; Roy H. age 18; Mildred age 14; Charles G. father, age 67, widower, carpenter

--CHILDREN of Charles G. Jacobus and Sarah (Graham?):

Charles G.   b. April 1874; m. Annie M. Jacobus

--1880 Census, p. 415A, Caldwell: Hetty M. Jacobus, widow, age 50, b. NY, parents b. NJ; Albert W., son, age 24, grocery store; Ella L., dau-in-law, age 27, b. NJ; Ella O., dau., age 22; Carrie E. dau., age 18; Charles G., other, age 6, b. NJ, mother and father b. NJ; Cornelius R. Jacobus, grandson, age 9 months b. NJ

--1900 Census: #102 Verona: Charles G. Jacobus, brother, b. April 1874, artist; at res. of brother, Herbert H. Jacobus

--1910 Census #122 Cedar Grove: George Jacobus, age 62, pumping site labor; Florence W. wife, age 61, 3 born 3 living; Charles G. Jacobus Jr., age 36, m. 9 yrs. artist; Annie M., wife, b. June 1879, 1 born 1 living; George, grandson, age 7

--1930 Census, #155, Cedar Grove: Charles G. Jacobus, age 56, engraver photographer, real estate $15,000;Anne M. age 51, b. NJ; Charles R. son, age 11(?)

Herbert H. b. April 2, 1866; m. Carrie E. Jacobus:dau. of William J. Jacobus,q.v.

--"About 1898, Herbert H. Jacobus started on the north side of Cedar Street, a business which was to develop into the well-known printing establishment." (Boardman, p.14)

--1900 Census, p.253, Verona: Herbert H. Jacobus, b. April 2, 1866, artist; Carrie E. b. February 1862; Ethel M., b. July 1889; Roy H. b. July 1891, works print shop; Mildred O. b. May 1895; Charles G. father, b. April 1841, widower, carpenter; Charles G. bro., b. April 1874, artist

--1910 Census, p.13A, Cedar Grove: Herbert H. Jacobus, age 44, artist photo engraving; Carrie E., age 48; Ethel M. age 20; Roy H. age 18; Mildred O., age 14; Charles G. Sr., age 67, father, carpenter house building

--1920 Census, #204, Cedar Grove: Herbert H. Jacobus, age 53, painter; Carrie, age 57; Ethel M. dau., age 30; Sidney Truman, son-in-law, age 24, b. Indiana, parents b. Ohio, private secretary Pennick Hodges Co.; Mildred J. Truman, dau, age 24

- - - - -

Jacobus, CHARLES H.   b.
                          d.

Notes:

--He served in the Civil War; private, Co. H, 39th Regiment, New Jersey Infantry;enlisted September 14, 1864;discharged June 29, 1865.

--Recruitment advertisement in the Newark Daily Advertiser, 1864:

"39th Regiment. Only one year! Recruits Wanted"
For the new regiment lately authorized to be raised, to whom the highest bounties will be paid. Look at the following figues: Bounty and pay $864...Cash paid on muster, $533.33. Capt. George W. Harrison (late of the 26th Regiment) having received authorization to recruit a company for the 39th Regiment, has established his headquarters in Main Street, near Centre, Orange, where recruits will be received. The pay for married men, in addition to rations and clothing, amounts to $16.00 per week. For single men, $15.60 per week. " (Capt. George Harrison was the H. Co. officer from September 1864 to his death at Petersburg, Virginia, April 2, 1865, the Regiment's "Day of Glory".)

--(?)1880 Census: #250 Caldwell: William B. Allen, age 66, b. NJ, farmer, father b. CT, mother b. NJ; Margaret, wife, age 60; b. NJ, parents b. NY; Charles H. Jacobus, age 34, farmer, son-in-law; Sarah S. Jacobus, daugher age 36, b. NJ; Charles A. Dougherty(q.v.), single, age 21, b. PA, parents b. Ireland; laborer on farm.

--(?)1900 Census, p.249A, Verona: Charles H. Jacobus, b. April 1845, age 55, widower, retired, boarder

- - - - -

Jacobus, C.H. JR.	b. December 20, 1828
(gmnj) (Cornelius H. Jr.)	d. April 22, 1863
wife, SARAH	b.
(gmnj)	d. April 18, 1874 (??)

"Aged 29.5.14"
"Our Sadie"

wife, HETTY M.(Jacobus)   b. February 14, 1830
(gmnj)(Will #27971G,1899)   d. January 18, 1899

son, AUSTIN   b. September 1, 1859
(gmnj)   d. May 29, 1864

Notes:
--Cornelius H. Jacobus, Jr. m. Hetty M. Jacobus, before 1860 Census.
--Hetty was daughter of William Jacobus (q.v.) and Rachel Egbertson.
--The death of Cornelius H. Jacobus was recorded as 'inflammation of the brain'.
--1850 Census: #104: Margaret Jacobus, age 48; Cyrus F. age 25, woodturner; Cornelius H. age 21, woodturner; Sarah C. age 19; Peter N. age 17, woodturner;Rebecca, age 14;Cornelia Brockaway.
--1860 Census: p. 111B, Caldwell/Cedar Grove: Cornelius Jacobus, age 31; Hetty M. age 30; William A.; Ella O.; Austin, 10 months; Anna Keen,age 34, servant, b. Ireland
--1870 Census, p.133A, Caldwell: William Jacobus, age 71, mason; Hetty M., dau., age 40, real estate $2500, widow; William J., age 14; Helen, age 12; Carrie E., age 7
--1880 Census, p. 415A, Caldwell: Hetty M. Jacobus, widow, age 50, b. NY, parents b. NJ; Albert W., son, age 24, grocery store; Ella L., dau-in-law, age 27, b. NJ; Ella O., dau., age 22; Carrie E. dau., age 18; Charles G., other, age 6, b. NJ, mother and father b. NJ; Cornelius R. Jacobus, grandson, age 9 months b. NJ
--CHILDREN of Cornelius Jacobus and Hetty M. Jacobus:
Albert William

           b. abt 1856;m. Ella L. Vreeland,dau. of John E. Vreeland(q.v.)
           --1880 Census, p. 415A, Caldwell: Hetty M. Jacobus, widow, age 50, b. NY, parents b. NJ; Albert W., son, age 24, grocery store; Ella L., dau-in-law, age 27, b. NJ; Ella O., dau., age

22; Carrie E. dau., age 18; Charles G., other, age 6, b. NJ, mother and father b. NJ; Cornelius R. Jacobus, grandson, age 9 months b. NJ

Ella O.'Helen' b. September 1857, m. Ehler O. Wettyen,"first successful land developer" (Boardman, p.10) in Cedar Grove. They had children: Alice (Mrs. William Blaine); and Harold who m. Grace Johnson, daughter of David and Alma Johnson.

--1870 Census #523 Caldwell: Conrad F. Wettyen, age 51, farmer, real estate $50,000, b. Hanover; Gennie, age 38, b. Hanover; Ehler, age 13, b. NY; Edina, age 7, b. NY; Anna, age 4, b. NJ; Joanna, age 5 months, b.

--1880 Census #322, Caldwell: Conrad Wetyen, age 60, b. Hanover, Germany; farmer; Gesane, wife, age 48, b. Hanover; Ehler O., son, age 23, b. NY, milkman; 4 other children

--1900 Census #121 Verona: Ehler O. Wettyen, b. Feb. 1857, m. 19 yrs., farmer/milkman; Ella O. b. Sept. 1857; Alice, age 12; Harold, age 5, 1 hired man

--1910 Census, #185, Verona: Ehler O. Wettyen, age 53, b. NY, own income; Ella O. age 52; Alice, age 22; Harold E., age 15

--1920 Census #177, Cedar Grove: Ehler O. Wettyen, age 62, b. NY, parents b. Germany Ella O., age 62, b. NJ; Alice, dau., age 32, single

Austin   b. September 1,1859; d. May 29, 1864
Carrie E.   b. February 1862;
m. 1888, Herbert H. Jacobus, son of Charles G. Jacobus (q.v.)
--1900 Census, p.253 Verona: Herbert H. Jacobus, b. April 1866, artist; Carrie E. b.

Feb. 1862; Ethel M. b. July 1889; Roy H., b. July 1891; Mildred, b. May 1895; Charles G. Jacobus, father, widower, b. April 1842, carpenter; Charles G. Jacobus, artist, single, brother, b. April 1874

--1910 Census, p.13A, Cedar Grove: Herbert H. Jacobus, age 44, m. 22 yr; artist,photo engraving; Carrie E. age 48, 3 born 3 living; Ethel M. age 20; Roy H. age 18; Mildred age 14; Charles G. father, age 67, widower, carpenter

- - - - -

Jacobus, Isaac Munson.**	b. (July 1833)
(gmnj)	d. (bef. 1910)
wife, Harriet** (Personett)	b.
(gmnj)	d. (after 1910)
daughter, LUCY ROSALIND	b. (September 11, 1858)
(gmnj)	d. March 4, 1862

"Aged 3 yrs. & 6 mos."

Notes:

--Isaac was son of Isaac I. Jacobus and Rachel VanNess.

--Isaac M. Jacobus, age 21,mechanic, m. 1854, at West Bloomfield, Harriet Personett, age 20.

--Harriet Personett was daughter of George Personett and Elsie Doremus.

--1850 Census: #71, Caldwell: Isaac M. Jacobus, age 17, farmer; at res. of his parents Isaac I. and Rachel Jacobus

--1860 Census: #402 Caldwell Twp./Cedar Grove: Isaac M. Jacobus, age 27; turner; Harriet, age 26; Elsy, age 5; George H. age 4; Lucy R. age 1.

--1870 Census #547 Caldwell: Isaac M. Jacobus, age 36, farmer, real estate $3000; Harriet, age 36; Elsie A., age 15;

George H., age 13; Frank, age 9; Warren I., age 7; Jennie, age 1;

--1880 Census #272, Caldwell: Isaac M. Jacobus, age 46, farmer; Harriet, wife, age 46; Elsie A., dau., age 25, single; George H., son, age 23, carpenter; Frank son, age 19, works in cotton mill; Warren I., son, age 17, at home; Jane, dau., age 11; Millard L., son, age 6

--1900 Census #149, Verona: Isaac M. Jacobus, b. July 1833, m. 46 yrs., no occup. listed; Harriet, b. February 1834; Jane J., b. Sept. 1868; Herbert M. b. Sept. 1888; Helen A. b. Jan. 1872; John Winker, age 22, b. Switzerland, hired hand; Benj. F. Gould, b. June 1848, hired man

--1910 Census p.17B, Cedar Grove: Harriet Jacobus, age 76, widow, 7(?) born, 7 living; adj. to son, Millard L. Jacobus

--CHILDREN of Isaac M. Jacobus and Harriet Personett:

Elsey Alida   b. February 9, 1855, d. 1892;
           m. Sebastian Cabot Taylor
           --1880 Census #320 Caldwell: Sebastian Taylor, age 43, b. NJ, farmer; Mary T. (Vreeland) (first wife) age 35; Edwin E., son, age 16; Hardy A. son, age 13 (m. Jane J. Jacobus,q.v.); George E., age 8, m. Mary P. Chesney; Edith M. dau., age 2, m. Frank Hill; Sarah Vreeland, age 71, b. NJ, mother-in-law
           --1900 Census #77 Verona: Sebastian Taylor b. April 1837, m. 8 yrs., retired; Elsie Alida, wife, b. February 1854, 0 born, 0 living;
           --1910 Census, #26, Cedar Grove: Sebastian Taylor, age 72, farmer, b. NY; Elise A., wife, age 55, 0 born, 0 living
           --1920 Census #229 Cedar Grove:Sebastian Taylor; Elsie A., age 64

George H.   b. October 1, 1856, m. 1883, Mary A. _____.
           --1910 Census, #22, Cedar Grove: George H. Jacobus, age 56, carpenter; Mary A., age 50; Maurice L., age 24 RR Clerk; Elise E., age 23, insurance clerk; Harriet P., age 21;

Everett, age 5

--1920 Census, #197, Caldwell Boro: George
H. Jacobus, age 63; Mary A., age 59; Everett
G. age 15

Daughter b. July 10, 1857, d. bef. 1860

Lucy Rosalind b. September 11, 1858, d. March 4, 1862
"consumption"

Frank V. b. May 19, 1861, m. 1889, Emma A.
Rickerich

--1880 Census #107 Caldwell: Louisa
Rickerich, age 36, widow, b. NY, farmer,
parents b. Germany; Emma, dau, age 11, b.
NJ; 6 other children

--1900 Census, #74 Verona: Frank Jacobus,
b. May 1861, m. 11 yrs, brushmaker; Emma
A., b. February 1869; Oscar P., b. November
1889; Clarence Easman, b. August 1891;
Albert L., b. January 1893; Emma Augusta, b.
August 1894; Henry S., b. February 1910

--1910 Census, #119 Cedar Grove: Frank
Jacobus, age 47, m. 21 yrs., brushmaker;
Emma A., age 41, 5 born 5 living; b. NJ;
father b. Germany, mother b. NY; Oscar
P. age 20, clerk at brush factory; Clarence E.,
(Easman?)age 18; Albert L., age 17; Emma
Augusta, age
15; Henry S., age 2 months

Warren I. b. April 19, 1863, d. 1932;
m. 1892, Minnie E. Coe
bur. Prospect Hill Cemetery, Caldwell

--1900 Census #58,p.250A, Verona: Warren I.
Jacobus, b. April 1863, m. 8 yrs. milkman;
Minnie, b. December 1866, 0 born 0 living;
Anna Hillman, servant, b. August 15, 1884
(m. James Winfield Price,q.v.)
William G. Lyon, age 32 labor

--1910 Census, p.16B, Cedar Grove: Warren

I Jacobus, age 47, bronze mill labor; Minnie, age 43; Ruth C., age 9; LeRoy Coe, nephew, age 14 (Ruth C. m. Edwin Johnson)
--1920 Census #39, Cedar Grove: Warren I. Jacobus, age 56, labor, Newark Reservoir; Minnie C., age 53, b. NJ; father b. NY, mother b. NJ; Ruth Jacobus, age 18, dau., steno, American Railway Express; Oscar Jacobus, age 30, nephew, supt. Westinghouse; Clarence Jacobus, age 28, nephew, painter; Albert Jacobus, age 26, nephew, Elect. Eng. General Electric; Robert Lindsley, nephew, age 30, photographer
--1930 Census #131, Cedar Grove: Warren I. Jacobus, age 67, real estate $9000; janitor, town hall; Minnie C., age 63; Ruth C. Johnson, dau.,age 29, secretary real estate office; Edwin Johnson, grandson, age 5

Forrest? d. July 27, 1864; age 1 week;
"son of Munson Jacobus"

Millard Lee b. May 1874, m. 1897, Alice _____.
partner with John H. Price in "Price and Jacobus, Painters and Decorators" at Cedar Grove.
--1900 Census #160,Verona: Millard L Jacobus, b. May 1874, m. 3 yrs., milkman; Alice, b. October 1873; Frederick Lockwood, boarder, b. July 1878, single
--1910 Census, #103, Cedar Grove: Millard L. Jacobus, age 36, m. 12 yrs.,painter/houses; Alice, age 38, 1 born 1 living; b. NJ, parents b. Germany; Mildred, age 9 (m. Frank Leslie Jacobus)
--1920 Census #59, Cedar Grove: Millard L. Jacobus, age 45, painter; Alice, age 47, b. NJ, parents b. Germany; Mildred Julia, age 19, bookkeeper, bank

--1930 Census Part 2, Sheet 2A, Cedar Grove; Millard R. Jacobus, age 55, real estate $10,000, tax collector;Alice, wife, age 58

Jane J.'Jennie' b. September 1868, d. aft. 1934;

m. Hardy A. Taylor;son of Sebastian Taylor
--She had two children: Herbert who m. Catherine Ninnis;, and, Helen, who m. David Carpenter.

--1910 Census #82,p.16B, Cedar Grove: Jennie J.Taylor, age 41, widow; Helen A., dau, age18; Maud Collins, age 25,boarder

--1920 Census #37, Cedar Grove: Jennie J. Taylor, age 51, widow, runs boarding house; Helen A., age 27, dau., single, cable trans- lator for China/Japan Trading Co.; Alonzo Jacobus, age 58, widower, cousin, carpenter Phebe Jacobus, age 25, 2nd cousin, single, secretary; James Cole, age 21, single, brush maker; Andrew G. Meeker, age 28, widower, blacksmith

--1930 Census, #130, Cedar Grove: Jennie J. Taylor, age 62, widow, b. NJ, boarding house keeper; real estate $8000; Alonzo A. Jacobus, age 69, widower, cousin(son of Henry and Frances Jacobus); Alida Taylor, age 75, sister; Phebe Jacobus, age 35, single, b. NJ, secretary in real estate office; 4 boarders.

- - - - -

Jacobus, JAMES   b.
(gmnj)   d. February 19, 1851

"Aged 45 (?) years"

Notes:

- - - - -

Jacobus, James*
daughter, Rachel Lutecia
m. Anthony Cisco (q.v.)

- - - - -

Jacobus, John W*   b. (abt. 1835)
                                  d. (June 18, 1900)
wife, MARY ESTHER (Monroe)
(gmnj)   b. (May 14, 1826)
                                  d. July 11, 1859

"Aged 33.1.28"

daughter, ABBY A.   b. (February 6, 1851)
(gmnj)   d. November 20, 1857

"Aged 6.9.14"

wife, Lucy* (Lindsley)   b.
                                  d.
son, JOHN   b.(1863)
(gmnj)   d.(June 8, 1865)
                                (small pox)

"Age 8 mos."

Notes:
--John W. Jacobus was son of William I.(T.?) Jacobus(q.v.)
and Rachel Egbertson.
--John W. Jacobus m. #2, Lucy Lindsley, b. abt. 1839, dau. of
Gabriel Lindsley and Lucy Harriman
--1870 Census #160 Caldwell: John W. Jacobus, age 48, real
estate $5000; Lucy, age 32; Rachel, age 16; Abby, age 18;
Ida Frances, age 14; Elmer, age 9; William age 7; John Hunt,

b. October 1864; Milton, age 4; Austin, age 2; Louis, age 8 months

--1880 Census, p.243 C, Newark: John W. Jacobus, age 58, b. NJ; Lucy, wife, age 41, b. NJ; Elmer L., son, age 19, teamster; William, son, age 17, button engraver; John M. son, age 13; Austin, son, age 12; Alice A., dau., age 8; Henry L., son, age 6; Charles W., son, age 1

--CHILDREN of John W. Jacobus and Mary Esther Monroe:

Abby A.	b. February 1851; d. November 20, 1857
Rachel	b. October 1852

--CHILDREN of John W. Jacobus and Lucy Lindsley:

Ida Frances	b. March 1856
Elmer L.	b. May 1861
William	b. abt 1862
	--(?)1910 Census, p.47A, 1 Wd Newark: William Jacobus, lodger, age 47, m.25 yr, house painter
John Hunt	b. 1863; d. June 8, 1865 (small pox)
John Milton	b. abt 1867
Austin	b. March 1868
	--1900 Census, p.10A, 1 Wd,Newark: Austin Jacobus, b. March 1868, bartender; Rose B., b. December 1869 Scotland, parents b. Ireland; Mildred b. October 1899
	--1910 Census, p.11A, 1 Wd.Newark: Austin Jacobus, age 42, m.15 yr, 2 born 2 living; clerk in store; Rose B. age 40; Mildred R. age 10
	--1920 Census, p.218B, 11th ED, Newark: Austin Jacobus, age 51; Rose, age 49
Louis	b. abt 1869
Alice A.	b. abt 1872
Henry Louis	b. abt 1874
Charles W.	b. abt 1879

- - - - -

Jacobus, Joseph G.*	b. (abt. 1815)
(gmnj)	d. (aft. 1910)
wife, JANE PERSONETT	b. (August 23, 1819)
(gmnj)	d. September 9, 1858

"Aged 39 yrs. & 17 days"

son, FRANK	b. (September 26, 1855)
(gmnj)	d. March 3, 1857

"Aged 1 yr & 6 mos." (?)

son, EDWARD	b. (May, 1858)
(gmnj)	d. June 7, 1858

"Aged 1 mo."

Notes:

--Jane Personett was daughter of George Personett and his wife, Elsie Doremus.

--Joseph Gould Jacobus was b. abt. 1815, son of ?Daniel P. Jacobus and Hannah Campbell

--Joseph Gould Jacobus continued to reside in New Jersey until abt. 1869.

--After the death of Jane, Joseph and the children were living at the houses of other residents.

--1850 Census: #113, Caldwell Twp./Cedar Grove: Joseph G. Jacobus, age 36, woodturner; Jane, age 32;Elijah B., age 12;Amzi P. age 10; William G. age 7;Theodore T. age 6;Cyrus T. age 4;Joseph L. age 1.

--1860 Census:p.109A, Caldwell Twp/Cedar Grove: Joseph G. Jacobus, age 46, labor;and, son, Walter Jacobus, age 6; at farm of William Wheaton

and:

--1860 Census, p. 120B, Caldwell: Joseph G. Jacobus, age 45 farmer; Walter, age 7; at farm of Leoanrd Corby

--(?)1870 Census, p.71A, Fenton Twp., Genesee Co.,
Michigan: Joseph Jacobus, age 59?, farmer; Deborah, age 58,
b. PA; Frances Griswold, age 16, b. Michian
--CHILDREN of Joseph Gould Jacobus and Jane Personett:

Lou	b. bef. 1838
Elijah B.	b. 1838, d. bef. 1900;
	m.(?)Mrs. Catherine Amelia (Bower) Jacobus
	m.(?)Catherine Amelia Sindle
	--1860 Census: #405, Caldwell Twp./Cedar Grove: Elijah Jacobus, age 21, brushmaker; at res. of Jonathan B. Ward, brush manufacturer
	--1870 Census #502 Caldwell: Elijah B. Jacobus, age 28, farmer; Amelia, age 20
	--1880 Census, #271, Caldwell: Elijah B. Jacobus, age 40, laborer; Catherine A., wie age 30; Eddie A., son, age 8; adj. to Isaac M Jacobus (q.v.) (The daughter of Edward A. Jacobus, Maude, m. John Vanderberg; The son of Edward A. Jacobus, Walter, m. Margaret Cully)
	--1900 Census: #175, Verona: John Bower/ Brower b. December 1829, widower, farmer; Amanda Lockwood, b. 1842, widow; Catherine Amelia, b. December 1850, widow
	--1910 Census, #129, Cedar Grove: Edward A. Jacobus, age 37, m. 15 yrs, brushmaker; Ada Belle (Howell), age 35, 2 born,2 living; Maud M., age 13; Walter E. age 11; Catherine A., mother, age 59, widow, 1 born, 1 living; Beulah B. Baldwin, cousin, age 18
	--1920 Census, #138, Cedar Grove: Edward A. Jacobus, age 47, brushmaker; Ada Belle, age 44; Maude M. age 22, single; Walter E., age 21; Catherine Amelia, mother, widow, age 70

Amzi P.

--1930 Census #218 Cedar Grove: Edward G. Jacobus, age 57, real estate $8,000; brush maker; Walter E., age 32, single, clerk, surgical supply co.; Amelia, mother, age 80 b. February 1841, m. Dec. 24, 1863, Rachel Ann Brooks.

--1850 Census #65 Caldwell: Rachel Ann Brooks, age 6, b. England; at res. of her parents William and Ellen Brooks

--1860 Census: p..112B, Caldwell Twp/Cedar Grove: Amzi Jacobus, age 20, turner; at res. of Lemuel Stagg, farmer

--1870 Census p.135A, Caldwell: Amzi P. Jacobus, age 28, works spoke factory; Rachel Ann, age 26; Minnie R., age 1 month

--1880 Census #308 Caldwell: Amzi P. Jacobus, age 40, farmer; Rachel A., wife, age 36; Minnie R., dau., age 10

--1900 Census #114, Verona: Amzi P. Jacobus, b. February 1841; m. 37 yrs., no occup. listed; Rachel Ann, b. March 1844; Minnie R. Baldwin, dau., b. April 1866; Harry R. Baldwin, son-in-law, b. April 1866(son of John B. Baldwin and Gertrude L. ____); Henry H. Jacobus, b. March 1886, b. NY

--1910 Census, p.14A, Cedar Grove: Amzi P. Jacobus, age 70, general farmer; Rachel Ann, wife, age 66, 1 born 1 living; Minnie R. Baldwin, age 40, dau.; Harry R. Baldwin, age 45, musician; James W. Gilson, age 44, boarder, musician

--1920 Census #225, Cedar Grove: Harry R. Baldwin, age 53, b. NJ, father b. NJ, mother b. NY; landscape gardener, Newark Reservoir; Minnie R., wife; Beulah, dau., age

27, stenographer; Gertrude Baldwin, mother, widow, age 83; Rachel Jacobus mother-in-law, age 75, widow, b. NJ; 1 boarder

William G.(q.v.)b. 1843, m. July 4, 1863, Caldwell, Sarah Ann Courter, daughter of John J. Courter and Ellen Jacobus.

--(?)1860 Census #447, Caldwell; William G. Jacobus, age 19, labor; at res. of Cyrus F. Jacobus, turner, age 34

--1870 Census, #497, Caldwell: William G. Jacobus, age 27, works spoke factory; Sarah C., age 27; Franklin P. age 4; Lucy R., age 2; Ada E., age 3 months; Mary Mullaney, age 45, housekeeper

Theodore F. b. 1844, d. December 25, 1892, Montclair; m. Emma A. _____

--his son, Frank Leslie Jacous m. Mildred Jacobus, dau. of Millard L. Jacobus. Frank was the first president of the Cedar Grove Historical Society.

--1860 Census #459, Caldwell: Theodore Jacobus, age 15, labor; at farm of his grand father, Isaac I. Jacobus

--(?)1870 Census, p.236B, 3Wd Newark: Theodore Jacobus, age 21, wood turner; at res. of Farrand K. Stagg, wood turner

--1880 Census p.33C, Montclair, NJ: Theodore F. Jacobus, age 37, b. NJ, brakeman, Emma A., wife, age 29, b. NJ, parents b. NJ; Gertrude, dau., age 5, b. NJ; Mabel, dau., age 3; Nettie, dau., age 1; John McTaggert, other, age 35, b. NJ, baggage master

Cyrus F. b. 1846, d. abt. July 1877, age 31. (1880 Mortality Schedule)

--1860 Census, p.608, Pequannock Twp,
Boonton P.O., Morris Co., NJ: David Young,
age 59, farmer, b. Morris Co., NJ: Mary, age
61, wife, b. Essex Co.; Cyrus Jacobus, age 12,
b. Essex Co., NJ
--1870 Census, p.132 A., Caldwell: Cyrus
Jacobus, age 24, team driver; at res. of
Lemuel Stagg, hub manufacturer

Joseph Sandford

b. June 2, 1849, aft. 1891, Michigan;
m. 1869, Diana Lucy Gilmore
In 1869 he was in Michigan and settled at
Sidney Twp., Montcalm County. He was a
miller of shingles and a farmer. He had a farm
of eighty acres and was a man of
"indomitable industry and perseverance."
(*Portrait and Biographical Album of Ionia
and Montcalm Counties, Michigan*, Chicago,
1891, (pp.378-379)
--1860 Census, p.113A, Caldwell: Joseph
Jacobus, age 10; at farm of John J. Courter
--1870 Census, p.173B, Sidney Twp.,
Montcalm Co., MI: Joseph Jacobus, age 22,
farm labor, b. NJ; Lucy D., age 17, b. Ohio
(adj. toHenry Gilmore age 60, farmer, b. NY
Lucy, age 56, b. NY)
--1880 Census, p.349B, Sidney, Montcalm
Co. Michigan: Joseph Jacobus, age 31, b. NJ,
farmer; Lucy, wife, age 27, b. Ohio, parents b.
NY; Jesse, son, age 8, b. Michigan; adj.
to Nobel Gilmore, age 40
--1910 Census: p.40A, Sidney Twp.,
Montcalm Co., MI: Joseph S. Jacobus, b. NJ,
m.40 yr, general farm; Lucy D. age 57, 1 born
1 living
--1910 Census, p.33A,Sidney, Montcalm
Co.,Michigan: Jessie G. Jacobus, age 39, m.

17 yr, b. Michigan, laborer; Eva E. age 39 b.
MI; Chester L. age 7, b.Michigan; Roy, age 5;
Kevin?, age 4; Alma, age 2; Cora B. Radey?,
age 32, single, b. MI, sister-in-law

Male   b. 1852

Walter K.   b. February 9, 1853; m. Georgia E. Winans
--1870 Census, p.107A, Caldwell: Walter
Jacobus, age 17, farm labor; on farm of John
H. Speer
--(?)199- Census, p.387D, Shohola, Pike Co.,
PA;Walter Jacobus, age 24, b. NJ,parents NJ,
laborer; Elmira, wife, age 21, b. PA, father b.
NJ, mother b. PA; 4 boarders
--1910 Census, p.111 Verona: W. Jacobus,
age 56, m. 25 yr; Georgia E. age 51, 1 born 1
living; Howard H., age 23; Mary P. Winans,
mother-in-law, age 81, widow

Frank   b. September 26, 1855, d. March 3, 1857

Edward   b. February 28, 1858, d. June 7, 1858

- - - - -

Jacobus, P.N.* (Peter N. Dr.)b. (December 1833)
                                d. (aft. 1900)

1st wife, OTTILIE E.   b. (April 17, 1834)

(gmnj)   d. December 27, 1868

"Aged 34.8.10"

Notes:
--Peter N. Jacobus was son of William G. Jacobus,q.v. and
Margaret Speer.
--1860 Census, p. 655, Independence, Warren Co., NJ: P.N.
Jacobus, age 26, physician; Otilia E., age 26, b. Prussia;
Julia, age 1 month, b. NJ
--1880 Census, p.138B, Newton, Sussex Co., NJ: Peter N.
Jacobis, age 46, b. NJ, doctor; Hannah E. wife, age 31, b. NJ;

Julia D. dau., age 20,works in shoe factory; Preston N. son,
age 16; Edith D. age 6; May E. age 3
--1900 Census, p.151, Washington Boro, Warren Co., NJ:
Peter N. Jacobus, b.Dec. 1833, m.29 yr,physician; Hannah E.
b. Nov. 1848, 3 born 2 living, b. NJ; Edith D. b. Sept. 1873;
May E., b. July 1879
--CHILDREN of Peter N. Jacobus and Ottilie E. .....:
Julia D.   b. 1860
Preston N.   b. abt. 1864
--CHILDREN of Peter N. Jacobus and Hannah E. .....:
Edith D.   b. abt. 1874
May E.   b. abt. 1877

- - - - -

Jacobus, Rachel Lutecia
m. Anthony Cisco (q.v.)

- - - - -

Jacobus, TUNIS   b. (July 4, 1779)
(gmnj)   d. December 16, 1848

"Aged 69.6.12"

wife, Leah A.**(Vreeland) b. (Abt. 1779)
(gmnj)   d. (July 4, 1865)

"Age 86"

daughter, ELEANOR   b. (December 26, 1811)
(gmnj)   d. July 16, 1838

"Aged 26.6.21"

daughter, ELEANOR   b. (March 27, 1811)

(gmnj)	d. September 13, 1811

"Aged 5 mos. & 17 dys."

son, JACOB	b. (November 16, 1806)
(gmnj)	d. September 13, 1814

"Aged 7.9.27"

son, JACOB	b. (August 17, 1817)
(gmnj)	d. July 14, 1820

"Aged 2.10.28"

son, RICHARD	b. (January 10, 1802)
(gmnj)	d. September 22, 1811

"aged 9.8.12"

Notes:

--Tunis was son of Derick/Richard Jacobus and Eleanor Speer of Peckman's River(Cedar Grove). In 1805, he inherited from his father "90 acres of old homestead, house and barns; also 1/2 of lands in the little Piece."(NJ Will #10416G,1805)

--Tunis Jacobus m. June 29, 1799, Caldwell, Leah Vreeland.

--Tunis' cause of death was recorded as "palsey".

--Leah's cause of death was recorded as "old age".

--1850 Census: #425, Caldwell: Leah Jacobus, age 72; Mary Ann Perkins, age 30 (Between Henry Jacobus, age 39, farmer and William J. Jacobus, age 50, farmer)

--1860 Census #408 Caldwell: Leah Jacobus, age 81, widow; at res. of son, Henry T. Jacobus

--CHILDREN of Tunis Jacobus and Leah Vreeland:

William T.(qv)b. abt 1800; m. Rachel Egbertson

Richard   b. January 10, 1802; d. September 22, 1811

Henry T.   b. abt. 1811; m. Mary Stager

--1850 Census #424 Caldwell: Henry Jacobus, age 39, farmer, real estate $5000; Mary, age 39; Amarintha, age 19;Harriet,(m.1852,Calvin Francisco) age 16; Mary E., age 12; Sarah M. age 10; Leah E., age 8; Charles, age 5; George, age 3(m. Florence W. ___); Henrietta, age 7 months ; adj. to Leah Jacobus, age 72

--1860 Census: #408, Caldwell Twp./Cedar Grove: Henry T. Jacobus, age 49, farmer; Mary, age 49; Mary E. age 22; Sarah M. age 19; Leah E. age 17; Charles, age 14; George age 13; Henrietta, age 10; Alice, age 8; Also, Leah Jacobus age 81.

--1870 Census, #470 Caldwell: Henry T. Jacobus, age 59, real estate $12,000; Mary, age 59; George, age 22; Henrietta, age 20; Mary E. Clark, dau.,age 21, no occupation

--1880 Census p.413A, Caldwell: Henry T. Jacobus, age 69, b. NJ, no occupation; Mary, wife, age 69, b. NJ; Mary E. Clark, daughter, widow, age 41, b. NJ, dressmaking; Henrietta, dau., single, age 30, b. NJ; Elizabeth C. Baldwin, other, widow, age 69, b. NJ, no occupation

Eleanor	b. March 27, 1811; d. September 13, 1811
Eleanor	b. December 26, 1811; d. July 16, 1838
Jacob	b. November 16, 1806; d. September 13, 1814
Richard T.(?)	b. abt. 1815; m. Asenath ___

--1860 Census, #415, Caldwell: Richard T. Jacobus, age 45, mason, Asenath, age 50, b. England; Wesley R. age 21, labor; catherine, age 22; Elizabeth B. age 14(m. Theodore G. Vreeland); Jonas, age 14
adj. to Tunis Jacobus, brother?
--1880 Census p. 38D, Montclair, NJ:

Richard T. Jacobus, age 65, b. NJ, brick mason; Asenoth, wife, age 69, b. England; Jonas T., son, widower,(m. Liz Tweedle) age 36, b. NJ, carpenter; Alice Jacobus, granddaughter, age 9, b. NJ, father b. NJ, mother b. Ireland; Burt L. Jacobus, grandson, age 3, b. NJ, mother b. Ireland;

Jacob
Tunis T.(?)

b. August 17, 1817; d. July 14, 1820
b. abt 1820; m. Leah Ann Jacobus,dau. of William I. Jacobus(q.v.)
--1860 Census, p.112B, Caldwell: Tunis Jacobus, age 40 carpenter; Leah, age 40; Anna C. age 15; Rachel E. age 13;; Helen M. age 11; Sarah E. age 9; Abraham E. age 6; Leah A. age 4; William age 2; adj. to Richard T. Jacobus, age 45; near #408, Leah Jacobus, age 81, widow of Tunis Jacobus
--1870 Census, p.369B,3Wd Orange: Tunis Jacobus, age 55, works boot/shoe factory; Leah A., age 50; Helen, age 20; Sarah, age 18; Abram age 16; Addie, age 13; Fannie, age 9; John Harrison, age 25, stone mason; Anna C. Harrison, age 25; Horatio Murry, age 25, b. NY, teamster, Emma Murry, age 23
--1880 Census p.171B, Orange, NJ: Tunis Jacobus, age 60, b. NJ, carpenter; Lea Ann, wife, age 60, b. NJ; Ellen, dau., age 29, b. NY; Addie, dau., age 20, b. NJ; Fannie, dau., age 17, b. NJ

- - - - -

Jacobus, W.E.   b.
(lfrc) (Lot #9)   d.
--W. E. Jacobus purchased Lot # 9 in 1882)

Notes:

--(?)1880 Census, p.184C, Little Falls: William Jacobus, age 60, b. NJ, farmer; Abby, wife, age 52, b. NJ
--(?)1880 Census, p.406C, Caldwell: Ellen Jacobus, age 66, b. NJ; Wesley, son, age 28, b. NJ; Alexander P. son, age 26, works brush factory; Margaret Miles, widow, age 82, b. NJ; Edward Gould, single, age 35, b. NJ, works brush factory

- - - - -

Jacobus, WILLIAM G.   b. (December 14, 1842)
(gmnj)   d.

"Co. D, 26th N.J. Inf" (Pvt.)

wife, Sarah* A. (Courter)   b. (December 1841)
(gmnj)   d. (after 1910)
daughter, Ada E.
m. Charles Dougherty(q.v.)

Notes:
--William G. Jacobus served in the Civil War;Co. D, 26th Regiment, NJ Volunteers. He enlisted September 3, 1862 and was discharged September 27, 1863. He lived in Cedar Grove.
--William G. Jacobus was son of James G. Jacobus and Sarah Bush.
--William G. Jacobus m. July 4, 1863, Sarah A. Courter, b. December 29, 1842; d. 1927. She was daughter of John J. Courter and Ellen VanRiper and is buried at Hillside Cemetery, Fairfield, NJ.
--1850 Census #317 Caldwell: James G. Jacobus, age 38, farmer, real estate $2500; Sarah, age 42; Thomas H., age 15, farmer; William, age 9; Samuel, age 7
--1880 Census #159,p.406D, Caldwell: William G. Jacobus, age 37, dealer in tobacco; Sarah A., wife, age 37; Franklin P., son, age 14; Lucy R. dau, age 12, b. Michigan; Ada E., dau., age 11, b. Penna; Theodore, F., son, age 7, b. NJ

--1900 Census #292 Caldwell Twp: Charles A. Dougherty, b.
June 1858, age 41, widower, farmer, b. PA, parents b.
Ireland; Ethel , dau., b. November 1894; Sarah A. Jacobus, b.
December 1841, m. 37yrs; 4 born 3 living

--1910 Census: p.12B West Caldwell: Charles A. Dougherty,
age 51, widower, farm labor; Ethel M., dau., age 15; Sarah
A. Jacobus, age 67, mother-in-law, m. 46 yrs, 4 children born
3 living

--CHILDREN of William G. Jacobus and Sarah A. Courter:

Franklin P.	b. April 1866
Lucy R.	b. September 12, 1867; d. February 26, 1949; m. William Allen Butler
	--1880 Census, p.176D, Acquackanonk, NJ: William Butler, son, age 12, b. NJ, father b. CT, mother b. Scotland; at res. of parents Josiah and Ellen Butler
	both bur. Hillside Cemetery, Fairfield, NJ
Ada E.	b. March 20,1870; d. December 5, 1899 m. Charles A. Dougherty (q.v.) He is buried Hillside Cemetery, Fairfield, NJ
Theodore F.	b. July 1, 1872; m. Laura Brown

- - - - -

Jacobus, WILLIAM G. (gmnj)	b. (August 8, 1795) d. April 8, 1840

"Aged 44.8.20"

wife, MARGARET (Speer) (gmnj)	b. (abt. 1802) d. May 15, 1864

"Aged 62 yrs. & 2 mos."

son, JOHN G. (gmnj)	b. (February 6, 1839) d. January 13, 1843

"Aged 3.11.7"

son, CYRUS F.   b. (abt. 1824)
(Inv. #15771G)   d. January 22, 1863

"Aged 39 yrs."

Notes:
--This stone was standing in 1993.
--William G. Jacobus is also recorded as buried at the
Presbyterian Church Yard, Caldwell: "d. April 18, 1840, ae
44 yrs. 8 mos."
--Son, John G. Jacobus,"son of William G. & Margaret", is
also recorded as buried at the Presbyterian Church Yard,
Caldwell. He is on the stone of William G. Jacobus "d. April
18, 1840, ae 44 yrs.8 mos.".
--1850 Census: #104, Caldwell/Cedar Grove: Margaret
Jacobus, age 49, Real estate value $1200; Cyrus F. age 25,
woodturner; Cornelius H., age 21, woodturner; Sarah C. age
19; Peter N. age 17, woodturner; Rebecca, age 14; and,
Cornelia Brockaway, age 7
--1860 Census: #447 Caldwell/Cedar Grove: Cyrus Jacobus,
age 34,woodturner; Margaret, age 58, (widow of Wm. G.
Jacobus);Rebecca, age 23; William G. age 19
--CHILDREN of William G. Jacobus and Margaret Speer:
Cyrus F.,   b. abt 1824; d. January 22,1863, 'hem. of the
               bowels';m. Mary _____
Cornelius H., b. abt. 1827, d. April 22, 1862. "Inflammation
               of Brain"
Sarah C.   b. abt. 1831
Peter N.(q.v.) b. abt. 1833; m. Ottilie E. _____
Rebecca   b. abt 1836
John G.   b. February 6, 1839; d. January 13, 1843
William G.   b. abt 1841
               --(?)1880 Census #166 Caldwell: William H.
               Jacobus, age 38, works brush factory; wife,
               Emma S.F. (Felty), age 24 (2nd wife); Burton

W., son, age 17; Frederick, son,a ge 11; Annie
E., dau.,age 10; Charles W., age 6; Arthur L.
b. November 1880; Josephine Felty, age 16,
wife's sister; Mary Felty, age 58,
mother-in-law, b. Canada

- - - - -

Jacobus, WILLIAM I.	b. January 26, 1799
(gmnj)	d. July 31, 1878
wife, RACHEL (Egbertson)	b. March 27, 1799
(gmnj)	d. March 26, 1870
daughter, ELLEN	b. (July 9,1828)
(gmnj)	d. June 15, 1833

"Aged 4.11.6"

Notes:

--Son of Tunis Jacobus (q.v.)

--William I. Jacobus m. Rachel Egberts, November 6, 1819,
Caldwell Presbyterian Church.

--1850 Census #426 Caldwell: William Jacobus, age 50,
farmer, real estate $3000; Rachel, age 50; Hetty M. age 20,
b. NY; Abraham E., age 18, mason; William A. Davis, age
11; Tunis T. Jacobus, age 31, carpenter, real estate $1000;
Lean Ann, age 30; Anna C., age 6; Rachel E., age 4; Helen
M. age 2; Ann Curran, age 22, b. Ireland

--1860 Census:p.111B, Caldwell Twp./Cedar Grove: William
I. Jacobus, age 61, farmer; Rachel, age 61; Abraham, age 28;
Edna, age 27(dau-in-law?); John B. age 2(grandson?); adj.
to Leah Jacobus, age 72

--In the 1870 Mortality Schedule, Rachel's cause of death
was recorded as 'consumption'

--1870 Census, p.133A, Caldwell: William Jacobus, age 71,
mason; Hetty M., dau., age 40, real estate $2500, widow;
William J., age 14; Helen, age 12; Carrie E., age 7

--CHILDREN of William Jacobus and Rachel Egberts:

Leah   b. abt.1819;d.March 22, 1890; m.Tunis
           Jacobus

Eliza Margaret b. January 19,1825; d. June 18, 1900
           bapt. Apr. 25,1825, Stone House Plains, NJ

Ellen   b. July 9, 1828; d. June 15, 1833

Hetty M.   b. abt. 1830; m. C. H. Jacobus(q.v.)
           --1870 Census, p.133A, Caldwell: William
           Jacobus, age 71, mason; Hetty M., dau., age
           40, real estate $2500, widow; William J., age
           14; Helen, age 12; Carrie E., age 7
           --1880 Census, p. 415A, Caldwell: Hetty M.
           Jacobus, widow, age 50, b. NY, parents b. NJ;
           Albert W., son, age 24, grocery store; Ella L.,
           dau-in-law, age 27, b. NJ; Ella O., dau., age
           22; Carrie E. dau., age 18; Charles G., other,
           age 6, b. NJ, mother and father b. NJ;
           Cornelius R. Jacobus, grandson, age 9 months
           b. NJ

Abraham E.   b. abt. 1832;d. 1900; m. Edna Bowden
           both bur. Prospect Hill Cemetery, Caldwell
           --1850 Census, #108, Caldwell: John
           Bowden, age 61, cotton mfr, b. Norwich,
           England, real estate $7000; Mary, age 57, b.
           Cheshire, England; Hannah, age 26; Anthony,
           age 22; Alice Ann,age 19; Edna, age 16;
           Elizabeth, age 36 (wid. of William Bowden;
           Rachel Bowden, age 15, (dau. of William
           Bowden); Mary, age 13; 4 boarders
           --1880 Census, p.226C, Newark, NJ:
           Abram E. Jacobus, age 48, b. NJ, sale &
           Exchange Stables, Edna, wife, age 46, b. NJ,
           parents b. England; Joseph, son, age 16, b.
           NJ, clerk
           --1910 Census, p.20A, Cedar Grove: Edna
           Jacobus, age 76, widow, 2 born 2 living;
           Franklin C. Courter, nephew, age 55,
           widower, engraving house artist

John(q.v.)   b. abt. 1835; m. Mary Esther Monroe

- - - - -

JARDINE

Jardine, Robert*   b. (abt. 1832)
                         d. (bef. 1910)
wife, Elizabeth*   b. (abt. 1843)
                         d. (aft. 1910)

daughter, MARY E.   b. (abt. 1860)
(gmnj)   d. November 25, 1889

"Aged 28 yrs. & 6 mos."

daughter, JENNIE M.   b. (May 25, 1861)
(gmnj)   d. July 8, 1885

"Aged 17 yrs. & 1 day"

daughter, SARAH E.   b. (May 24, 1875)
(gmnj)   d. July 16, 1883

"Aged 8.1.23"

Notes:
--Robert Jardine served in the Civil War; Co. K, 25th Regt. NJ Inf. Vol. He enlisted August 15, 1861 and was discharged December 20, 1865.
--1880 Census, p.162D, Matteawan, Duchess Co., NY:
Robert Jardine, age 48, b. Scotland, carpet printer; Elizabeth, wife, age 44, b. Scotland; Thomas R.(q.v.), son, age 24, b. MA, carpet weaver; George, son, age 21, b. MA, carpet weaver; Mary, dau., age 18, b. RI, works in carpet factory; Martha, dau., age 16, b. RI, works in carpet factory; Annie,

dau., age 14, b. RI; Jennie, dau., age 11, b. MA; Lilly, dau.,
age 7, b. NJ; Sarah, dau., age 5, b. NJ
--1900 Census #29,p.249 Verona/Cedar Grove: Robert
Jardine, b. July 1830, age 69, b. Scotland, m. 76 yrs., retired:
Elizabeth, b. September 1836, Scotland, age 63; Annie E.
Stevens, dau., age 33, b. NJ, m. 1 year; James Stevens,
son-in-law, b. March 1822,Scotland; 'retired'?;Agnes L.
Ross, dau., age 26, b. NJ; William Ross, son-in-law, b.
March 1870 NJ, age 30, farmer; Elizabeth Richardson,
granddaughter, b. September 1897; 6 boarders, farm labor
--1910 Census: p.210A,Little Falls Twp: Elizabeth Jardine,
age 67, widow, b. Scotland,12 born, 2 living; Annie
Thompson, dau., age 45, widow, b. RI, parents b. Scotland,5
born 5 living; Lillie Ross, dau., age 34, m. 11 yrs, 1 born 0
living; William Ross, age 38, b. NJ,parents b.
Scotland,son-in-law; Oliver Jardine, age 10, grandson,b. NJ,
father b. Scotland, mother b. RI; Bruce Jardine, age 7,
grandson; Annie Thompson, age 4, granddaughter; Jennie
Thompson, age 2, granddaughter; Elizabeth Jardine, age 14,
granddaughter
--CHILDREN of Robert Jardine and Elizabeth.....:

Thomas R.(q.v.)b. May 23, 1856	
George	b. abt. 1859
Mary	b. abt 1860; d. November 24, 1889
Jennie M.	b. May 25, 1861; d. July 8, 1885
Martha	b. abt. 1864
Annie E.	b. abt. 1866; m. ..... Thompson and, m. James Stevens;
Jennie	b. abt. 1869
Agnes Lilly	b. abt.1874;m.William Ross --1900 Census, #29, Verona, NJ
Sarah E.	b. May 24, 1875; d. July 16, 1883
Daughter	m. _____ Richardson

- - - - -

Jardine, THOMAS R.   b. (May 23, 1856)

(gmnj)(Plot #13)   d. November 20, 1888

"Aged 32.5.28"

Notes:
--Son of Robert Jardine (q.v.)
--(?)Military records show Thomas R. Jardine,"private,
Chapman's Battery, N.J. Miltitia.
--1880 Census, p.162D, Matteawan, Duchess Co., NY;
Thomas R. Jardine, age 24, b. MA, parents b. Scotland,
carpet weaver; at res. of parents, Robert and Elizabeth
Jardine (q.v.)

- - - - -

JOHNSON

Johnson, Alice
m. Dan Pilling (q.v.)

- - - - -

KERN

Kern, CHARLES   b.
(npfh)   d. August, 1913
                         (bur. August 16, 1913)

Notes:
--(?)1910 Census, p.150A, Manchester Twp.,Passaic Co:
Fred Kern, age 38, b. Switzerland, silk weaver; Ida, age 37,
b. Germany; Fred, age 12; Adolph age 11; William age 10;
Minnie, age 7
--(?)1910 Census, p.110B, 1 Wd Paterson: John Kern, age
45, b. Switzerland, silk mill weaver; Louise, age 40, b.
Switzerland; Louise, age 11, b. NJ; John, age 4, b. NJ

- - - - -

KENNEDY

Kennedy, Andrew*   b.
                        d.
wife, JANE   b. (January 6, 1793)
(gmnj)   d. January 11, 1858

"Aged 64 yrs. & 5 dys."

Notes:

- - - - -

KOPPE

Koppe, L. HENRIETTE   b. April 22, 1860
(gmnj)   d. September 13, 1860

Notes:
--Henriette was b. Brooklyn, NY and d. Little Falls, NJ
--See: Constance A. and N.C. Kopp, plot owners at Cedar
Lawn Cemetery, Paterson, as of 1917.
--(?)1910 Census, p. 278A, 3 Wd.Paterson: Joseph Kopp, age
69, b. Germany, helper; Annie, age 61, 12 born 2 living;
Adolph, age 36, b. Germany, driver; Elizabeth age 30,b.
Switzerland (dau-in-law) Florence?. age 13, b. NJ; Mildred
age 5 months b. NJ

- - - - -

KRANZAK

Kranzak, ANNIE   b.
(npfh)   d. May, 1916
                        (bur. May 8, 1916)

Notes:
--(?)1910 Census, p.207A, Little Falls: John Kramshoch, age
38, b. Hungary, carpet mill finisher; Bertha, age 30, b.
Hungary, 3 born 3 living; John, age 3, b. NJ; Margaret, age
2; Helen, age 9 months
--(?)1920 Census, p.121B, Little Falls: John Krancsek, age
46, b. Poland; Bertha, age 43, b. Hungary; John, age 12, b.
NY; Margaret, age 11, b. NJ; Helen, age 10, b. NJ
--(?)1930 Census, p. 240A, Singac, Little Falls: John
Kranscak, age 58, b. Austria, labor at silk mill; Bertha K. age
56, b. Austria; John Jr. age 22, b. NY, weaver; Margarite,
age 20, b. NJ, weaver; Helen, age 18, b. NJ, weaver

- - - - -

LANATI

Lanati, PASQUILE   b.
(npfh)   d. May, 1913
                          (bur. May 10, 1913)

Notes:
--(?)1910 Census, p.199A, Little Falls Twp: Pasquale
DeLonato, age 37, b. Italy, railroad labor, m. 9 yrs; Natale,
wife, age 36,b. Italy, 2 born 1 living; Caroline, age 8, b. Italy
--(?)1920 Census #194, Giovanni "Linnato"; age 36;
Lav...,wife, age 50; Livia Gianello, orphan daughter, age 6,
two boarders
--(?)1920 Census, p.130B, Little Falls: Dominick Leonitti,
age 25, laborer, b. Italy; Jennie, age 16, b. Italy
--(?)1920 Census, p.143B, Little Falls: John Lanetta, age 45,
b. Iraly, labor at stone quarry; Mary A., age 35, wife, b. Italy;
Joseph Alessio, age 39, b. Italy, labor,road contractor; wife,
Minnie, age 32, b. Italy; Jennie, age 12, b. NJ; Mildred age
10; Julia age 8; Patrick age 6; Caroline, age 3 yr 9 months;

Gladis, age 4 months; Angeline Croak, sister, age 26, widow,
b. Italy; Charles Croak, age 2, grandson, b. NJ
--(?)1930 Census, Part 2, Sheet 7B, Cedar Grove: John
Linnato

- - - - -

LORIGAN

Lorigan, GEORGE T.　　　　b. February 16, 1842
(gmnj)　　　　　　　　　　d. May 14, 1904

Liet. Col.
9th Regt. N.G.N.Y.
Aged 62 years
2 mo. and 28 days

"A thoughtful and loving father"

1st wife, Mary A.*(Wells)　　b. (October 20, 1842)
　　　　　　　　　　　　　　d. (June 8, 1875)
　　　　　　　　　　　　　　bur. (Mattituck, LI, NY)

2nd wife, EVA P.(Courter/Wells)
　　　　　　　　　　　　　　b. May 8, 1858
(gmnj)　　　　　　　　　　　d. April 6, 1928

His Wife

Notes:
--George and Eva are on the same stone as Elmer E. Wells
(q.v.) and Cornelius Supenor.(q.v.)
--George T. Lorigan served in the Civil War: Lt. Colonel, 9th
Regt., New York National Guard. "The 9th was New York's
original Irish regiment."

--George T. Lorigan m. #1, December 4, 1865, Mary A.
Wells; dau. of Benjamin F. Wells and Jane Teed of
Mattituck, Suffolk co., NY. She died in childbirth.
--1870 Census, p.239B, Southold, Suffolk Co., NY: George
Lorigan, age 28, farmer, b. Ireland; Mary, age 26, b.
Pennsylvania(??)
--1870 Census, p 94A, 18 Wd, New York City: George C.
Wells, age 53, b. NY, restaurant; Marietta P., age 33, b. NJ;
Eva Courter, age 11, b. NJ; Elmer Courter, age 7, b. NJ; 5
other persons
--1880 Census, p.630A, Manhattan, New York City: Marietta
P. Wells, age 40, widow,b. NJ, boarding housekeeper,
parents b. NJ; Eva P., dau., age 21, b. NY, parents b. NJ;
Edgar C., son, age 19, b. NY, bookkeeper; Elmer E. son, age
17, b. NY, clerk in store; George T. "Lougan", widower, age
35, b. Ireland; Nellie Lougan, age 9, b. NY; 2 servants
--1900 Census, p.258A, Manhattan Boro: George T. Lorigan,
b. February 1842, Ireland, journalist; Eva P., b. May 1858
NY, parents b. NJ; Nellie E. dau., b. November 1871
--CHILDREN of George T. Lorigan and Mary A. Wells:

Nellie	b. November 2, 1870
	--1910 Census, p.15A, 22Wd.Brooklyn: Nellie E. Lorigan, age 39, single, b. NY, parents b. NY?; 'own income'; boarder at res. of Duch? E. Daniels.
Mamie	b. June 8, 1875; d. September 13, 1875 (bur. Mattituck Parish Cemetery, LI, NY)

- - - - -

M.

M., A. A.	b.
(gmnj)(simple fieldstone)	d.

Notes:

--(??)1900 Census, p.81, Little Falls: James Madden, (q.v.)b. August 1859, insurance, m. 5 yrs. b. NY, father b. England, mother b. Ireland; Freda A., b. June 1868, Vermont, 1 born 1 living; Allene A. b. 1897

- - - - -

MADDEN

Madden, James*   b. (August 1859)
                               d. (aft. 1920)
(gmnj)
1st wife,MAGGIE JACOBUS (VanNess)
(gmnj)   b. May 30, 1860
                               d. February 22, 1887

2nd wife, Freida* (Andrews) b. (June 1868)
                            d. (aft. 1920)
Notes:
--Maggie was daughter of Elias VanNess(q.v.) and Mary E. Marley.
--James Madden m. #2, abt. 1895, Freida B. Andrews; dau. of Edmond E. Andrews and Lucy A. .....
--1880 Census, p.184C, Little Falls: Elias VanNess, age 55, b. NJ, storekeeper; Mary, wife, age 38, b. Ireland; Maggie, dau, age 18, father b. NJ, mother b. Ireland, assistant P.M.; Cyrus, son, age 16, b. NJ, clerk in store;Mary Gilmore, age 46, b. Ireland; Thomas Peer, age 18, b. NJ, servant
--1880 Census, p.29A, Berlin, Washington Co., VT: Edmond E. Andrews, age 56 b. VT farmer; Lucy A., wife, age 49, b. VT; Freida B. Andrews, dau., age 11, b. VT; 4 other children;
--1900 Census, p.81, Little Falls: James Madden, b. August 1859, insurance, m. 5 yrs. b. NY, father b. England, mother b. Ireland; Freda A., b. June 1868, Vermont, 1 born 1 living; Allene A., b. 1897

--1910 Census, p.196B, Little Falls Twp: James Madden, b. NY, parents b. England, age 50, m. 15 yrs., insurance company agent; Frieda, age 42, 2 born 2 living, b.Vermont, parents b. Vermont; Allene, dau., age 13, b. NY; Elizabeth dau., age 8, b. NY

--1920 Census, p.199A,Ridgewood, Bergen Co., NJ: James Madden,age 62, b. NY, father b. England, mother b. Ireland, insurance manager; Fredia, age 52; Alline M. age 22; Elizabeth age 17

--CHILDREN of James Madden & Maggie J. VanNess:

James. b. April 1876; m. Edna .....
1900 Census: p.83A, Little Falls
James Madden, b. April 1876; Edna, b. September 1876, 3 born 1 living; Charles G., b. May 1898

--CHILDREN of James Madden and Freda Andrews:

Alline A. b. December 1897
Elizabeth b. abt. 1902

- - - - -

MAKEPEACE

Makepeace, CHARLES W.
(npfh) b. (abt. 1851)
d. August, 1907
(bur. August 15, 1907)

wife, Margaret** b. (abt. 1859)
d. (aft. 1910)

Notes:
--(?)1880 Census, p.145A, Paterson: William Makepiece, widower, age 47, b. NJ: Charles, single, age 21; Lorenzo, age 19; George age 17; Laura age 13; Eava, age 9
--(?)1880 Census, p.319D, Paterson: Wm. H. Makepiece, age 40, b. VA, clerk D.G.store, parents b. NJ: Margret, wife, age 38, b. NJ; Marry, dau., age 13, b. NJ; Anna Armstrong,

mother, widow, age 75, b. NJ; Charles Makepiece, son, age 16, b. NJ, clerk D.G.store
--(?)1880 Census, p.417A, Caldwell: Hugh Stewart, age 67, b. Ireland, blacksmith; Jane, wife, age 63, b. Ire; William, age 39; Henry age 35; Isabella Walters dau.,a ge 29; James Stewart son,a ge 19; Charles Walters, grandson, age 4, b. NJ, father b. France, mother b. Ireland; Christina Sevus, grandau., age 6, b. NY, father b. Germany, mother b. Ireland; Willimatha Stewart, grandson, age 4, b. England, father b. Ireland, mother b. England
--1900 Census #11,p.248, Verona: Jane Stewart age 86, widow, b. Scotland; Henry Stewart, age 44, single, farmer: Margaret Makepeace, dau., age 41, married; Charlie Makepeace, age 49, tinman at RR; Mattie Makepeace, age 9, granddaughter
--1910 Census #159 Cedar Grove: Henry Stewart, age 47, single, b. NJ, laborer; M.... Makepeace, sister, age 45, widow, housekeeper; Mattie Makepeace, niece, age 16
--1920 Census #81,p.167A, Cedar Grove: Henry Stewart, age 60, single; Margaret Makepeace, age 55, sister, widow; b. NJ, parents b. Scotland; Mattie Makepeace, niece, age 24, b. NJ, parents b. NJ
--CHILDREN of Charles W. Makepeace and Margaret .....:
Mattie   b. abt. 1896

- - - - -

MARLEY

Marley, Mary E.
(dau. of Patrick Marley,q.v.)
m. Elias VanNess (q.v.)

Marley, PATRICK   b. (abt. 1800) Ireland
(gmnj)   d. August 3, 1885

"Aged 85 yrs."

wife, RUTH b.January 18, 1818 Ireland
(gmnj) d. January 18, 1894
daughter, SARAH A. b. (November 4, 1851)
(gmnj) d. February 1, 1869

"Aged 17.2.27"

Notes:

--The Marley brothers' saw mill had machinery for hub and spoke turning. The mill was built early in the 19th century by K. Perry.

--1850 Census: #98 Caldwell: Patrick Marley, age 40, labor, b. Ireland; Ruth, age 31, b. Ireland; Mary, age 11, b. Ireland; James age 9, b. Ireland; Thomas age 5, b. Ireland; Francis, age 1, b. New York.

--1860 Census: #419 Caldwell/Cedar Grove: Patrick Marley, age 50, farmer, b. Ireland; Ruth, age 40, b. Ireland; Mary, age 20; Margaret age 1 month; J. Thomas, age 12, b. Ireland; Francis, age 10, b. NY; Sarah H. age 8, b. NJ;Charles S. age 5, b. NJ

--1870 Census: #485 Caldwell/Cedar Grove:Patrick Marley, age 55, b. Ireland; farm labor, real estate $6000; Ruth, age 50; Margaret VanZile, age 17, works cotton mill; Thomas Marley, age 25, hug mfg., $2000, b. Ireland; Francis Marley, age 21, hub mfg., b. NY

--1880 Census:p.415B, #299 Caldwell/Cedar Grove: Patrick Marley, age 78, b. Ireland, no occupation; Ruth, wife, age 60, b. Ireland. (Adj. to William E. Pierce)

--"Since about 1860, Patrick Marley (and after his death, his heirs) had owned all the low land between the highway and the Peckman River (roughly speaking), extending from Grove Avenue on the north to the west Supenor strip on the south, except fo a piece at the south sold to ex-Governor Marcus L. Ward, just west of the Public Hall purchase. Patrick Marley died without leaving a will, leaving several

134

heirs. One of them, his son, James, had been trough
bankruptcy but had forgotten to list among his assets his
interest in the Marley properties in Cedar Grove. The
bankruptcy proceedings were reopened and James' interests
here sold by the trustees to the highest bidder, hiswife, Maria
Marley. At last, title was perfected and transaction
completed conveying the land in question (175.48 ft.
frontage) from all the Marleys to the Public Hall
Association. The erection of the hall was soon begun and
was finished by the end of 1910." (Boardman, p.17)
--"An auction sale of Marley land in numerous parcels took
place at the end of 1912. The low land between the Post
Office and the Public Hall was sold in lots of 50 ft. frontage
to several buyers, while the Marley upland across which
Love Lane (now Bowden Road) ran, was bought by Anthony
Frick - south parcel, and George F. Hutter -north and
narrower piece. A tract of Marley land on the east side of
Pompton Avenue was acquired then or shortly afterwards by
the Episcopal Diocese." (Boardman, p.18)
--There was an F. J. Marley, "Trap Rock Stone Crushing
Works: Macadamizing Streets a Specialty" located at
Bloomfield Aveue, Verona and Valley Road, Great Notch,
NJ.
--CHILDREN of Patrick Marley and Ruth .....:

Mary   b. October 15, 1839,Ireland; m. Elias
              VanNess(q.v.)

James   b. abt 1841, Ireland; m. Maria ____
              --1860 Census, p.471, 4 Wd.Newark:
              Jas. Marley, age 19, clerk, b. NJ?,boarder
              --1870 Census, p.339A, 10 Wd.Newark:
              James Marley, age 29, shirt mfg, b. NY;
              Maria, age 25, b. NJ; Frances age 6; Louisa
              age 4; William, age 3 months
              --1910 Census, p.283A, 9 Wd Newark: James
              H. Marley, b. Ireland, age 68, m.47 yr;
              secretary,print mfg.;Maria L., b. NJ, 10 born 5
              living

Thomas   b. abt 1845, Ireland; ?m. Elizabeth Piper
--1880 Census, #300 Caldwell: Thomas
Marley, son-in-law, age 32, woodturner, b.
NJ; parents b. Ireland; Elizabeth Marley,
dau., age 26, b. NY; at res of Ellen Piper,
age 49, widow, b. England

Francis   b. abt 1849. NY; m. Louise .....
--1880 Census, p.187A, Little Falls, NJ:
Francis Marley, age 30, b. NY, parents b.
Ireland, hub manufacture; Louise, wife,
b. NJ, parents b. Germany; James C., son,
age 1, b. NJ; Minnie Cook age 13, b. NJ,
servant, parents b. Germany; Emaline Bone,
age 29, b. NJ, servant.
--1900 Census, p.103, Little Falls: Francis
Marley, b. NY, parents Ireland, boat?
contractor, b. March 1849; Louisa, b. Nov.
1857; James C. b. Jan 1879, foreman roads;
Ethel b. 1888; Francis G. b. April 1892;
Wilhelmina Marshall, aunt, b. June 1838,
Germany, widow; Mary Hanky, autn, b.
September 1830, widow, b. Germany
--1910 Census, p.224A, Little Falls Twp:
Francis J. Marley, age 61, b. NY, parents b.
Ireland, m. 33 yrs, contractor; Louisa, age 54,
b. NJ, parents b. Germany, 3 born 3 living;
Frank G. age 18, clerk; James C. age 31,
insurance agent
--1920 Census, p.111A, Little Falls: Francis J.
Marley, b. NJ, parents Ireland, age 73,
deputy collector,US Gov't; Louise, age 64, b.
NJ, parents b. Berlin

Sarah A.   b. abt 1852, b. NY
Charles S.   b. abt. 1855, NJ
--(?)1900 Census, p.250, Verona: Scharle
Marley, b. March 1854, widower, b. NJ,
parents Ireland; salesman;

--(?)1910 Census, p.125B, 8 Wd Newark:
Charles Marley, age 54, m.20 yr, b. NJ
Mary, age 45?, b. Ireland; Ruth, age 15, b. NY
--(?)1920 Census, p.123A, 8 Wd.Newark;
Charles S. Marley, age 66, widower, boarder,
commercial traveler,furniture

Margaret   b. 1860, NJ

- - - - -

Marley, THOMAS   b.
(gmnj)   d.
On Elias VanNess stone (q.v.)

Notes:
--(?)Brother of Patrick Marley
--(?)Son of Patrick Marley
--(?)1860 Census, #728, East Ward, Paterson: Thomas
Marley, age 40, labor, b. Ireland; Bridget, age 30, b. Ireland;
Thomas age 3 and Mary age 1.
--(?)1880 Census, #300 Caldwell: Thomas   Marley,
son-in-law, age 32, woodturner, b.NJ; parents b. Ireland;
Elizabeth Marley,dau., age 26, b. NY; at res of Ellen Piper,
age 49, widow, b. England

- - - - -

MAS
(MAAS?)

Mas, DIRK   b. _____ 14, 18__(gmnj)
     d.
(partially destroyedwooden marker)

Mas, HESSELTJE   b. February 1, 1907
(gmnj)   d. February 11, 1907
(wooden marker)

Mas, WILLEM   b. 1897
(gmnj)   d. 1898

Notes:

--See: Willem Maas, b. November 2, 1858, the Netherlands; son of Cornelius Maas and Maartje Koorn; d. June 30, 1940, Paterson, N.J. He sailed from Rotterdam on November 17, 1892 for New York (Ellis Island) with wife and four children. He m. May 17, 1883, Texel, Netherlands, Ariaantje Huisman, b. May 18, 1863.

--This family may be descendants of the Maas family of Texel, Netherlands who emigrated to the Passaic County area.

--(?)*MAAS:* "Willem Cornelisz Maas, a grandson of Hendrik Pietersz Maas, was farmer in the village DeKoog. He sold his 7 cows, 52 sheep, 18 young cows, 2 horses, 4 goats, 60 chickens and his inventory, and left Texel (The Netherlands) in November 1892 with his wife Ariaantje Huisman and their four children:Maartje, Cornlis Bernardus, Bernardus Cornelis and Hendrik. They sailed from Rotterdam November 17, 18?? to New York. Ariaantje was very pregnant of her son Jacob, who was born in December. The doctor who examined them before leaving, told them he doubted if the little Cornelis would survive the trip. He was a very fragile child. The doctor at Ellis Island hesitated about giving permission to enter the United States. Cornelis survived and became 82 years old.

"The family of Willem Maas and Ariaantje Huisman settled down in Totowa, NJ. Soon three of the children died: Maartje died of cerebro-spinal in 1893, and in the same year baby Jacob and the five year old son, Bernardus died. Later the family moved to Paterson, NJ. They got two more children, Martha and John Bernard. Ariaantje never spoke English. She died October 31, 1924.

"The sons Henry James (Hendrik) Maas and Cornelius Maas registered in Paterson for the WW I Draft and was married

with Emma Nutt. Together they got two children. Henry
James was disabled, because he had a 'stiff arm'. He died
March 14, 1923 Paterson, only 32 years old.
"Cornelius Bernardus Maas married December 19, 1915
(Paterson) Anna Cummings. They had one child at the time
of the draft registration, but afterwards they got another four
children. He worked as a silk weaver most of his working
life. He made labels for the more prestigious stores in the
area of Paterson and retired from the place he started as a
weaver. Cornelius died March 17, 1968, and his wife Anna
July 1, 1968.
"There were also other members of the Maas-family
emigrating to the US. Cornelis Pietersz Maas left (Texel) in
1909 with his wife Jantje Cornelia Pieters Huisman and
seven children. They followed their oldest   Pieter who left
already in 1908. Their destination was also Paterson. There
are a lot of descendants of this couple still living in New
Jersey."*(Texelse geslachten; Hijijij..is naar Amerika;
Boerderijenboek; Stamboom MaesTexel 1785-1985.)*
(Miriam Klaasen, RootsWeb.Com)
--Other families from Texel who settled in the Passaic
County area: Bakelaar; Barhorst;DenBleijker; DeBlock;
DeBoer; Breen;Daalder;Eelman; Van Es; VanHeerwaarden;
Hoogheid; Janssen; Kievit; Klaasen; Kranenburg; Kuiper;
Liedmeijer; Mantje; Meijer; Mulder; Pippeling; DeRidder;
Sandifort; Schagen; Sikkelee; Stark; Steenland; Tanis;
Verbaarschot; Vlaming;
--Cornelius Bernardus Maas was a "label weaver for 50 years
and was employed for 42 years by Central Woven Label
Company, retired in 1960. ...attended St. Joseph's grammar
and high schools. (RootsWeb. Com)
--(?)1880 Census, p.383C, Paterson: Garret Van Der Mass,
age 50, b. Holland, laborer; Mary, wife, age 63, b. Holland;
--(?)1900 Census #186, Caldwell Twp: Max Mass
--(?)1910 Census, p.224B, Little Falls Twp: Ernest Maass, b.
Germany, age 42, m. 17 yrs, carpenter; Dorothy, age 42, b.
NY, parents b. Germany, 5 born 4 living; Ernest son, age 12,

b. NY; Harold, age 10, b. NY; Magdaline, age 4, b. NJ;
Marie, age 6, b. NY; Marie Gloeckner, b. Germany,
mother-in-law, age 67, widow, 4 born 3 living
--(?)1920 Census, p.137B, Little Falls: Earnest M. Maass,
age 52, b. Germany, printer; Dorothy F. age 52, b. NJ;
Harold J. age 20, b. NY; Marie E. age 16, b. NY; Madeline,
age 14, b. NY; Marie E. Glockner, age 76, widow, born
Germany

- - - - -

MATCHES

Matches, Charles W.*	b. (abt. 1859)
	d. (aft. 1920)
1st wife, Lillie J.*	b.
(gmnj)	d.
daughter, LILLIE	b. May 10, 1889
(gmnj)	d. May 11, 1889

Notes:
--Charles W. Matches was son of Robert Matches (q.v.) and
Agnes Voorhees.
--1st wife should read "Lizzie J."??
--1870 Census, p.203A, 8Wd.Newark: Robert Matches, age
56, works stone quarry, b. Scotland; Agnes, age 44, b. NJ;
Jane, age 21; Robert, age 15; Charles, age 13
--1880 Census: p.145A, Newark, NJ: Charles W. Matches,
age 22, single, clerk in store, b. NJ; res. with his parents.
--1900 Census: p.84 Little Falls: Charles Matches, b.
February 1860, m. 17 yrs.; Elizabeth, b. February 1862, 3
born 2 living; Meredith son, b. June 1886; Jeanette b. June
1889 (1890)
--1920 Census, p.117B, Little Falls:Charles W. Matches, b.
NJ, insurance agent, age 61; Imogene, wife, age 38, b. NJ

--1930 Census, p.265B, Little Falls: Charles W. Matches, age 72, b. NJ, father b. Scotland, mother b. NJ: Imogene S., age 50, b. NJ, father b. NJ, mother b. NY

--CHILDREN of Charles W. Matches and Elizabeth ....:

Robert Meredith	b. June 1886
	--1920 Census, p.111A, Little Falls: Robert M. Matches, age 34, b. NJ, parents NJ; stationary engineer; Marietta, age 31, b. NJ; Lillian K. age 11; Charles W. age 9; Robert M. age 7; Marietta, age 5
	--1930 Census, part 2, Sheet 5A, Cedar Grove:Levi E. Mosher, age 43, b. NJ, blacksmith shop; Mary E. age 41, b. NJ; Lillian K. Matches, dau., age 21, restaurant waitress; Charles W. Matches, son, age 19; Robert M. age 17, chauffeur trucking; Mary E. Matches, dau., age 15
Lillie	b. May 10, 1889; d. May 11, 1889
Jeanette A.	b. June 1890
	--1910 Census, p. 202B, Little Falls: Isaac M. VanNess, age 55, wood engraver; Evelyn H. age 53, 2 born 2 living; Howard E., age 31, civil engineer RR; Jeanetta A. Matches, niece, age 21

- - - - -

Matches, ROBERT (gmnj)	b. (1813-1816) d. October 28, 1884

"In 71st yr."

wife, AGNES (Voorhees) (gmnj)	b. (Abt. 1826) d. May 12, 1889

"In 63rd yr."

son, STEPHEN V.   b. (Abt. 1850)
(gmnj)   d. October 31, 1867

"In 17th yr."

daughter, JENNIE A.   b. (Abt. 1849)
(gmnj)   d. July 10, 1889

"In 37th yr." (should read 39th year?)

Notes:
--Robert was a farmer at Little Falls 1871-72. (Boyd)
--Robert was b. Orkney Islands, Scotland. (*World Family Tree*, Vol. 21)
--Agnes was daughter of Stephen Voorhees and Margaret .....
--1850 Census, p.360A, Acquackanonk: Robert Matches, age 34, b. Scotland, quarryman; Agnes, age 24, b. NJ; Jane A. age 1, b. NJ (adj. to John Spence,q.v.)
--1860 Census: p.1030, Acquackanonk, Passaic Co.: Robert Matches, age 44, quarryman, real estate value $10,000, b. Scotland; Agnes, age 33; Jane, age 11, Stephen, age 8; Robert, age 4; Charles age 2.
--1870 Census, p.203A, 8Wd.Newark: Robert Matches, age 56, works stone quarry, b. Scotland; Agnes, age 44, b. NJ; Jane, age 21; Robert, age 15; Charles, age 13
--1880 Census: p.145A, Newark, NJ: Robert Matches, age 62, b. Scotland, stone mason, father b. Denmark, mother b. Scotland; Agnes, wife, age 57, b. NJ; Jennie A. dau., age 30, b. NJ; Robert J., son, age 24, bookkeeper; Charles W. son, age 22, clerk in store; Margaret Nevine, mother, widow, age 88, b. NJ
--CHILDREN of Robert Matches and Agnes Voorhees:
Jane A.'Jennie' b. abt. 1849; d. July 19, 1889
Stephen V.   b. abt. 1852;named for his grandfather

d. October 31, 1867

Robert James b. abt 1856; m. Ida Elizabeth Strong
m. Margaret .....
--1920 Census, p.155A, Summit, Union Co.,
NJ: Robert Matches, age 63, b. NJ, salesman
for rubber?co.; Margaret age 61, b. NJ; Ida,
dau., age 19, b. NJ, mother b. NY

Charles W.(q.v.) b. February 1860
--1900 Census: p.84 Little Falls:
Charles Matches, b. February 1860, m.
17 yrs.; Elizabeth, b. February 1862, 3
born 2 living; Meredith Son, b. June
1886; Jeanette b. June 1889
--1920 Census, p.117B, Charles W. Matches,
b. NJ, insurance agent, age 61; Imogene, wife,
age 38, b. NJ
--1930 Census, p.265B, Little Falls: Charles
W. Matches, age 72, b. NJ, father b. Scotland,
mother b. NJ; Imogene S., age 50, b. NJ,
father b. NJ, mother b. NY

- - - - -

MEYERS

Meyers, ANTJE   b.
(npfh)   d. January 1913
                (bur. January 8, 1913)

Notes:
--(?)1900 Census, p.86 Little Falls:Annie Mayer, b. Holland
July 1836, widow, 2 born 2 living; George b. September
1873, Holland; Ella, b. Feb. 1881, Holland
--(?)1910 Census #114, p.166A,Cedar Grove: William S.
Myers, age 42, b. NJ, house carpenter; Magdelena, age 43, b.
NJ, parents b. Germany; William M. age 12, b. NJ; John, age

10; Anna E., age 9; Clifford, age 8; Seymour, age 7; Harry, age 6; James, age 1

--(?)1910 Census #114, Cedar Grove: William S. Myers, age 42, b. NJ house carpenter; Magdelena, age 43, b. NJ, parents b. Germany; William M. age 12, b. NJ; John, age 10; Anne E., age 9; Clifford, age 8; Seymour, age 7; Harry, age 6; James, age 1

--(?)1920 Census, Family #67,Cedar Grove: William Myers, age 52, contractor; Magdalena, age 54, b. NY, parents b. Germany; William, age 22; John, age 21; Anna, age 19; Clifford J., age 18; Seymour, age 16; Henry W., age 14; James S. age 11

--(?)1920 Census, p.139A, Little Falls: George S. Myers, age 46, widower, felt finisher, b. Holland

--(?)1930 Census, Part 2, Sheet 5A, Cedar Grove: William S. Myers, age 61, b. NJ, father b. PA, mother b. NY, carpenter for building contractor; Lena, age 63, b. NY, parents b. Germany; John E., son,age 30, plumber; Clifford J., son, age 28, carpenter; Henry W., son, age 24, mason; James S. son, age 22, chauffer

- - - - -

MILLER

Miller, HENRY   b. April 15, 1849
(gmnj)   d. May 20, 1896

Notes:
--(?)1880 Census p.37A, Paterson, NJ: Henry Miller, age 29, b. PA, painter, parents b. Germany; Elvira wife, age 27, b. PA; Jennie, dau., age 9, b. PA; George H., son, age 10 months, b. PA

- - - - -

MOON

Moon, JOHN   b. 1815
(gmnj)   d. 1896

"Co. H, 3rd Regt. Inf. Vol." (Pvt.)
Grand Army of the Republic Marker

wife, JANE (Doremus)   b. (February 13, 1817)
(gmnj)   d. February 22, 1892

"Aged 75 yrs. & 9 days"
"Our Mother"

Notes:

--John Moon served in the Civil War: Private, 3rd Regt.,
Infantry Volunteer.

--John Moon m. December 22, 1828, Jane Doremus. She was
daugher of Abraham Doremus and Elsje Bush.

--He was born and "brought up on the north side of the Little
Falls Road, immediately west of the East Jersey water supply
pipe-line; was a shoemaker by trade. He subsequently lived
in various western states, but returned to the old homestead."
(Eberhart, p.180)

--1870 Census, p.222b, Orangeville, Barry Co., Michigan:
John Moon, age 60, farmer b. NY: Martha(?), age 55, b. NY;
William, age 25, b. NY; John, age 14, b. NY; Ella age 8 b.
NY

--1880 Census:p.219B, Prairieville, Barry Co., Michigan:
John Moon, age 65, b. NJ, boot & shoe maker, father b. NY,
mother b. NJ: Jane, wife, age 63, b. NJ; Georgia E. daughter,
age 17, b. NY

--CHILDREN of John Moon and Jane Doremus:

Charlotte A.   b. October 18, 1840;m#1 August Schieber
                #2,George Sindle(q.v.)

--1880 Census, p.116C, Newark, NJ: August
Schreiber, age 37, b.Germany, wholesale
produce; Lottie, wife, age 39, b. NJ; Jennie,
dau.,age 10, b. NJ; Lottie B., dau., age 8, b.
NJ; George A., son, age 6, b. NJ; Lauretta,
dau., age 1, b. NJ; Jennie Moon (sis. of wife),
age 27, b. NY dressmaker; Christena
Schreiber, niece, age 13, b. NJ, servant

Elsie Emma   b. December 18, 1842; m. Abraham
Armstrong
--1870 Census, p.222B, Orangeville, Barry
Co., Michigan; Abram Armstrong, age 35,
farmer, b. NY; Elsie, age 26, b. NY; Eva age
8 b. NY; Aaron G. age 3, b. MI; Violetta A.,
age 11 months b. MI
--1880 Census, p.219B, Prairieville, Barry
Co., MI: Abraham Armstrong, age 40, b. NY,
winds engine; Elsie M. wife, age 37,b. NY,
parents b. NJ;Evie A., dau., age 17, b. NY;
Aaron J., age 13, b. MI; Violetta A, age 10,
b. MI; Henry A., son, age 9 months, b. MI

William L.   b. May 19, 1844; m. Etta Waters
--(?)1900 Census, p.45A, Cleon
Twp.,Manestee Co., Michigan: Wm. Moon, b.
Oct. 1845, NY; Ettie b. Jan 1861, MI, 7 born
6 living; John, b. Aug 1883, MI; Nettie b.
May 1889 MI; Vera, b. June 1898, MI

Susan   b. October 1, 1846; m. Charles Tunnell
--1860 Census, p.730 Harrison Twp., Hudson
Co., NJ: Chas. Tunnel, age 49, boatman, b.
Delaware; Mary, age 39, b. England,
'tayloress'; Charles, age 17, apprentice segar
maker, b. NJ; Isaac, age 15, apprentice segar
maker
--1870 Census, p.401B., Harrison, Hudson
Co., NJ: Charles Tunnel, age 27, boatman;

Susan, age 24, b. NJ; Charles age 8 months;
Adelia Moon, age 22, b. NY, domestic
--1900 Census, p.201, 1Wd Kearny, Hudson
Co., NJ: Charles Tunnell, engineer,b. March
1843, (2nd) marriage 23 yrs; Elizabeth, b.
England, Sept. 1859; Hannah, b. Aug 1878

Adelia   b. April 5, 1849; m. Adam Stahl
--1870 Census, p.401B., Harrison, Hudson
Co., NJ: Charles Tunnel, age 27, boatman;
Susan, age 24, b. NJ; Charles age 8 months;
Adelia Moon, age 22, b. NY, domestic
--(?)1900 Census, p.119A, 14 Wd Newark:
Adam Stahl, b. Sept. 1848, espressman, b. NJ,
parents b. Germany; Barbar, b. Dec. 1850
NY; Clarence b. Sept. 1886;

Kate   b. May 1890

Laura M.   b. February 18, 1851; m. James Burr
--1870 Census, p.75A, Barry, Barry Co., MI:
James Burr, age 25, farm labor, b. NJ; Laura,
age 19, b. NY; Jenny age 9 months

Jennie E.   b. August 10. 1853; Wm. E. Storey as
his second wife. They resided at her paternal
homestead on Little Falls Road
--1880 Census: p.116C, Newark, NJ: Jennie
Moon, age 27, single, b.NY, dressmaker,
parents b. NJ; at house of August and Lottie
(her sister) Scheiber.
--1900 Census, p.89, Little Falls: Wm. Story,
b. August 1853, m. 16 yr, labor at felt mill;
Jennie E. b. Aug 1853, NY; Acenath, adopt.
dau., b. April 1898
--1910 Census, p.192A, Little Falls: Wm.
H. Story, age 57, m.twice, 26 yr, b. NJ; Jennie
E. age 57, b. NY 0 born 0 living; Acenath M.
niece, age 10, b. NJ

--1920 Census, p.139B, Little Falls: William Story, age 67, miller at feed mill; Gennette, age 67; Acenath E.(niece), age 20

--1930 Census, p.279A, Little Falls: Arthur W. Davenport, radio repair, age 34, b. NJ; Acenath E.(Story), age 30, b. NJ; William H. Story, father-in-law, (age blurred) widower, odd jobs at laundry (adj. to Gordon E. Story, age 40, b. NJ, electrician; Margaret m. age 38; Gordon E., age 9)

John A.   b. May 19, 1855; m. Rubie Valentine

--1880 Census, p.219B, Prairieville, Barry Co., MI: Maria Smith, widow, age 56, b. NY; Ruby Valentine, grand daughter, age 16, b. MI, parents,b. Michigan

--1900 Census, p.82, Little Falls: John Moon, b. NJ, parents b. NJ, b. May 1855, widower, stationary engineer; Vern?, son, b. August 1882, Michigan,father b. NJ, mother b. Michigan, labor at carpet mill; Susie, b. May 1884, Michigan; Laura b. August 1886 Michigan; James b. April 1890 Michigan; Beatrice b. Feb. 1884, Michigan; John, b. March 1895, Michigan

--1910 Census: p.222B, Little Falls Twp: John Moon, age 56, widower, b. NJ, parents b. NJ, carpenter; boarder at res. of Charles Margeson

Melissa'Lissie'b. June 17, 1858 d. June 9, 1863

Georgia Ella   b. September 27, 1862; m. William Neer

- - - - -

MORRELL

Morrell, William M.*	b. (abt. 1801)
	d. (aft. 1880)
wife, CATHARINE (Bone)	b. January 8, 1820
(gmnj)	d. November 22, 1892
daughter, EMELINE	b. (July 5, 1859)
(gmnj)	d. March 5, 1865

"Aged 5 yrs. & 8 mos."

Notes:

--William M. Morrell m. #1 .....

--William M. Morrell m. June 26, 1851, Acquackanonk, Catherine Bone, widow of Isaac Evert VanNess; she was daughter of Benjamin Horton Bone and Lydia Riker.

--William M. Morrell owned plot #449 and plot #450, First Reformed Church Cemetery, Paterson, Passaic County, New Jersey.

--1850 Census, p.360A,#410 Acquackanonk, Passaic Co., NJ: Wm. M. Morell, age 58, farmer, real estate $3500; Thomas, age 21; Catherine Bush, age 21

--(?)1850 Census, #429 Acquackanonk, Passaic Co., NJ: Benjamin H. Bone, age 53, hotel keeper; Lydia, age 48; John E., age 15; Emeline, age 12; Horace, age 10

--1860 Census: p.1022, #496, Acquackanonk, Passaic Co.: William Morrell, age 58, farmer b. NY; Catherine, age 39, b. NJ; Mary, age 4; Emeline age 1; William VanNess, age 18, farm labor.

--1870 Census: p.242B, Little Falls: Wm. M. Morrell, b. NY; age 69, farmer, real estate $35,000; Catherine, age 49; Mary F. age 17

--1880 Census:p.182D,Little Falls, NJ: Asher Brower, age 32, b. NJ, sawyer; Sarah age 28, b. NJ, father b. NY, mother b. NJ; Alace, dau., age 7; Irene, age 4; Nettie age 1;

Catherine Morrell, widow, age 60, b. NJ, father b. NJ, mother b. NY

--CHILDREN of William M. Morrell and _____:

Thomas   b. abt. 1829

> --1860 Census, p.1035, Acquackanonk:
> Thomas Morrell, age 31, b. NY; Hester, age 22, b. NJ; Susan age 2, b. NJ
> --1880 Census, p.187B, Little Falls, NJ:
> Thomas Morrell, age 51, b. NY, hotel keeper, parents b. New York; Ester, wife, age 45, b. NJ, parents b. NJ: Susan, dau., age 20, b. NJ, father b. NY, mother b. NJ

--CHILDREN of William Morrell and Catherine Bone:

Sarah(?)   b. abt. 1852;(possible child) m. Asher Brower

> --1880 Census:p.182D,Little Falls, NJ:
> Asher Brower, age 32, b. NJ, sawyer; Sarah age 28, b. NJ, father b. NY, mother b. NJ; Alace, dau., age 7; Irene, age 4; Nettie age 1; Catherine Morrell, widow, age 60, b. NJ, father b. NJ, mother b. NY

Mary F.   b. abt 1853

Emeline   b. July 5, 1859; d. March 5, 1865

- - - - -

MOWRY

Mowry, JOHN	b. (July 1838)
(npfh)	d. September 1911
	bur. September 27, 1911
wife, ANNA	b. (April 1836)
(npfh)	d. May, 1911
	bur. May 13, 1911

Notes:

--(?)1860 Census, p.1020, Acquackanonk, Passaic Co: John H. Moorey, age 20, shawl maker; Ann, age 24; Sarah Scott, age 6; Peter Sheppard, age 76

--1870 Census, p.236, Little Falls: John Mowry, age 30, b. PA; works wollen mills; Anne M. age 30, b. NJ; Sarah J. age 17; James age 19

--1880 Census, p.192D, Little Falls, NJ: John "Mowery", age 42, b. NJ, parents b. NJ, laborer; Ann, wife, age 40, b. NJ, parents b. NJ; David, son, age 2, b. NJ

--1900 Census, p.79, Little Falls: John Mowery, b. July 1838, m. 42 yrs., b. PA; Ann, b. April 1836, 4 born, 0 living

--1910 Census, p.194A, Little Falls Twp: John Mowery, age 72, m. 45 yrs; b. NJ, parents b. NJ; Anna M., age 73, 7 born, 1 living, b. NJ, father b. France, mother b. Germany

--CHILDREN of John and Ann Mowry:

David   b. abt. 1878

- - - - -

MUIR

Muir, Margaret
m. James Brash (q.v.)

- - - - -

NEAFIE

Neafie, JOHN R.   b. (January 3, 1792)
(gmnj)   d. September 27, 1867

"Aged 75 yrs. & 9 mos."

wife, SARAH (Doremus)   b. (June 15, 1797)
(gmnj)   d. October 15, 1869

"Aged 72 yrs. & 4 mos."

Father and Mother
In Memory of
John R. Neafie

(and)

Sarah Doremus
wife of John R. Neafie

Notes:

--John was b. at Two Bridges, NJ the only child of Richard Nevius/Neafie and Maria VanSaun.

--John m. May 15, 1814, Caldwell Presbyterian Church, Sarah Doremus, daughter of Thomas Doremus(q.v.) and Elizabeth VanHouten.

--He served in 1814 in Capt. Crane's Company of Essex County Militia. In 1822 he was commissioned first lieutenant in the Caldwell Cavalry Company, of which he became Captain, June 15, 1822. He was a Constable of Caldwell Township in 1829-34; he was justice of the the peace for fifteen years.

--He learned the trade of tanner/currier. About 1820 he moved to Little Falls and took charge of the tollgate on the Newark and Pompton Turnpike. He settled estates, drew wills and deeds, and was a general auctioneer.

--1830 Census: #226, Caldwell Twp:

--1840 Census, p.102A,Acquackanonk: John R. Neafie

--1850 Census: p.364A,#471, Acquackanonk, NJ: John R. Neafie, age 59, farmer; Sarah, age 53; Aaron B., age 28, teamster; Emeline, age 20; Eugenia, age 17; Jeptha F., age 14

--1860 Census: #590,p.1035, Acquackanonk, Passaic Co.:
John R. "Naffie", age 68, farmer; Sarah, age 64; Aaron, age
34, farm labor

--CHILDREN of John R. Neafie and Sarah Doremus:

Maria VanSaun b. April 21, 1815, d. October 15,
1875,NYC; m. Ogden Hall.
--1860 Census, p.622, 16 Wd,NYC:
Peter N. Grant age 33, cloth cutter, b.
Scotland; Emeline (nee Neafie) age
30, b. NJ; Isabella N. age 6 b. NY;
Elizabeth, age 2, b. NY; Sarah Hall,
age 19, b. NJ

Thomas Doremus
b. November 29, 1816;d. July 8, 1876;
m. Mrs. Jane Wight

James Orton   b. May 1, 1819, m. Emily Peters
--1880 Census, p.271C, Jersey City,
NJ: James Neafie, age 61,
b. NJ, carpenter; Emily, wife, age 57,
b. NY; Emily, dau., age 33,b. NY,
single

Aaron Baldwin
b. December 11, 1822, Little Falls, d.
Dec. 4, 1898, Little Falls
--1880 Census, p.187A, Little Falls,
NJ: Aaron B. "Nathey", single, age 55,
b. NJ, laborer, parents b. NJ; at res. of
Henry L. and Harriet Crane.

Frances Elizabeth
b. August 12, 1825, Little Falls, m.
Theodore F. Snover

Stephen Personett
> b. March 4, 1828, Little Falls, m.
> Sarah Elizabeth Acker
> --1880 Census, p.499C, New York
> City: Stephen "Neafir", age 50,
> b. NJ, carpenter; Sarah, wife, age 45,
> b. NY; John, son, age 23;
> Mary, dau., age 20, b. NY; Maggie,
> dau., age 17, b. NY

Jane Emeline b. May 23, 1830 Little Falls, m. Peter
> M. Grant
> --1870 Census, p. 622, 16 Wd,NYC:
> Peter M. Grant, age 33, cloth cutter, b.
> Scotland; Emeline, age 30, b. NJ;
> Isabella N., age 6, b. NY; Elizabeth,
> age 2, b. NY; Sarah Hall, age 19, b. NJ
> --1880 Census, p.157A, New York
> City: Peter M. Grant, age 56,
> b. Scotland, wholesale clothing;
> "Emma", age 45, b. NJ; Elizabeth,
> dau., age 20, b. NY; Frederick, son,
> age 16, b. NY; Reeta H.,dau., age 16,
> b. NY

Catharine Eugenia
> b. July 3, 1833, Little Falls, d. Aug. 7,
> 1865, m. George VanNess

Jeptha Frederick
> b. March 2, 1836, Little Falls, m. Jane
> Lush
> --1880 Census, p.126A, New York
> City: Fredrick "Nephie", age 45,
> b. NJ, carpenter; Jane, wife, age 35, b.
> CT, father b. England,
> mother b. NY; Lorenzo C., son, age 4,
> b. NY

- - - - -

NIX

Nix, JOHN H. Cpl.	b. (November 1837)
(gmnj)	d. (August 18, 1911)

"Co. K, 25th NJ Inf. Vol." (Cpl.)

wife, HESTER C. (Brower)	b. (February 1844)
(npfh)	d. November 1907
	(bur. November 5, 1907)

Notes:
--John Henry Nix was b. Germany, son of Johann Heinrich Ferdinand Nix and Catherine Elizabeth Weyel, and d. Little Falls. He arrived in the United States in 1852. John was also known as F.W. John Henry Nix.
--John Nix m. Hester C. Brower December 2, 1861, Acquackanonk.
--Hester Brower was daughter of Cornelius Brower and Sarah Ann Doremus. 'Esther' was "born on the Singack road about a mile above Little Falls".
--John H. Nix was a blacksmith.
--John Nix served in the Civil War. He enlisted September 1, 1862; was promoted to Corporal June 1, 1863 and was discharged with the rank of 'chaplain',June 20, 1863. He enlisted the same day as George Personett.
--John Nix was a blacksmith at Little Falls, NJ
--1860 Census: #563 Little Falls: John Nix, age 22, blacksmith, b. Germany; Res. with family of William Jacobus, blacksmith.
--1870 Census: p.246A&B, Little Falls Twp:Wm. M. Brower, farmer, age 45; Mary A. age 29; Cornelilus, age 5; William age 3; John, age 1; John H. Nix, age 30, b. Germany, blacksmith; Hester Nix, age 26; John W. Nix, age 5; Lizzie S., age 3; Emma, age 4 months

--1880 Census:p.188D, Little Falls Twp: John Nix, age 41, works carpet factory; Hester, age 31(sic); John, age 15, clerk; Lizzie, age 12; Jennie, daughter, age 8; Charles, age 7; Carrie, age 8 months.

--1890 State Census: p.001, Little Falls Twp:

--1900 Census: p.80,#89 Little Falls. John Nix, blacksmith, b. Germany, b. November 1837, m. 38 yrs; Hester C., b.February 1844, NJ, parents b. NJ; '10 children born, 5 living'

--CHILDREN of John H. Nix and Esther Brower:

John William b. August 1864, d. 1956, m. 1892, Elizabeth Personett, daughter of George Personett (q.v.) and Caroline Smalley

--1900 Census, p.83, Little Falls: John W. Nix, b. August 1864, m. 8 yrs;mgr of grocery store; Elizabeth b. July 1874, 4 born 2 living; John M. b. Oct. 1892; Harold b. August 1895

--1910 Census p.197A, Little Falls Twp.:John Nix, age 43, b. NJ, father b. NJ, mother b. Germany, m. 18 yrs., lumber yard; Elizabeth age 35, 6 born, 4 living, b. NJ, parents b. NJ; John, age 17; Harold, age 14; Clarence, age 8; Elizabeth age 2

--1920 Census, p. 118B, Little Falls: John W. Nix, age 53, buyer,Erie R.R.Co.; Elizabeth A. age 45; John M. age 27, post office clerk; Harold age 24, chauffeur; Charles C. age 17, labor at felt mill; Elizabeth C. age 11; May, daughter-in-law, age 28?

--1930 Census, p.268A, Little Falls: John W. Nix, age 64; lumber inspector; Elizabeth A., age 55; Russell E. age 10; Noah G. Krieger, age 25, b. NJ, son-in-law; Elizabeth C.

Krieger, age 22, dau; Jennie Frank, boarder,
age 92, widow
Elizabeth "Lizzie" b. abt. 1868
--(?)1880 Census, p.189A, Little Falls,
NJ: Eliza Nix, single, age "28", b. NJ,
parents b. Germany, servant; at res. of
Henry and Catherine Stanley.
Emma J...ice   b. abt. 1872; d. (before 1880?)
Fred. Charles b. abt. 1873
Caroline "Carrie" b. abt. 1879

- - - - -

NORWOOD

Norwood, Hannah
m. Peter C. Doremus(q.v.)]

- - - - -

P.

P., D.   b.
(gmnj)   d.
(fieldstone)

Notes:

- - - - -

PASKIEWZ

Paskiewz, ISYDON   b.
(npfh)   d. March, 1908
      (bur. March 20, 1908)

Notes:
--not found

- - - - -

PEER
(Pier)

Peer, JACOB B.   b. (February 4, 1822)
(gmnj)   d. November 4, 1886

"Aged 64 yrs. & 9 mos."

wife, MARY C. (Redman)   b. (abt. 1829-1831)
(gmnj)   d. February 1, 1889

"aged 58 yrs."

Notes:
--NJ Will of Jacob Peer, #21792G, 1886
--Mary was daughter of Barney Redman and Catherine Garrabrant.
--1850 Census: #81, Caldwell: Barney Redman, age 54, carpenter; Catherine, age 56; Mary C., age 21; James Garrabrant, age 36, tanner/currier.; adj. to Cornelius H. Jacobus, age 49
--1860 Census:p.116B, #473 Caldwell/Cedar Grove; Jacob B. Pier, age 39, labor, $1000; Mary C. age 31; Elizabeth, age 1; Catherine Redman, age 66

--1870 Census: p.134A, #512, Caldwell/Cedar Grove; Jacob
Peer, age 46; Mary C., age 40; near Robert and Eliza
(Kinsey) Redman
--1880 Census:p.414C, #261 Caldwell,NJ: Jacob Peer, age
58, b. NJ, farmer;Mary C., wife, age 50, b. NJ;Lizzie,
daughter, age 21, b. NJ
--CHILDREN of Jacob B. Peer and Mary C. Redman:
Elizabeth   b. abt. 1859

- - - - -

PERSONETT

Personett, GEORGE   b. (March, 1834)
(gmnj)(death certificate)   d. (July 20, 1908)
(Undertaker:A.C.Derby)

'Geo. Personett
Co.K
25 N.J. Inf.' (Pvt.)

wife, CAROLINE (Smalley) b. August 27, 1837
(npfh)   d. August 20, 1916

Notes:
--George was son of John Personett and Fannie Harrison;
grandson of John Personett, Esq.(q.v.) and Elenor Doremus.
--Caroline was daughter of Abraham Smalley and Elizabeth
Doremus.
--George served in the Civil War;Co. K, 25th Regiment, NJ
Volunteers. He enlisted September 1, 1862 and was
discharged June 23, 1863. He enlisted the same day as John
Nix(q.v.) His pension states: "cronic sour throat not able to
work romatic"
--1850 Census: p.074, Caldwell Twp: John Personett, age 45,
hatter; Ellen, age 38; Almira, age 17; George, age 14;
Charles age 12; Ellen, age 10; John, age 5; Stephen, age 3;

Sarah, age 2; Alfred age 5 months; Alonzo...(b. January 10, 1849; son of dau., Almira)

--1860 Census:p. 378A, 3Wd Orange,George Personett, age 24, hatter, b. NJ; Caroline, age 23, b. NJ

--1870 Census, p.241A, Little Falls Twp: George Pursonett, hatter; Caroline age 34; Charly, age 4; Lizzy Brower, age 7 (niece)

--1880 Census, p.179B, Orange, NJ: George Persanett, age 45, b. NJ, hat maker; Caroline S., wife, age 44, b. NJ; Charles H. son, age 14, b. NJ; Elizabeth, dau., age 6, b. NJ

--1900 Census: #73 Verona/Cedar Grove: George Personett, retired; wife, Caroline; at res. of son, Charles.(q.v.)

--CHILDREN of George Personett and Caroline Smalley:
Charles Hopson

> b. April 7,1866, d. 1934;bur. Hanover Cem.
> m. #1Jessie Gertrude Simmonds;dau. of
> Stanley Simmonds and Rosalie DeFarbech
> m. #2 Phebe Catherine Sprigg, widow of
> John Edwin Brower; dau. of Thomas A.
> Sprigg and Arminta C. Meeker
> --1880 Census, p.179B, Orange: George
> Personett, age 45, hat maker; Caroline S. age
> 44; Charles H., age 14; Elizabeth, age 6
> --1900 Census #73, Verona: Charles
> Personett, b. April 1866, age 34, m.
> 14 yrs., pedlar; Jessie G. wife, b.
> November 1865, England; Rosalie M.,
> dau., b. September 1886; George S.
> son, b. October 1890; George
> Personett, father, b. March 1834,
> retired; (Caroline Personett, mother,
> not listed?)
> --1910 Census #146,p.20A, Cedar Grove:
> Charles H. Personett, age 44, m.24
> yrs., no occup. listed; Jessie G., 4 born
> 3 living, b. England; George S., age

19, carpenter; Clifford W., age 7;
Caroline Personett, mother, age 72,
2 born 2 living;(George Personett
not recorded?) Charles W. Mills,
age 9, b. NJ (son of Charles Mills and
Margaret Personett.)
--1920 Census #108, Cedar Grove:
Charles H. Personett, age 53, labor,
Newark Water Co.; Jessie, age 54;
b. England, father b. England, mother
b. France
--1930 Census Part 2, Sheet 4B, Charles
Personett (Personett Place), age 64, widower;
real estate $1,000; m. first at age 20; watch
man at waterworks

Elizabeth   b. June 1874, m. 1892, John Nix (Jr.)q.v.
--1910 Census: p.197A, Little Falls Twp;
John Nix, age 43, m. 18 yrs, b. NJ, father b.
Germany, mother b. NJ;works lumberyard;
Elizabeth, age 35, b. NJ, 6 born 4 living;
John, age 17; Harold, age 14; Clarence age 8;
Elizabeth age 2

- - - - -

Personett, George**   b. (1795)
                              d. (September 27, 1853)
wife, Elsie** (Doremus)   b. (Abt. 1797)
                              d. September 21, 1863

"Age 66"

Notes:
--NJ Will of George Personett #14406G
--NJ Will of Elsie Doremus Personett #15812G
--George was son of John Personett, Esq.(q.v.) and Elenor
Doremus.

--George m. Elsie Doremus, October 25, 1815, Caldwell Presbyterian Church; dau. of Pieter Doremus and Hannah Norwood.

--George's cause of death was recorded as "Fever".

--1830 Census, p.456 Caldwell Twp: George Personett, wife and 3 daughters at the residence of his father

--1840 Census, p.331, Caldwell Twp: George Personett, wife, and 1 daughter

--1850 Census: p. 074,#110, Caldwell/Cedar Grove: George Personett, age 55, farmer; Real estate value $600? or $1600?; Harriet, age 16

--CHILDREN of George Personett and Elsie Doremus:

Jane   b. August 24, 1819, d. September 9, 1858, m. Joseph Gould Jacobus(q.v.)

Amzi**   b. unk. d. age 9 or 10

Harriet   b. February 1834, d. aft. 1910, m. 1854, Isaac Munson Jacobus(q.v.)

- - - - -

Personett, Jane
m. Joseph Gould Jacobus (q.v.)

- - - - -

Personett, John, Esq.** b. abt 1751
         d. May 1844
         "In his 94th year"

1st wife, Elenor** (Doremus)b. January 9, 1757
         d. bef. October 1814
2nd wife, Mary*(Baldwin) b. (abt. 1762)
         d.

Notes:
--John Personett was son of George Personett, Esq. and Mary Condit. Both parents are buried at The Old Burying Ground, First Presbyterian Church, Caldwell.

--John Personett, Esq. died "Suddenly, at his residence in Cedar Grove, Essex County, on the 8th instant, John Personett, a soldier of the Revolution, in the 94th year of his age."*Newark Daily Advertiser, May 9, 1844*

--John Personett m. Elenor Doremus, dau. of Abr. Doremus and Helena VanHouten

--John Personett m. #2, October 12, 1814, Orange, NJ, Mary Baldwin, b. abt. 1762, Orange, NJ; dau. of Benjamin Baldwin and Abigail Lindsley; widow of Joseph Cone.(Joseph Cone was b. November 18, 1770, Tomkins, NY)

--John Personett was a Justice of the Peace; he was in the tanning and currying business in Cedar Grove. He also had a mill for the "grinding of bark; sawing of lumber; and, provided machinery for wood-turning."

--The Personett family owned a "double strip of land west of the patent line. (Boardman, p.6)

--1830 Census: p.94, Acquackanonk.

--1840 Census, #247, Caldwell Twp: John Personett

--CHILDREN of John Personett, Esq. and Elenor Doremus:

Stephen	b. abt 1781, Cedar Grove; d. bef. Nov. 1811; m. Rachel Simonson
Sarah	b. February 11, 1782; d. January 21, 1844; m. Ephraim S. VanNess
	--Ephraim served in the Essex Co. Militia
	--1830 Census, #229, Caldwell Twp.
	--1840 Census, #236, Caldwell Twp:
Jane	b. abt 1782; m. Daniel Allen
	Daniel Allen was a mill builder; "while engaged in Mexico in the construction of a water-wheel, he accidentally fell into the wheel pit and was seriously injured. He immediately returned to his home, where gangrene followed his injury, and he died soon afterward. He married Jane Personett, who survived him, and was the mother of five children."(Lee, p.766)

--(?)1850 Census, p.372, Manchester, Passaic Co., NJ: Alexander Barnes, age 37, labor, b. NY; Abigail, age 36, b. NJ; Nathaniel, age 15, labor, b. NY; Harriet, age 12, b. NY; Samuel Concklin, age 23, blacksmith, b. NY; Lydia A. Haycock, age 16, b. NY; Jane Allen, age 70, b. NJ (mother of Abigail Barnes?)

Joseph** b. March 5, 1786; d. March 19, 1872; (NJ Will #17674G) m.Alletta Doremus; dau. of Goline Doremus and Catherine Farver. Her cause of death was 'acute fever'. (Alletta was buried Prospect Hill Cemetery, Caldwell;NJ Will #21066G,1883)

--1830 Census, p.458, Caldwell Twp.

--1840 Census, #315, Caldwell Twp.

--1850 Census #62,p.332, Caldwell: Joseph Personett, age 64, farmer, real estate $5000; Alletta, age 57; Jeptha C. age 28, farmer; Catherine Pryme,(dau.) age 35, widow; Anna L.Pryme, (granddau.)age 8

--1860 Census #431,p.113, Caldwell: Joseph Personett, age 74, farmer, real estate $6000; Jeptha age 38; Catherine Prime, age 45; Anna L. Prime, age 18

--1870 Census, #457, p.131,Caldwell/Verona: Joseph Personett, age 84, no occup; Alice, age 77; Jeptha C., age 48, farmer, real estate $18,000; Anna L. Prime, age 25, no occup.;

--1880 Census, #227,p.411A; Alletta Personett, age 87, widow; Anna L. Pryme, age 38, widow, dau., 1 servant

Mary "Polly" b. abt 1787; d. aft 1850; m. Areson McCloud

--(?)1840 Census #256, "Aaron McCloud"

--(?)1860 Census, #399 Bloomfield: Aaron McCloud, age 63, laborer; Polly, age 61

--daughter, Lavinia, d. January 3, 1851, aged 9.6.23; bur. Ref. Dutch Cemetery, Brookdale, NJ

Abraham D. b. January 31, 1790; d. May 5, 1881; m. Joanna Williams;dau. of Jeniah Williams bur. Old Burying Ground, Caldwell: cause of death "consumption"

--1840 Census, #390 Caldwell;Abram Personett

--1850 Census #230 Caldwell: Abraham Personett, age 60, tanner and currier; Joanna, age 54; Anna Maria, age 10

--1860 Census #310 Caldwell: Abr. D. Personett, age 70, tanner & currier; Joanna, age 64; Charlotte Williams, age 84, widow, mother-in-law; Mary Bond, age 40

--1870 Census: #132, p. 112; Caldwell: Abraham Personett, age 80, no occup; real estate $3500; Charlotte Lockward Backus, age 53, personal $7000; Mary K. Backus, age 33,personal $7000; James A. Backus, age 23, $8000; Edmund P., age 19; Fannie Backus, age 16; Clara L., age 13; Lewis G. Lockward, age 31, tobacconist, personal $9000.

--1880 Census: #51, Caldwell: Abram Personett, age 90, retired tanner; Abram D. son, age 47, works tobacco factory; Sarah E.(Gould)(wife of Abram D.) age 45; Emma, age 23, granddau; George D., age 17, grandson, works tobacco factory; Eliza B., age 21, granddau; Bertha, age 14, granddau; Frederick, age 7, grandson

Lydia b. November 17, 1791;
m.#1,Joseph VanGiesen;m.#2 ..... Yorks

Nancy b. abt. 1794; m. Artemas Brundage
--1830 Census, #88, Caldwell

George(q.v.) b. 1795; d. October 1853; "fever"

m. Elsey Doremus

--1850 Census, #110 Caldwell: George
Personett, age 55, farmer, real estate $800;
Elsy,age 55; Harriet, age 16

John   b. March 3, 1805; d. August 17, 1886
bur. St. Mark's Episcopal Cemetery,Orange.
m. #1, Fannie Harrison; bur. Caldwell Presb.
m. #2, Ellen/Elenor ____

--1830 Census, p.442A, Orange Twp: at res.
of James "Boss Jimmy" Condit, hatter

--1840 Census, #247, Caldwell Twp: at res. of
his father, John Personett, Esq.(q.v.)

--1850 Census, p.074, Caldwell Twp: John
Personett, age 45, hatter; Ellen, age 38;
Almira, age 17; George, age 14; Charles, age
12; Ellen, age 10; John, age 5; Stephen, age 3;
Sarah age 2; Alfred, age 5 mos.; Alonzo, b.
Jan. 10, 1849(son of dau. Almira)

--1860 Census #401 Caldwell: John
Personett, age 55, hatter; Elinor, age 47, b.
NJ; John age 15; Stephen, age 13; Sarah, age
12; Alfred, age 10; Mary, age 7; Robert, age
4; adj. to Cornelius H. Jacobus Jr.(q.v.); adj.
to Isaac M. and Harriet Jacobus

--1870 Census, p.350A, 2Wd Orange: James
Lennox, age 40, carpenter, b. Ireland; Ellen,
age 29, b. NJ; Wm. age 10, b. NJ; Harry, age
8, b. Canada?;Elmer, age 6, b. NJ; Frank, age
3; Almira, age 7 mos; Mary Personett, age 16,
b. NJ; Alonzo Lennox, age 21, carpenter;
Alfred Personett, carpenter; Robert Personett,
age 14; John Personett(q.v.), age 65, b. NJ,
works hat factory

--1880 Census, p.474A, East Orange: George
Gardner, age 34, painting; Sarah M., wife, age
27; Frederic W.,son, age 7; John Personett,
father-in-law, age 75, works hat shop

- - - - -

Personett, John S.**   b. (November 30, 1803)
(gmnj)   d. (January 8, 1845)
wife, ELLEN (Post)   b. October 21, 1809
(gmnj)(obituary)   d. November 21, 1861

"Age 52.1.0"

daughter, AMARINTHA   b. (August 22, 1830)
(gmnj)   d. February 22, 1832

"Aged 1 yr. & 6 mos."

Notes:
--NJ Will #161P, Intestate 1845
--John S. Personett was son of Stephen Personett and Rachel
Simonson; grandson of John Personett, Esq.(q.v.)
--John S. Personett m. November 2, 1827, Caldwell
Presbyterian Church, Ellen Post.
--Ellen was daughter of Capt. Francis R. Post and
Leah/Elenor Doremus. Her cause of death was recorded as
consumption.
--"Died. Suddenly in this town on Wednesday afternoon the
8th instant, after a few days illness, Mr. John S. Personett,
age 41 years. His death was as unexpected in this community
of which he has been for several years a valuable and
deserving member, as it has been very generally and
sincerely regretted." *Paterson Intelligencer*
--(?)He may be the 'G.S. Personett' who purchased Lot #68
with T. B. Dunkerly, at the Cemetery of the First
Presbyterian Church of Paterson. The plot was in the 'second
purchase' made by the church in 1826.
--1830 Census: #346, Caldwell: John S. Personett; between
Francis Post and Jacob Courter
--1840 Census, p.45A,Paterson: John S. Personett,(tax
accessor at Paterson); 2 males 15-20; 3 males 20-30;2 males

30-40; Females: 1 und. 5; 1 10-15; 1 20-30; 1 30-40; 1 50-60
(2 families?)
--1860 Census #423, Ellen Personett, age 50?; at res. of
Cornelius Supenor; with parents Francis and Leah Post.
--1860 Census:,p.271, 20th Wd, Dist 2, New York City:
James M. Courter, age 25, porter, b. NJ; Mary, age 23, b. NJ;
Eva, age 2, b. NY; Edgar, age 4 months b. NY; Adelia
Personette, age 15, b. NJ; Ellen Personett, age 47, b. NJ,
nurse
--CHILDREN of John S. Personett and Ellen Post:

Amarintha	b. (August 22, 1830); d. February 22, 1832
Mary(?)	b. abt. 1836
Julia(?)	b. abt. 1837
Adelia	b. abt. 1844

- - - - -

PFIZENMAYER

Pfizenmayer, William.J.*	b.(abt. 1827, Germany)
	d.
wife, JOHANNA	b. June 21, 1821
(gmnj)	d. August 7, 1896

"Aged 75.1.17"

son, OTTO E.	b.
(gmnj)	d. (no dates)

"Aged 1 mo."

Notes:
--Stone for Johanna 'erected by W. J. and J. E. Pfizenmayer'.
--1860 Census: p.11A, Caldwell Twp:William Fitzmayer,
age 33, cabinet maker, b. Wertenberg; Joanna, age 39, b.
Wertenberg; Caroline, age 9, b. NY; Charles age 7, b. NY;

Barbara age 6, b. NJ; Louiza age 4, b. NJ; Jacob, age 1, b. NJ.

--1870 Census, p.137B, Caldwell: William Pitzmyer, age 40, farmer, b. Germany; Hannah, age 47, b. Germany; Charles, age 18, farm labor, b. NY; Barbara age 15, b. NJ; Louisa, age 14, b. NJ; Jacob, age 12, b. NJ; John, age 5, b. NJ

--1880 Census: p.415A,#282 Caldwell/Cedar Grove, NJ: William Fitzmeyer, age 53, b. Wirtemberg, farmer; Joanna, wife, age 58, b. Wirtemberg; Barbara, dau., age 26, b. NJ; Jacob, son, age 21, wood turner; William, son, age 14, at home.

--CHILDREN of William Pfizenmayer and Joanna ___:

Otto E.	d. age 1 month
Caroline	b. abt. 1851
Charles	b. abt. 1853

--1880 Census, Caldwell: Charles Pfitzmayer, age 28, works in factory, father b. Wirtemberg; Caroline, wife, age 26, b. NJ, parents b. Hanover, Germany; Daisy Evelyn, dau., age 3

--1900 Census,p.247A, Caldwell: Charles Pfizenmayer b. Dec. 1852, carpenter, b. NY; Caroline b. May 1855 NJ, parents b. Germany; Daisy E. b. March 1876; Frank G. b. July 1880; Benjamin H. b. March 1883; Charles A. b. Feb. 1885; Arthur E. b. May 1895; Florence M. b. May 1895,twin

--1910 Census, #72, N. Caldwell Boro: Charles Pfizenmayer, age 57, m. 33 yrs,; Caroline, age 54, 7 b. 6 living; Daisy, dau., age 33; Arthur age 14; Florence age 14

--1920 Census, p.4B, North Caldwell: Charles W. Pfitzenmayer, b. NY, carpenter, age 68, widower; Daisy, dau., age 42, single, b. NY; Benjamin, age 36, single; Arthur age 24 single; Florence, dau., age 24 single

Barbara	b. abt. 1854

Louisa   b. abt 1856
Jacob E.   b. abt. 1859
William John(q.v.)
      b. abt. 1866; m. Anna _____ ;
      --1920 Census, p.166A, Cedar Grove:
      WilliamPfizenmayer, age 54, carpenter;
      Anna, age 44, b. Germany; Albert, age 24,
      farmer; William E. age 20, farmer; Carl L.
      age 17, farm labor; Otto H. age 14; Arthur age
      11

- - - - -

Pfizenmayer, WM. J.* b. (abt. 1866)
(gmnj)   d.
wife, ANNA   b. March 30, 1872, Germany
(gmnj)   d. December 29, 1890(?)

Notes:
--William John was son of Wm. H. Pfizenmayer (q.v.)
--NJ Will of Anna Pfizenmayer #24209G
--1880 Census: #282 Caldwell: William Fitzmeyer, age 53, b.
Wirtemberg, farmer; Joanna, wife, age 58, b. Wirtemberg;
Barbara, dau.,age 26, b. NJ; Jacob, son, age 21, b. NJ, wood
turner; William, age 14, b. NJ
--1910 Census: #113 Cedar Grove: House carpenter, age 44,
m. 16 yrs., b. NJ, parents b. Germany; Johanna, age 35, b.
Germany; Albert F. age 15; William E. age 10; Carl L. age 6;
Otto H. age 4; Arthur R. age 2 (Son Otto, was Cedar Grove
Fire Chief, 1938-39)
--1920 Census, p.166A, Cedar Grove: WilliamPfizenmayer,
age 54, carpenter; Anna, age 44, b. Germany; Albert, age 24,
farmer; William E. age 20, farmer; Carl L. age 17, farm
labor; Otto H. age 14; Arthur age 11
--1930 Census, Part 2, Sheet 5A, Cedar Grove: Wm. J.
Pfitzenmayer, real estate $9,000, age 64, carpenter retired;

Johanna, age 55, b. Germany; Albert F., son, age 34, single, farmer; William, son,age 29, single, farmer
--CHILDREN of William J. Pfizenmayer and Anna _____, and/or Johanna___:

Albert F.	b. abt 1885
William E.	b. abt 1890
Carl L.	b. abt 1894
Otto H.	b. abt. 1896; Cedar Grove Fire Chief, 1938-1939
Arthur R.	b. abt. 1898

- - - - -

PIERCE
(Pearce)

Pierce, MR. (ougheltree)	b. d. (abt. 1920-22)
Pierce, MRS. (ougheltree)	b. d. (abt. 1920-22)
Pierce, SARAH (npfh)	b. d. December, 1914 bur. December 26, 1914

Notes:
--(?)1880 Census, p.429B, Dist. 2, Caldwell, NJ: Marcus Pierce, age 28, b. NJ, segar maker, parents b. NJ; Sarah, wife, age 26, b. NJ, parents b. NJ; Minnie, dau., age 7, b. NJ
--(?)1880 Census, p.23B, Montclair, NJ: Francis H. Pierce, age 30, b. NJ, mason; Sarah, wife, age 27, b. NJ; Lottie F., dau., age 5; Benjamin C., son, age 2; George Bush, brother, age 20, b. NJ, plumber

- - - - -

Pierce, William E.*   b.
(gmnj)   d.
wife, MARY (Sindle)   b. (October 23, 1848)
(gmnj)   d. December 24, 1915

"Aged 66.3.1"

Notes:

--Mary Lavinia Sindle was daughter of Peter Sindle and Elizabeth _____ .

--(?)1850 Census, #367 Caldwell: William Pierce, age 5; at res. of his parents Joseph and Nancy Pierce

--1860 Census, p.89B, Caldwell Twp: Joseph Pearce, age 46, farmer; Nancy, age 40; Rachel, age 18; William, age 14; Margaret A., age 12; Francis H., age 10; Sylvanus, age 6; Mary L., age 3; Albert W., age 10 months

--1870 Census, p.37B, Boonton Twp: William Pearce, age 24, mason; Mary L., age 21

--1880 Census: p.415B,#282 Caldwell/Cedar Grove,NJ: William E. Pierce, age 34, b. NJ, stone mason; Mary S. wife, age 32, b. NJ; Lilly B. dau., age 10, b. NJ

--1900 Census: #44 Verona/Cedar Grove.Peter Sindle, age 76 widower, retired; Mary S. Pierce, dau., age 51; William E. Pierce, son-in-law, b. October 1845

--1910 Census: #154 Cedar Grove, Little Falls Rd:William E. Pierce, age 65, mason; Mary S., age 61, b. NJ

--CHILDREN of William E. Pierce and Mary Sindle:

Lilly B.   b. abt. 1870; m. Louis W. Jacobus
        --1910 Census
        --1920 Census #101, Cedar Grove: Louis W. Jacobus, age 53, salesman,Hahne & Co.; Lily B. age 49; May E. age 23; William E. Pierce, father-in-law, age 74, widower
        --1930 Census, Part 2, Sheet 2B, Cedar Grove: Lillie B. Jacobus, age 59, widow,

mother-in-law; at res. of Frederick L. and
May J. Long

Munson J.?   --1900 Census #266, Caldwell

- - - - -

PILLING

Pilling, DAN   b. June 14, 1794,
England(gmnj)   d. April 8, 1871

"Aged 78.9.24"

wife, ALICE (Johnson)   b. (1793) England
(gmnj)   d. August 12, 1868

"Aged 75 yrs."

Notes:
--Dan Pilling was bapt. August 3, 1794, Royton, Lancashire,
England; son of John Pilling and Ann _____.
--1850 Census: #284 Caldwell: Daniel Pilling, age 56,
farmer, b. Lancastershire, England, Real estate $3000; Alice
(Johnson), age 58, b. England; Mary Woolsingcroft, age 77,
b. England.
--1860 Census: #215 Caldwell: Dan Pilling, age 66, b.
England; Alice, age 67, b. England. Also, Emmons Courter,
age 15, b. NJ
--1870 Census, p.242A, Little Falls: John Smalley, age 31,
harness maker; Ann, age 31; Ada, age 6; Daniel Pillen, age
76, b. NJ

- - - - -

PINCONCET

Pincocet, AUGUST   b.
(npfh)   d. July 1907
                          (bur. July 12, 1907)

Notes:
--(??)1900 Census, p.5A, Acquackanonk Twp: Francis
Poncet b. May 1844, France, milk man; Charlotte, b. April
1840, France, 0 born 0 living

- - - - -

POHLMAN

Pohlman, MABLE   b.
(npfh)   d. July 1914
                          (bur. July 27, 1914)

Notes:
--(?)John Pohlman; William B. and wife Pohlman: plot
owners at Cedar Lawn Cemetery, Paterson, New Jersey, as
of 1917.
--(?)1880 Census, p.107D, Paterson: .....Pohlman, widow,
age 66, b. Bavaria; Herman Hagan, son-in-law, age 25, b.
Prussia; Sophia Hagan, dau., age 23, b. NJ, parents b.
Bavaria
--(?)1880 Census: p.68B, Paterson, NJ: John Pohlman, age
38, b. Bavaria, moulder; Mary, wife, age 35, b. NY, parents
b. Bavaria;John, son, age 17, b. NJ, moulder;James, son, age
15, works in cotton mill; William, son, age 13, works in
cotton mill;Elmira, dau., age 9;Charles, son, age 5, b.
NJ;George, son, age 6;Joseph, son, age 4, b. NJ;Herbert, son,
age 8 mos.
--1900 Census, p.44, 2nd Ward, Paterson: John Pohlman, b.
April 1836, age 64, m. 39 yrs, b. Germany, iron moulder;

Mary b. Oct. 1849, 11 born 8 living; Lidia b. Dec 1881;
Robert b. April 1878; Gene b. Oct. 1883, age 17
--(?)1910 Census, p.166B, 3rd Ward Paterson: John
Pohlman, age 67, b. Germany, m. 49 yrs.'pattern cutter'?;
Mary, age 65, b. NY, parents b. Germany, 11 born 8 living:
Lottie, age 24; Walter, age 23; John age 20; Jane age 16;
Mary age 15; adj. to Herman Hagen age 55, b. Germany,
mgr. of commission house; m. 30 yrs; Sophie, age 53, b. NJ,
parents b. Germany, 3 born 3 living; Lizzie, age 29; Margaret
age 27; William age 17
--(?)1930 Census, p.241A, Singac, Little Falls: Wm. B.
Pohlman, age 41, b. NY, father b. Germany, store mgr;
Lillian E. age 40, b. NY; Ellanor L. age 15, b. NY; Wm. B.,
age 12, b. NY; Lillian E. Bail, age 17, niece, b. NY
--(?)1930 Census, p.241A, Singac, Little Falls: Margaret
Pohlman, age 64, widow, b. NY, parents b. Germany; Lloyd
F. age 38, widower, son, b. NY, plumber; Lloyd F.,Jr. age16,
b. NJ, grandson; Francis, grandson, age 13; Margaret,
granddau., age 11; Dorothy, granddau., age 9

- - - - -

PORTER

Porter, JOHN   b.
(npfh)   d. November 1924
                         (bur. November 24, 1924)

Notes:
--(?)1920 Census, p.123 A, Little Falls: John Porter, age 53,
b. Holland, carder at felt mill; Jennie, age 52, b. Holland;
John, age 25, b. NJ; Marcus, age 21; Jennie, age 15; Henry,
age 13; all children b. NJ

- - - - -

POST

Post, FRANCIS R. (Mjr.)	b. 1786
(gmnj)	d. 1877
wife, LEAH (Doremus)	b. 1787
(gmnj)	d. 1860

Notes:
--Francis R. Post was son of Roelif Post and Marretje Post.
--Leah Doremus was daughter of Egbert Doremus and Geesje Jacobus. Her sister Elsy m. Garret Yorks, q.v. She was mentioned in her father's will NJ#11044G, 1817.
--Francis sold Paterson land to William Sandford in 1826; and, land to John S. Personett(q.v.) in 1832.
--1830 Census: #345 Caldwell/Cedar Grove: Adj. to Rynear VanGiesen and John S. Personett who m. Post's daughter
--1840 Census: #285 Caldwell/Cedar Grove:
--1850 Census: #119, Caldwell: at res. of Cornelius Supenor, son-in-law (q.v.)
--1860 Census: #422 Caldwell/Cedar Grove: Francis Post, age 74, carpenter; with daughter Mary and her husband, Cornelius Supenor.
--1870 Census: #500 Caldwell/Cedar Grove: Francis Post, age 83, no occupation.Mary, age 54; Cornelius Supenor, age 59, farmer, $2000; Cleveland Courter, age 10; James Doremus, (q.v.) age 40, no occup., $3000
--CHILDREN of Francis R. Post and Eleanor Doremus:

Ellen (?)	b. abt 1810 d. aft. 1860, m. November 2, 1827,John S. Personett (q.v.)
	--1860 Census, p.271, 20Wd NYC: James M. Courter, age 25, b. NJ, porter; Mary, age 23, b. NJ; Eva, age 2, b. NY; Edgar, age 4 mos. b. NY; Adelia Personett, age 15, b. NJ; Ellen Personett, age 47, b. NJ, nurse
Mary	b. Dec. 1815, m. Cornelius Supenor(q.v.)

--1880 Census, p.417A, Caldwell Twp:
Cornelius Supenor, age 70, farm; Mary, wife,
age 64; James Doremus, single, age 52, no
occupation; Henry A. Jacobus, single, age 71,
b. NJ, laborer

--1900 Census, #55, Verona: George
Ougheltree,b. April 1862, m. 9 yrs., salesman;
Elizabeth b. Sept. 1867 1 born 1 living; Olive,
b. November 1892; Mary (Post) Supenor, b.
December 1815, widow (of Cornelius
Supenor,q.v.)

Margaret   b. February 24, 1823
bapt. April 27. 1823, Stone House Plains,NJ

- - - - -

POULSSON
(Paullison)

Poulsson, HALVOR   b. (abt. 1804)
(gmnj)   d. February 1, 1854

"Aged 40 yrs."

wife, RUTH ANN (Mitchell) b. (abt. November 1822)
(gmnj)   d. March 29, 1872

"His widow & wife of John Dent"
"Aged 49 yrs. & 4 mos."

son, PAUL H.   b. (abt. July 1845)
(gmnj)   d. September 10, 1854

"Aged 9 yrs. & 2 mos."

Notes:

--Ruth Ann Mitchell, widow of Halvor Poulsson, m.#2, John
Dent (q.v.) March 11, 1859, Newark, NJ.

--CHILDREN of Halvor Poulsson and Ruth Ann Mitchell:

Paul H.	b. abt. July 1845; d. September 10, 1854
Ingeborg	b. abt. 1847
Laura	b. abt. 1852
Anna Emile	b. September 8, 1853, Cedar Grove, NJ.

- - - - -

PRICE

Price, GLADYS	b. 1902
(death certificate)	d. 1902

Notes:

--Gladys was daughter of James Winfield Price, Sr. and
Anna N. Hillman; granddaughter of John Henry Price and
Hannah Wilhelmina Lindquist who lived at 178 Grove
Avenue, Cedar Grove.

--James Winfield Price was a Cedar Grove fireman in 1909.

--1900 Census: #58, Verona:Anna Hillman, servant, b.
August 1884; at res. of Warren L Jacobus (q.v.)

--1910 Census: #182, Lindsley Road, Cedar Grove: James b.
August 1880, Cedar Grove; m. 1901; plumber; Anna N, wife,
age 26, b. Germany; Vera Ann, age 7; Belva W., age 5;
Winfield, age 1

--1920 Census: #163, Bradford Road, Cedar Grove: James
Price, age 41, master plumber; Anna, age 35, b. Bremen,
father b. Germany, mother b. England; Very, age 16; Belva,
age 14; Winfield, age 10; Helen, age 8; Dorothy, age 6

--1930 Census: #199, Caldwell Boro: James W. Price, real
estate $10,000; age 49, plumber; Anna, age 45, b. Germany,
father Germany, mother England; Winfield, age 20, clerk,

gas/electric co.; Helen, age 18, stenographer; Dorothy, age 16; Gloria, age 3

- - - - -

Price, WALTER   b. May 30, 1889
(death certificate)   d. January 22, 1890

Notes:

--Walter was son of John Henry Price and Hannah Wilhelmina Lindquist (who lived at 178 Grove Avenue, Cedar Grove. The Price family were renters of the "Jacobus house".

--John H. Price as partner with Millard Lee Jacobus in "Price and Jacobus, Painters and Decorators" at Cedar Grove.

--Walter's sister, Helen Marie Price, m. George Personett, great great grandson of John Personett, Esq.(q.v.) and Elenor Doremus. Helen was b. at 178 Grove Avenue and George was b. at 727 Pompton Avenue., the Personett homestead.

--1880 Census: #295 Caldwell/Cedar Grove: John Price, age 22, painter, b. NJ: Hannah, age 22, b. Sweden

--1900 Census: #100 Verona/Cedar Grove: John Price, b. NJ, painter, b. September 1860; Hannah, b. May 1858, Sweden; James W.(q.v.), b. August 1880, plumber; Laura O., b. September 1882, bronze mill packer; John E., b. October 1884, labor at dye works; Ella E., b. July 1886; Leester A., b. June 1891; Helen M., b. January 1894 (m. George S. Personett; Frederick W., b. May 1896; Alma M. b. May 1899; Clifford T. b. 1902; Albert A. Garrabrant, boarder, b. September 1871, painter; Mary Olivia Wells, boarder, b. January 1889

--1910 Census: #120 Cedar Grove: John Price, age 50, painter, m. 31 yrs., Hannah, age 51, 10 born, 5 living; Lester, age 18, carpenter; Helen, age 16, bronze mill packer (m. George S. Personette, son of George Personett (q.v.) and Caroline Smalley) Frederick, age 13; Alma, age 10; Clifford, age 8

--1920 Census: #128 Cedar Grove: Hannah Price, age 61, widow, b. Sweden; Alma, age 20, dau., typist Montclair Bank; Clifford, age 17, sheet metal worker; Fred, age 23, plumber; George Personett, age 29, son-in-law, auto mechanic, Packard Motor Co. (son of Charles Hopson Personett,q.v.) Helen Personett, dau. age 25; Stanley Personett, grandson, age 5; Verna Personett, granddaughter, age 1 yr and 4 months

- - - - -

PRZYBYLINSKI

Przybylinski, JAN   b. January 6, 1867
(monument)   d. July 2, 1927
wife(?), MICHALINA   b.
     d. 194?

Notes:

- - - - -

RAY

Ray, JAMES, JR.   b. (January 4, 1840)
(gmnj)   d. January 14, 1873

"Aged 33 yrs. & 10 dys"

Notes:
--(?)James Ray was a farmer at Singac Gate, Little Falls, 1870-71. (Boyd)
--(?)James M. Ray m. Margaret Riggs, 1834, at Essex Co.
--(?)1860 Census, p. 1035, Acquackanonk Twp: James Rea, age 54, b. Ireland, carpet weaver; Elizabeth age 50, b. Ireland; Nancy, age 15, b. NJ

--(?)1870 Census, p.244A, Little Falls: James Ray, age 65, b. Ireland, carpet weaver; Elizabeth G., age 60, b. Ireland
--(?)1880 Census, #235, Caldwell: Catharine Ray, widow, age 60, b. NY, keeping house; at res. of Henry I. VanNess

- - - - -

REDMAN

Redman, Mary C.
m. Jacob B. Peer (q.v.)

- - - - -

REVERET

Reveret, JOHN E.	b. (1841)
(military records)	d. (1867)
	(also recorded as buried at Prospect Hill Cemetery)

10th Regt. Inf., NY Vol., Co. H

wife, Ann J. (Sanderson)	b. (1844)
	d. (1922)
	bur. Prospect Hill Cemetery

Notes:
--Served in the Civil War: Private, 10th Regt. Infantry, NJ Volunteers, Co. H. Enlisted April 23, 1861; discharged May 7, 1863. Res. of Cedar Grove
--John E. Reveret, b. 1841; d. 1867; m. Ann J. Sanderson, b. 1844; d. 1922. Both 'buried' at Prospect Hill Cemetery, Caldwell, NJ.
--Ann Sanderson was dau. of George and Ann Sanderson (1860 Census, #453, Caldwell)
--1870 Census, p.137A, Caldwell: Wm. A. Smith, age 32, brushmaker, b. Canada; Margaret, age 21, b. Ireland; Alice,

age 1, b. NJ; Ann Reveret, age 24, works brush factory, b. Ireland; Mary R. age 3, b. NJ

--1880 Census #273, Caldwell: Ann Reveret, sister, widow, age 34, b. Ireland, works in cotton mill; Mary Reveret niece, age 13, b. NJ; at res. of her sister, Margaret Smith, widow, age 29, b. Ireland, making brushes

--1910 Census, #90 Cedar Grove: Margaret Smith, age 64, widow, (?of William Smith,q.v.)b. Ireland, sewing mops; Alice A., age 41, single; Susan B. age 37, single; Annie A., age 35, single, dressmaking at store; Ann J. Reveret, sister, age 65, widow, b. Ireland, sewing mops.

--1920 Census, #51, Cedar Grove: Mrs. Ann J. Reveret, age 85, widow; Alice Smith, niece, age 50 single; Anna L. Smith, niece, age 44 single

--CHILDREN of John Reveret and Ann Sanderson

Mary   b. 1867; d. 1915;bur. Prospect Hill Cemetery
m. Andrew Webster Mitchell
He was son of John M. Mitchell and Jane E. Taylor.
--1870 Census #503, Caldwell: John M. Mitchell, age 41, farm labor; Jane E. (Taylor), age 30; Andrew W., age 8; Mary E., age 7; Charles W., age 5
--1900 Census, #126, Verona; Andrew Mitchell, b. June 1861, no occup. listed; Mary, wife, 'birth date unknown'
--1910 Census, #134, Cedar Grove; Andrew W. Mitchell, age 45, m. 23 yrs., expressman, own business; Mary, age 43
--1920 Census, #143, Cedar Grove: Andrew W. Mitchell, age 58, chauffeur; Nellis, age 39 Naomi, age 1 yr and 3 monts; Jane, mother, age 80, widow
--1930 Census, #198, Cedar Grove: Andrew W. Mitchell, real estate $10,000, age 69, b. NJ, parents b. NJ, general trucking, driver;

Nellie N., age 50, wife, m. at age 37, b. NJ;
Naomi, daughter, age 11, b. NJ

- - - - -

RIKER

Riker, GEORGE   b.
(npfh)   d. March 1907
                                 (bur. March 4, 1907)

Notes:
--(?)1850 Census: #133, Caldwell/Cedar Grove: John Riker,
age 45, labor; Catherine (Canfield), age 50; Clarissa, age 16;
Maria, age 13; Elizabeth, age 8; George, age 6; Margaret,
age 4
--(?)1860 Census, p.1037, Acquackanonk Twp: John Riker,
age 50, labor; Catherine, age 60; Jane, age 22,
washerwoman; Elizabeth age 18, washerwoman; Martha, age
20, servant; George age 14; Margaret age 13; Charles
Smalley age 4; Laura? Smalley, age 8 months; Emma
Slingerland, age 4 months
--(?)1870 Census, p.238 Little Falls: Catherine Riker, age 70;
Jane Smalley age 33; Charles H. Smalley, age 14; Susan
Smalley age 9; George Smalley age 5; Martha Stager, age
32; Lorene? Stager, dau. age 10; Jenny Stager age 9; John
Stager age 7; Mary Stager age 4; Julia B. Stager, age 2
--(?)1880 Census: p.495A, Paterson: Jacob VanRiper, age 41,
b. NJ, carpenter; Ellen, wife, age 40, b. NY; James E., son,
age 10, b. NJ, laborer; William, son, age 10, b. NJ; George
Riker, son-in-law, age 20, b. NJ, stone mason; Jemima
Riker, dau., age 16, b. NJ; Ella Riker, granddaughter, age 1
month, b. NJ; David Riker, other, widower, age 50, b. NJ,
stone mason, parents b. England (sic)
--(?)1880 Census, p.30B, Paterson: George Riker, age 47, b.
NJ, brick mason; Mary A., wife, age 52, b. Ireland; Jennie,

dau., age 22, b. NJ; Sarah, dau., age 18, b. NJ; Ulysses, son, age 15, b. NJ; Samuel, age 12, b. NJ
--(?)1900 Census, p.77, Little Falls: George Riker, b. May 1865, age 35, single, bartender

- - - - -

Riker, JOHN   b.
(npfh)   d. June 1916
                                     (bur. June 28, 1916)

Notes:
--(?)1840 Census, p.103A,Acquackanonk: John Riker
--(?)1850 Census, #145, Acquackanonk, NJ: Jacob Riker, age 38, blacksmith; Margaret, age 37; Abraham age 6; John P. age 4 months
--(?)1850 Census, p.365A, Acquackanonk: John H. Riker, age 8; John Riker, age 11
--(?)1870 Census: p.243 B, Little Falls: John Riker, age 29, stage driver; Carry, age 22; Netty, age 3; Viola, age 1
--(?)1880 Census, p.181B, Little Falls, NJ: John Riker, age 43, b. NJ; Carrie, wife, age 32, b. NJ; Viola, dau.,age 11; Emma, dau, age 3
--(?)1900 Census, p.86A, Little Falls: John Riker, b. Feb. 1838, m. 33 yrs, coal dealer; Carry, b. October 1850, 6 born 3 living; Florence b. 1887; Viola Stager, daughter, b. April 1870, m. 11 yrs. 2 born 2 living; Chester Stager, grandson, b. April 1890; Russell Stager b. Dec. 1891
--(?)1910 Census, p.192B, Little Falls Twp: John Riker, coal dealer, age 70, m. 43 yrs., b. NJ; Caroline, age 59, 6 born, 3 living, b. NJ; Florence, age 22, b. NJ; Russell Stager, grandson, age 17; 2 hired men
--(?)1910 Census, p.191B, Little Falls Twp: John Riker, age 49, widower, labor at carpet mill, b. NJ, parents b. NJ; Thomas, son, age 15, box? boy, carpet mill; George, son, age 20, picker at felt mill

--(?)1920 Census, p.138A, Little Falls: John Riker, age 79; Louis R., age 62; adj. to Russell A. Stager, age 27 and his wife, Louise A., age 26

- - - - -

ROBERTS

Roberts, JOHN   b.
(npfh)   d. October 26, 1909
                                 (bur. October 26, 1909)

Notes:
--(?)1880 Census: p.306B, 2Wd.Paterson: John Roberts, age 30, b. England, painting machinery; Maggie,a ge 29, b. England; Clara age 7; Annie age 6;Edna age 50; James Stout age 31, wood engraver; Sarah Stout age 28; Alice Roberts age 26,shirt maker; George H. Roberts, age 14; all b.England
--(?)1900 Census, p.87A, Little Falls: John Roberts, b. January 1842, NJ, father b. Wales, mother b. NY, day labor, m. 22 yrs; Sarah S. b. January 1862 NJ, parents b. NJ, 5 born 5 living; John b. Dec. 1879; Samuel b. July 1886; Hattie b. August 1888; William b. June 1892; Charles b. Jan. 1896
--(?)1910 Census, #73,Cedar Grove: Barbara Roberts, age 80, widow, b. Scotland
--(?)1930 Census, p.244A, Singac, Little Falls: John Roberts, age 50, road labor, b. NJ; Elsie M. b. PA; William, brother, age 32, single, b. NJ, private chauffeur

- - - - -

ROFFELO

Roffelo, JIMMIE   b.
(npfh)   d. September 1908
                                 (bur. September 28, 1908)

Notes:

--(?)1910 Census, p.3B,#64, N. Caldwell Boro: Anthony Ruffalo, age 35, labor, m. 5 yr; b. Italy; Fannie?, age 26, 2 b 2 liv; Jasper, age 3; Anthony age 7 months

--(?)1910 Census,p.3B, #65, N. Caldwell Boro: Dominic Ruffalo, age 26, m. 3 yr, laborer, b. Italy; Mary, age 25 0 b 0 liv;b. NY, parents b. Italy

--(?)1910 Census,p.3B #66, Frank Ruffalo, age 22, m. 2 yr, carpenter, b. Ialy; Julia, b. NJ, age 24, 1 b 1 liv; Maria, age 5 months

--(?)1920 Census, p.130B, Little Falls: Frank Ruffalo, age 31, b. Italy, carpenter; Julia, age 33, b. Italy; Mary, age 10, b. NJ; Joseph, age 9, b. NJ

--(?)1920 Census, p.131A, Little Falls: Joseph Ruffalo, b. Italy, age 39, labor at pumping station; Rose, age 30, b. Italy; Mary, age 7, b. NJ; Samuel, age 25, brother, b. Italy, labor on pipe line

--(?)1930 Census, Sheet8B, Cedar Grove: Alfred C. "Rosselo", real estate $8000, b. NJ, father b. Nebraska, mother b. NJ, salesman at real estate office; Mabel S., wife, age 23, parents b. NJ, teacher at public school

--(?)1930 Census, p. 246A, Singac, Little Falls: Frank Ruffalo, age 41, b. Italy, carpenter; Julia, age 42, b. Iraly; Margie, age 19, b. NJ, clerk; Frank J., age 17, b. NJ

--(?)1930 Census, p.246A, Singac, Little Falls: Samuel Ruffelo, age 35, b. Italy, weaver; Rose M. age 32; Louise R. dau age 9; Samuel Jr. age 1 month

--(?)1930 Census, p.248A, Singac, Little Falls: Joseph Ruffalo, age 50, b. Italy, labor,pick and shovel; Rosie, age 40, b. Italy; Mary, age 18, b. PA; Clara, age 9, b. NJ; Louis, age 7, b. NJ

- - - - -

S.

S., C.   b.
(gmnj)   d.

Notes:
--"date on fieldstone is 1775."

- - - - -

SCHMONSKI

Schmonski, MICHAEL   b. 1832
(gmnj)   d. 1923
wife, ELIZABETH   b. 1828
(gmnj)   d. 1907

Notes:
--1920 Census, p.126B, Little Falls: Charles Dirk, age 56, b.
Prussia, labor at carpet mill; Augusta age 55 b. Prussia; Otto,
son, age 24, b. NJ; Rosa dau., age 21, b. NJ; Charles, age 16,
b. NJ; Michael Schimonski, father-in-law, age 88, widower,
b. Prussia
--CHILDREN of Michael Schimonski and Elizabeth ....;
William   b. August 1852
                 --1900 Census, p. 101A, Little Falls:
                 William Schimonski, b. August 1852, m. 14
                 yr., b. Germany; Minnie, b. November 1869,
                 Germany; Elizabeth b. November 1889, NJ;
                 Carry, b. January 1893; Minnie b. March
                 1894; Otto b. February 1897
                 --1910 Census: p.193B, Little Falls Twp:
                 William Schimonski, age 48, m. 24 yrs., b.
                 Germany; Minnie, wife, age 41, b. Germany,
                 9 born, 5 living; Lizzie VanNorden, b. NJ,
                 dau., age 21, m. 3 yrs, 1 born 1 living, Alfred
                 VanNorden, son-in-law, age 24, m. 3 yrs.;

Caroline, dau., age 17, b. NJ; Minnie, dau,
age 16; Arthur, age 13, son; Freddie, age 7,
son
--1920 Census, p.141B, Little Falls: William
Schmonski, age 57, b.Germany,gate tender
RR; Minnie, age 50, b. Germany; Otto, age
23, b. NJ; Frederick, age 17, b. NJ
--1930 Census, p.275A, Little Falls: William
Schmuskie, age 74, b. Germany, RR flagman;
Minnie, age 62, b. germany; Frederick, age
27, labor contracting; Hazel, dau-in-law, age
23, b. NJ, laundry ironer; Carrie Keating, age
37, dau, works laundry; William Keating,
son-in-law; Wilhelmina, granddau.,age 11;
Daniel, grandson, age 8; Marie, granddau.,
age 6; Norma Schmuskie, granddau., age 1 yr
and 5 months; Robert W. Schmuskie,
grandson, age 1 month

Augusta   b. abt. 1865; m. Charles Dirk/Durk(q.v.)
Prussia, labor at carpet mill; Augusta age 55
b. Prussia; Otto, son, age 24, b. NJ; Rosa dau.,
age 21, b. NJ; Charles, age 16, b. NJ; Michael
Schimonski, father-in-law, age 88, widower,
b. Prussia

August   b. abt. 1870
--(?)1910 Census p.205B, August Shimski, b.
Germany, age 43, m. 21 yrs, grocer at store;
Mary, age 39, b. Germany, 6 born, 6 living;
Charles, age 21, b. NJ; Martin, age 18, b. NJ;
Lizzie, age 14, b. NJ; Joe, age 4, b. NJ; Gus,
age 15/12, b. NJ; Annie, age 10
--1920 Census, p.126B, Little Falls: August
Schimonski, widower, age 50, b. Germany,
railroad flagman; Charles, son, age 32, b. NJ;
Elizabeth age 22, b. NJ
--1930 Census, p.244A, Singac, Little Falls
Twp; August Schmonski, age 63, b. Germany,

RR watchman; Charles, son, age 41, single, b.
NJ, foundry watchman
--(?)1930 Census, p.257B, Singac: August
Schmonski, age 68, b. Germany; Mary, age
55, b. Bohemia; August Jr., age 21

- - - - -

SCHOONMAKER

Schoonmaker, DANIEL	b. 1816 (November 20, 1814)
(gmnj)	d. 1898
wife, SARAH (VanNess)	b. 1821
(gmnj)	d. 1911
son, MONROE	b. 1841
(gmnj)	d. 1868
daughter, SARANNA	b. 1857 (January 20, 1857)
(gmnj)	d. 1878

"July 23, 1878, Aged 21.6.3."

son GEORGE	b. 1850
(gmnj)	d. 1898
son, ELIAS	b. 1852
(gmnj)	d. 1910
daughter, EMELINE	b 1848
(gmnj)	d. 1915
daughter, HESTER	b. 1839
(gmnj)	d. 1921
daughter, HENRIETTA	b. 1843
(gmnj)	d. 1922

Notes:
--Daniel Schoonmaker (Sr.) was son of John Schoonmaker.
--Daniel Schoonmaker was a farmer at Centreville,
Acquackanonk, 1871-71.(Boyd)
--NJ Will of Sarah Schoonmaker, #27646G

--1840 Census, p.103A, Acquackanonk: Daniel Schoonmaker

--1850 Census,p.364B, #477, Acquackanonk, NJ: Daniel Schoonmaker, age 33, carpenter; Sarah, age 27; Hester, age 11; Monroe, age 11; Henrietta, age 11;Winslow, age 4; Emeline, age 2;

--1860 Census: #441 Caldwell/Cedar Grove; Daniel Schoonmaker, age 46, carpenter; $1500; Sarah, age 39; Hester, age 20; Monroe, age 18, clerk; Henrietta, age 16; Winslow, age 14; Emeline, age 12; George, age 10; Laura, age 7; Jefferson,age 6; Sarah, age 4; Daniel age 1

--(?)1870 Census:p.200A, Acquackanonk Twp: ...Schoonmaker, age 45; famer; david, age 20; Anne E., age 18; Henry, age 16; Matilda, age 13

--1880 Census:p.415A, #283 Caldwell/Cedar Grove:Daniel Schoonmaker, age 65, b. NJ, carpenter; Sarah, wife, age 59, b. NJ; Hester, dau., age 41; Henrietta, dau., age 36;Emeline, dau., age 32;Jefferson, son, age 25, wood engraver;Charles, son, age 21, farm laborer.

--1900 Census: #25 Verona.Cedar Grove.Sarah Schoonmaker, Widow, age 78, widow; Elias, son,a ge 47, single; Henrietta C., age 56, single; Emeline, age 32, single; Charles Lines, age 14, grandson, printer at carpet mill;Lucia Lines, granddau.,age 7

--1910 Census: #115,p.18A, Cedar Grove: Sarah Schoonmaker, age 88, widow;Hester age 62, single; Emeline, age 58 single; Elias, age 56, single.

--CHILDREN of Daniel Schoonmaker and Sarah VanNess:

Hester b. 1839, d. 1921
  --1920 Census, #69,p.166AmCedar Grove: HesterSchoonmaker, age 80; Henrietta, age 75 sister, single

Monroe b. 1841, d. 1868; Served Civil War, 25th Reg't;NJ Volunteers
  --1860 Census: #601 Acquackanonk, Passaic Co.: Monroe Schoonmaker, age 18, clerk; (at res. of Henry VanNess, age 50)

Henrietta   b. 1843; d. 1922, unm.
              --1920 Census #69 Cedar Grove: Henrietta
              Schoonmaker, age 75, sister, single; at res.
              of Hester Schoonmaker, sister
Emeline   b. 1848, d. 1915
              --(?)1880 Census, p.198C, Manchester, NJ:
              Emma C. Schoonmaker, single, age 30, b. NJ,
              seamstress; at res. of William F. and Dora I.
              Heins
              --(?)1910 Census, p.210B, 11 Wd. Paterson:
              Samuel S. Sherwood, age 79, b. NY, real
              estate agent; Emily C. Schoonmaker, age 64,
              single, housekeeper b. NJ
David   b. abt. 1849
              --1880 Census, p.164C, Acquackanonk, NJ
              David A. Schoonmaker, age 30, b. NJ,
              farming; Louisa, wife, age 25, b. NJ; Mabel,
              dau., age 2, b. NJ; E. Schoonmaker, dau., age
              9 months b. NJ
              --1910 Census, p.4A, 3Wd,Bayonne, Hudson
              Co.: David A Schoonmaker, age 60, b. NJ,
              merchant tea & coffee; A. Louise, age 54, b.
              Iowa, parents b. NY; Edna S. age 29, single,
              b. NJ; Clifford D., age 27, single, b. NJ; Grant
              P. age 25, single, b. NY
Winslow   b. abt. 1850
              --1880 Census, p.187A, Little Falls: Winslow
              "Schoemaker", single, age 30, b. NJ, keeping
              store
              --1910 Census, p.163B, 8Wd.Newark:
              Winslow Schoonmaker, b. NY?, retail
              lumber; Alice?. b.NJ; Nelda?. age 19; earle?
              age 17; Alva C, age 10
George   b. 1850/55, b. 1898
              --(?)1880 Census, p.577C, 22nd Ward,Dist.
              31, New York City: George Schoonmaker,
              single, age 28, b. NJ, parents b. NJ, car-

penter
--(?)1900 Census, p.77, Little Falls Twp;
.....Schoonmaker, lumber dealer, b. October
1856, m. 18 yrs; Lillie, b. 1856, 4 born, 4
living; b. NJ, parents b. Germany; Leon, b.
March 1882; Hilda, b. June 1890; earle, b.
Dec. 1892; Alva, dau., b. June 1899

Josiah	
Eliza	b. 1852, d. 1910
Henry	b. abt 1854

--(?)1880 Census, p.85B, 3rd Ward, Paterson:
Henry Schoonmaker, age 23, b. NJ, clerk in
store; Stella, wife, age 21, b. NJ,parents NJ
--(?)1920 Census, p.36A, Paterson, 11th Wd:
Henry Schoonmaker, age 62, merchant;
Stella. age 57

Jefferson	b. abt 1855
Matilda	b. abt 1856
Saranna	b. January 20, 1857, d. 1878
Charles	b. abt. 1859; m. Elizabeth_____

--1910 Census:p.20B, #162 Cedar Grove:
Charles Schoonmaker, age 50, grocer;
Elizabeth, age 36; Mabel, age 13; Gladys M.
age 11;Mildred E., age 10; Charles H., age 4;
Elizabeth A., age 1
--1920 Census #75,p.166B, Charles
Schoonmaker, age 59; Elizabeth, age 45, b.
NJ, parents b.Germany; Gladys M. age 20;
Mildred, age 19;Charles H. age 14; Elizabeth
A., age 11
--1930 Census, Part 2, Sheet 6A, Cedar
Grove: Charles Schoonmaker, age 71, retired,
real estate $10,000; Elizabeth, wife, age 56;
Charles H., age 24, pharmacist; Elizabeth A.,
age 21, teacher at public school

Alida(?)	m. Albert VanHouten

- - - - -

SEAMAN

Seaman, JOSEPH   b. (Abt. 1746)
(gmnj)   d. September 9, 1811

"In 65th yr."

Notes:

-- (?)Joseph Seaman, m. Claertje VanHouten, b. June 15, 1755, daughter of Roelof VanHouten. Children: Catharina, b. 1776, Grietje, b. 1778, Maria b. 1782, Cornelis b. 1784, Elisabeth b. 1787, Roelof, b. 1789. Hendrick b. 1791, Roelof, b. 1795.

- - - - -

SEUGLING

Seugling, August*   b. (February 1867)
                         d. (aft. 1930)
1st wife, WILHEMINE C. "Minnie" (Schieber)
(gmnj)   b. May 1, 1872
                         d. March 10, 1903

"born Scheuber"
"gen von ihrer mutter W. Scheuber"

2nd wife, Pauline C.* (Klimback)
                         b. (abt. 1874)
                         d. (bef. 1930)
3rd wife, Anna Martha* (Dorn)
                         b.
                         d.

Notes:
--August Seugling was son of John Frederick Seugling (q.v.)

--Wilhelmina was daughter of Edward Schieber and Wilhelmina _____.

--1880 Census, p.422A, Newark: Edward "Schreiber", age 46, b. Prussia, works in lead factory; Christina, wife, age 41, b. Prussia; Matilda, dau., age 16, b. Prussia, tailoress; Flora, dau.,age 12, b. Prussia;Charles, son, age 9, b. Prussia; Wilhelmina, dau., age 8, b. Prussia; Mary, dau., age 6, b. NJ; Henrietta, dau., age 4, b. NJ;

--1880 Census: #348 Caldwell: Pauline Klimbach, age 6, b. NJ, parents b. Wirtemberg: at res. of her parents, Frederick Klimbach, and Sophia.

--1900 Census, p.101, Little Falls: August Seugling, b. Feb. 1867, b. Germany, butcher; Minnie b. May 1872 NJ; Frederick b. Sept 1892; August b. June 1895; Charles b. Sept. 1896; Margaret b. Oct. 1898

--1910 Census: p.193B, Little Falls Twp: August Seugling, butcher at store; age ....; 2nd marriage 6 yrs, b. Germany; Pauline, wife, age 36, 4 born 4 living; b. NJ, parents b. Germany; Fred, age 17; August, age 15; Charles age 14; Margaret, age 12; Edward, age 7; Earle, age 5; Clarence, age 3; Theodore, age 2; Helen, age 2 months; David Smith, age 22, b. Russia, hired man; Mary Klimbach, sister-in-law, age 23, single, b. Hanover

--1920 Census, p.1424A, Little Falls: August Seugling, age 52, b. Germany, butcher; Pauline, age 46, b. NJ; Edward, age 17, butcher; Earl, age 16, butcher; Clarence, age 13; Theodore, age 11; Helen, age 9; Erving, age 7; Dorothy age 5; Robert and 2 yr and 2 months

--1930 Census, p.290B, Singac, Little Falls: August Seugle, age 65, widower, proprietor,butcher shop; Edward, age 28, butcher; Earl, age 25, prop. of radio store;Clarence, age 23, driver at butcher shop; Theodore, age 22, driver at butcher shop; Irving, age 17; Dorothy, age 14; Robert age 10

--1930 Census, #107, Cedar Grove: Wilhelmina, Scheiber, age 86, widow, b. Wirtemberg; at res. of son, Edward J. Scheiber.; adj. to son Louis Scheiber, age 52

--CHILDREN of August Seugling & Wilhemine C. Schieber:

August Frederick	b. September 1, 1892; d. Feb. 1920; m. Anna _____
Charles August	b. June 14, 1895; d. 1968
Charles Hobert	b. September 1, 1896; d. Feb. 1920
Margaret W.	b. October 18, 1898; d. August 1981
Edward L.	b. December 16, 1902; d. August 1970

--CHILDREN of August Seugling and Pauline C. Klimback:

Earl Wilhelm	b. October 3 1904; d. April 1972; m. Laura _____
Clarence Paul	b. July 16, 1906; d. May 1958
Theodore Arthur	b. March 21, 1908; d. May 23, 1993; m. Catherine Derby
Helen Pauline	b. February 20, 1910
Irving Kenneth	b. Nov. 14, 1912; d. Dec.13, 1932
Dorothy Lillian	b. October 27, 1914; d. June 19, 1988
Robert John	b. July 14, 1917; d. July 1978

- - - - -

Seugling, JOHN FREDERICK
(gmnj)   b. 1832 Germany
              d. 1894
wife, MARGARET   b. (abt. 1836)
(lfrc)   d. (December, 1912)
              bur. (December 6, 1912)

Notes:
--John Frederick Seugling d. at Little Falls.
--1880 Census, p.193A, Little Falls, NJ: "Hohn F. Serkling", age 49, b. Germany, farmer; Margret, wife, age 44, b. Germany; August, son, age 14, b. Germany; Mary, dau., age 12, b. Germany; Augusta, dau., age 9, b. NJ; Charles son, age 7, b. NJ; Edward, son, age 5, b. NJ; Lewis, son, age 2, b. NJ; Lizzie, dau., age 3 months b. NJ(adj. to John T. Sigler)
--1910 Census, p.194A, Little Falls Twp: Marguerite Seugling, b. Germany, age 74, widow, 8 born 7 living; Charles son,age 37, m. 5 yr., b. NJ; Susan, dau.-in-law, b.

NJ, 2 born 2 living; Lester, grandson,age 4; Raymond, grandson, age 1 yr and 8 months; Annie, daughter age 30, single.

--CHILDREN of John Frederick Seugling and Margret.....:

Christian Fred.b. May 6, 1861, Hamburg, Germany; d. May
19, 1959, Caldwell;
m. Vezena Frances Monagan.
--1900 Census, p.223, Caldwell Twp:
Christian Seugling, b. May 1869,Germany,
butcher; Vezena b. April 1869 Mass;
Christian, b. Sept 1891; Charles b. Aug 1893;
Augusta b. Nov 1895; Vezena b. Feb. 1898;
Estella Bixbee,stepdau., b. Apr 1884; Edgar
Bixbee stepson b. Jan. 1896
Christian Seugling
--1910 Census, #34, Caldwell Twp: Christian
Seugling, b. Germany, farmer, age 48, m. 20
yrs; Vezena F., b. Mass., age 46, 9 born 8
living; Christian, age 18; Augusta, age 14;
Vezena, age 12; Margaret age 8; Helen age 4

August   b. Feb. 1867, Germany;
m. #1 Minnie Schieber;dau. of Edward J.
Schieber and Emily C.___.
--1900 Census, #68, Verona: Frederick
Schieber, b. April 1828, age 72, b. Germany,
gardener; Wilhelmina C., age 56, 6 born, 4
living; Edward J., age 25, b. NJ, gardener;
Emily C., dau-in-law, age 24, b. Germany;
Minnie C., granddau., age 6
m. #2 Pauline C. Klimback;
m. #3 Anna Martha Dorn

Mary   b. abt. 1868, Germany
Augusta   b. abt. 1871, NJ; m. John Ziegler (Sigler?)
--(?)1880 Census, p.192D, Little Falls,
NJ:(adj. to John F. Seugling)John T. Sigler,
age 82, b. NJ, farmer; Maria (Brooks), wife,
age 78, b. NJ; Henry, son,age 32, b. NJ,

carpenter; Sarah E. (dau-in-law) age 31, b.
NY; John, son, age 13, b. NJ; Mary Sigler,
dau., age 3, b. NJ; Henry H. Knapp, other,
age 14, b. NJ

Edward   b. 1874, NJ; d. 1880, NJ

Charles   b. Nov. 1872, NJ; m. Susan (Ploch?)
--1910 Census, p.194A, Little Falls Twp:
Marguerite Seugling, b. Germany, age 74,
widow, 8 born 7 living; Charles son,age 37,
5 yrs, b. NJ; Susan, dau.-in-law, 2 born 2
living, b. NJ, parents b. NJ; Lester, grandson,
age 4; Raymond, grandson, age 1 yr and 8
months; Annie, dau., age 30
--1920 Census, p.139A, Little Falls: Charles
Seugling, age 47, cattle dealer; Susie, age 39;
Lester, age 13; Raymond, age 11
--1930 Census, p.280B, Little Falls: Charles
Seugling, age 57, cattle dealer; Susan,age 50;
Lester, age 24 farmhand, cattle; Raymond,
age 21, farmhand, cattle; William, age 9

Louis   b. August 12, 1877, Little Falls; m. 1901,
Eliza Vreeland daughter of John Milton
Vreeland and Ida Jacobus
--1910 Census, #69, Caldwell Twp: Louis
Seugling, age 31, m. 9 yrs; Elsie, age 3,
3 born, 1 living; Milton S., age 2

Elizabeth   b. 1880

Anna   b. March 1880; m. William Jackson

- - - - -

SHATTER

Shatter, FRANCES A.   b.
(npfh)   d. February 1909
                            (bur. February 2, 1909)

Notes:
--(?)1900 Census, p.43A, Boonton: Stephen Shatter, b. April 1863, single, b. NY, carpenter, boarder

- - - - -

SHERMAN

Sherman, G. W. *   b.
(gmnj)   d.
wife, E.J.*   b.
(gmnj)   d.
son, INFANT   b.
(gmnj)   d.
son, INFANT   b.
(gmnj)   d.
(no dates)

Notes:
--(?)1900 Census, p.107, 3Wd, Passaic: George W. Sherman, b. June 1852, NJ, m. 24 yr; rubber stamp man; Jennie E. b. October 1859, NY, 1 born 1 living; Thomas W., b. March 1883, Maryland

- - - - -

SINDLE

Sindle, Catharine
m. Barnabus Belding (q.v.)

- - - - -

Sindle, GEORGE	b. 1821
(gmnj)	d. (blank)
1st wife, SOPHIA	b. 1823
(gmnj)	d. 1895
daughter,MARGARET ANN	b. 1846
(gmnj)	d. 1885
daughter, HESTER (Esther)	b. 1848
(gmnj)	d. 1874
daughter, RACHEL	b. 1850
(gmnj)	d. 1876
daughter, ELIZABETH	b. 1853
(gmnj)	d. 1874
son, WILLIAM H.	b. 1855
(gmnj)	d. 1887
daughter, REBECCA	b. 1857
(gmnj)	d. 1883
daughter, MARY	b. 1863
(gmnj)	d. 1895
son, CHARLES	b. 1865
(gmnj)	d. 1884

Notes:
--(?)NJ Will of George Sindle, #17710G, 1872
--(?)NJ Will of Sophia Sindle, #4559P, 1895
--George Sindle married #1, Sophia ....
--George Sindle married #2 Charlotte A. Moon, daughter of John Moon. She was widow of August Schieber.
--George Sindle was a farmer at Little Falls, 1873-71. (Boyd)

--1850 Census:p.359A, #364, Acquackanonk, Passaic Co.,
NJ: George Sindle, age 28, shoemaker; Sophia, age 24;
Margaret A., age 3; Esther, age 1
--1860 Census: #509,p.1024, Acquackanonk, Passaic Co.:
George Sindle, age 41, shoemaker; Sophia age 32; Margaret
age 14; Esther age 11, Rachel, age 9; Betsey, age 7; William
age 5; Rebecca, age 3; Thomas age 2 months.
--1880 Census:p.186C, Little Falls, Passaic Co., NJ: George
Sindle, age 55, b. NJ, stage proprietor; Sophia, wife, age 57,
b. NJ; Margret, age 32; William, age 23, works in carpet
factory; Thomas, age 18, works in carpet factory;Mary, age
17, works in carpet factory;Charles, age 15, works in carpet
factory;Ralph, age 8, at school; George Gibson 'other', age
8, at school;Emma Roberts, 'other' age 16, b. NJ, works in
carpet factory;Laura Roberts, 'other', age 14, works in carpet
factory; William Mays, 'other' married, age 32, b. NJ,
factory laborer.
--1900 Census, p. 81A, Little Falls: George Sindel, b. August
1820, age 79, landlord, m. 4 yrs; Lottie, wife, b. October
1840; Lottie B. (Ritz) stepdau., b. Dec 1872, NJ;
Retta,(Loretta Hopper) stepdau b. Oct. 1878; Frederick
Hopper stepson-in-law, b. July 1877; William G. Hopper,
step grandson b. October 1899; Fred Ritz, stepgrandson b.
July 1892
--1910 Census, p.9A, 4Wd,Newark: Lottie Sindle, age 69,
widow, 8 born 3 living; Lottie Ritz, age 38; Loretta Hopper,
age 31; Fred Ritz, age 17, grandson, age 17; Wm. G. Hopper,
garndson, age 10
--1920 Census, p.7B, 2Wd.Newark: Loretta Hopper, age 41;
Wm. G. Hopper, son, age 20; Lottie Sindle, mother, age 79,
widow
--CHILDREN of George Sindle and Sophia _____:
Margaret Ann b. 1846; d. 1885
Esther   b. 1848; d. 1874
Rachel   b. 1850; d. 1876
Elizabeth   b. 1853; d. 1874
William H.   b. 1855; d. 1887

| Rebecca | b. 1857; d. 1883 |
| Thomas | b. 1860/62 |

--1900 Census, p.17, Boonton: Thomas Sindle, b. Nov. 1860; night watchman at iron mill; Celia, b. Sept. 1861; George b. Mar 1883; Mary b. Dec. 1884

--1910 Census, p.203B, Little Falls: Wm. Osborne, age 47, b. NY, RR Engineer; Ida, age 46; Irving, age 25; Albert age 17; Cecelia Sindle, sis-in-law, age 47, m.28 yr.,8 born 3 living; Albert Sindle, age 9; Margaret Conklin, mother-in-law, age 78, widow

--1910 Census, p.3B, North Caldwell: Robert Sanderson, age 53; Anna, age 53; Ethel H. age 24; Thomas C. age 22; Celia Sindle, age 45 (sister?)-in-law

--1910 Census, p.32A, Boonton: Nancy Voorhees, age 51, b. NJ; Earnest Sherwood, age 20, grandson, b. NJ; Thomas Sindle, age 49, boarder, watchman at rolling mill

--1920 Census, p.112A, Little Falls: Thomas Sindle, age 59, labor; Cecelia, age 58; George age 35 single; Mary Quinn/Quick??, dau., age 34; John Quinn, grandson, age 14; Cecelia, granddau. age 13; Thomas, grandson, age 10; William, age 8,grandson; Albert Sindle, son, age 18, single

Mary	b. 1863; d. 1895 (? NJ Will #4558P, 1895)
Charles	b. 1865; d, 1884
Ralph	b. abt. 1872

- - - - -

Sindle, Peter* b.
(gmnj)   d.
wife, ELIZABETH b. (April 29, 1825)
(gmnj)   d. March 10, 1883

"Aged 57.10.11"

eldest daughter, ANNIE E."Libbie"
(gmnj)   b.
        d. May 31, 1864

"Aged 17.10.8"

youngest daughter, EMMA L.b. (July 22, 1853)
(gmnj)   d. June 7, 1871

"Aged 17.10.16"

Notes:
--Peter Sindle was b. abt. 1822 and d. after 1900; son of Jacob Sindle and Rebecca Demarest.
--1850 Census: #105, Caldwell/Cedar Grove:Peter Sindle, age 26, wheelwright,Real estate value $500; Elizabeth, age 25; Ann E., age 4; Mary, age 1. (Adj. to Jacob Sindle)
--1860 Census: #455, Caldwell/Cedar Grove: Peter Sindle, age 38, carpenter; Elizabeth age 35; Anne E. age 14; Mary, age 12; Emma, age 7; Jacob Vreeland, age 45, labor
--1870 Census: #483,p.132, Caldwell/Cedar Grove:Peter Sindle, age 46; Elizabeth, wife, age 45; Emma L. dau., age 17; adj. to Hester (Sindle) Jacobus
--1880 Census: p.415B,#297 Caldwell/Cedar Grove,NJ:Peter Sindle, age 56, b. NJ, wheelwright; Elizabeth, wife, age 55, b. NJ, parents b. England; adj. to William E. Pierce(q.v.)
--1900 Census: #44,p.250, Verona/Cedar Grove: Peter Sindle, age 76, b. February 1824; widower, retired; Mary S.

Pierce, dau., b. September 1848, 1 born 1 living; Wm. E. Pierce, son-in-law, b. October 1845

--CHILDREN of Peter Sindle and Elizabeth _____:

Annie E.'Libbie'	b. ; d. May 31, 1864
Mary Lavinia	b. October 23, 1848;d.Dec. 24, 1915;m.William E. Pierce(q.v.) Peter Sindle, age 56, b. NJ, wheelwright; Elizabeth, wife, age 55, b. NJ, parents b. England; adj. to William E. Pierce(q.v.) --1900 Census: #44,p.250, Verona/Cedar Grove: Peter Sindle, age 76, b. February 1824; widower, retired; Mary S. Pierce, dau., b. September 1848, 1 born 1 living; Wm. E. Pierce, son-in-law, b. October 1845
Emma L.	b. July 22, 1853; d. June 7, 1871 --1870 Census, p.132B, Caldwell: Peter Sindle, age 46, carpenter and farmer; Elizabeth, age 45; Emma L. age 17

- - - - -

SIPMA

Sipma, MAGGIE	b. July 5, 1877
(gmnj)(wooden marker)	d. October 23, 1903

Notes:
--Maggie Sipma d. at Little Falls, New Jersey.

- - - - -

SLOAT

Sloat, ISAAC	b. January 27, 1814
(gmnj)	d. August 15, 1875
wife, CATHERINE (Doremus)	
(gmnj)	b. October 29, 1808
	d. January 28, 1880
daughter, Emma**	b. September 1846
	d. August 15, 1875

Notes:

--NJ Will of Isaac Sloat, #18615G

--Isaac Sloat was son of Petrus Sloat and Katy Allen.

--Isaac Sloat m. Catherine Doremus, April 29, 1841, Passaic Co., NJ

--Catherine was bapt. January 1, 1809, Dutch Church, Stone House Plains, NJ, daughter of Peter C. Doremus,q.v. and Hannah Norwood.

--"About 1850, Isaac Sloat, a son-in-law of Peter Doremus, joined with two or three others in opening a cemetery in Cedar Grove."

--(?)1840 Census, p.45A, Paterson: Catherine Sloat; 1 male 20-30; 1 female age 20-30; female age 30-40; 1 female age 50-60

--1850 Census: #68, Caldwell/Cedar Grove: Isaac Sloat, age 36, carpenter,Real estate value $2000; Catherine age 41; Emma, age 4; Thodore age 3

--1860 Census: p. 136B, Caldwell/Cedar Grove: Isaac Sloat, carpenter, age 45. $2000; Catherine, age 51; Emma, age 13; Theodore, age 11; Lavinia, age 9

--1870 Census: #539 Caldwell/Cedar Grove: Isaac Sloat, age 56, farmer; Catharine, age 61; Emma, age 23; Theodore, age 21; Lavinia. Also, Elizabeth Doremus, age 75(unm. sister of Catherine)

--1880 Census:p.416D, #311, Caldwell/Cedar Grove,NJ:Theodore Sloat, age 32, b. NJ; wife, Hester A., age

38, b. NJ; Emma Sloat, sister, single, age 34; Lavinia Sloat, sister, age 30, b. NJ.

--1900 Census: #156 Verona/Cedar Grove: Emma Sloat, age 53, single

--CHILDREN of Isaac Sloat and Catherine Doremus:

Emma**	b. September 1846; d. 1900-1906,unm., Doremus homestead, 32 Peckmantown Rd.,Cedar Grove.Through her mother, she inherited the homestead of Pieter C. Doremus and Hannah Norwood.
	--1900 Census #156, Verona: Emma Sloat, b. September 1846, age 53, single;adj. to Ella L. Jacobus, b. May 1853, widow
	--1910 Census, p.193b, Little Falls Twp: Lavinia Ferguson, widow, age 59, m. 19 yrs., 1 born 1 living, b. NJ, parents b. NJ; Emma M., dau., age 17, b. NJ, father b. NY, mother b. NJ; Emma Sloat, sister, age 60, single, b. NJ, parents b. NJ
Theodore	b. abt. 1847, m. Hester Ann VanNess
	--1880 Census: #311 Caldwell: Theodore Sloat, age 32, farmer; Hester Ann, age 38, b. NJ; Emma, sister, age 34, single; Lavinia, sister, age 30, b. NJ
Lavinia	b. abt. 1851, m. Joseph Ferguson q.v.

- - - - -

SLOCKBOWER
(Slodbower)

Slockbower, SIDNEY (npfh)	b.
	d. September 1923
	(bur. September 2, 1923)

Notes:
--1920 Census, p. 118A, Little Falls: Robert Slockbower, age 44, labor at felt mill; Anna J. age 35; Robert, age 19, plumber's helper; Maude M. age 14; Daniel age 12; Carl? age 7

- - - - -

SMALLEY

Smalley, JOHN H.   b. (November 1839)
(npfh)   d. (May 27, 1909)

wife, ANN (Pilling?) b. (September 1839)
(npfh)   d. April 1912

Notes:
--John was son of Abraham Smalley and Elizabeth Doremus.
--John was a farmer at Peckman River, 1873-74.
--John's sister, Caroline, m. George Personett, son of John Personett; grandson of John Personett, Esq. (q.v.)
--He may be the John Smalley of Essex County who served in the Civil War.
--(?)His wife may be daughter of Dan Pilling,q.v.
--1850 Census, p.357A, #366, Acquackanonk, NJ: Abraham Smalley, age 39, laborer; Elizabeth, age 41; Caroline, age 13; John, age 12; David, age 10; Sarah A., age 4
--1860 Census: #486, Acquackanonk, Passaic Co, NJ: Abraham Smalley, age 50, farmer; Elizabeth, age 44; John, age 20, farm labor; Sarah, age 14; David, age 3; and, Catherine Doremus, age 78
--1870 Census, p.240B, Little Falls: Abraham Smalley age 59; laborer; Elizabeth age 54; David D. age 14
--1870 Census:p. 242A, #142, Little Falls, Passaic Co: John Smalley, age 31, harness maker; Ann, age 31; Ada, age 6; Daniel Pillen, age 76, b. NJ

--1880 Census: p.181A, Little Falls, NJ: John Smalley, age
40, b. NJ, carpenter; Ann, wife, age 40, b. NJ, parents b. NJ;
John F. son, age 3, b. NJ.

--1880 Census, p.187A, Little Falls: Abram Smalley, age 70,
laborer; at res. of John and Mary Burns.

--1900 Census, p.86, Little Falls: John Smalley, carpenter, b.
Nov. 1839, m. 37 yrs; Ann, b. Sept. 1839, NJ, parents b. NJ,
1 born 0 living; John F. Smalley, adopted son, b. Feb. 1888
NJ, father b. NJ, mother b. NY, barber (adj. to John
Copeland, q.v.)

--1910 Census, p.195A, Little Falls Twp: Anna Smalley, age
70, widow, b. NJ, 1 born, 0 living; Esther, niece, age 11, b.
NJ, father b. unknown, mother b. NJ

--CHILDREN of John H. Smalley and Ann (Pilling?):

Ada	b. 1864, d. bef. 1880
John F.	b. abt 1877;(d. bef. ....)
John F.	b. February 1888 (adopted son)
	--1900 Census, p.86 Little Falls: John
	Smalley, b. November 1839; Ann, b. Setp.
	1839; John F., son, adopted, age 22 single, b.
	NJ, mother b. NJ, father b. NY, barber

- - - - -

SMITH

Smith, EDWARD	b.
(npfh)	d. December 1907
	(Bur. December 26, 1907)

Notes:

--(?)1930 Census, p. 287B, Singac,Little Falls Twp: Mary J.
Smith, age 79, widow, b. England; Allen A., son, age 53,
single, proprietor of straw hat factory, b. NJ, father b. NY,
mother b. England; Edward D. son, age 50, widower, realtor

- - - - -

Smith, Elias*   b.
(gmnj)   d.
wife, SARAH (Koach/Kock) b. (Abt. January 2, 1751)
(gmnj)   d. July 2, 1794

"SACRED
To the memory of
Sarah Wife of
Elias Smith who
departed this Life
July 2,1794 aged 43
Years and 6 months"

son, ELIAS   b. (September 9, 1783)
(gmnj)   d. September 8, 1793

"Aged 9.11.29"

daughter, ELIZABETH b. (March 16, 1793)
(gmnj)   d. June 22, 1794

"Aged 1.3.6"

Notes:
--Son Elias was baptised at Acquackanonk December 12, 1784.
--See Deed, Bergen County, March 28, 1804: Gen'l Richard Dey of Saddle River conveyed to Elias Smith & Francis Smith of Acquackanonk for $300, 7 and 68/100 acres.
CHILDREN of Elias Smith and Sarah _____:
Elias   b. September 9,1783;d.September 8, 1793
Elizabeth b. March 16, 1793; d. June 22, 1794

- - - - -

Smith, GUSSIE   b.
(npfh)   d. August 1916
       (bur. August 31, 1916)

Notes:
--(?)1880 Census, p.288C, Passaic, NJ: M. B. Smith, age 47,
b. PA, clergyman, parents b. PA; Agusta, wife, age 42, b.
NY; Agusta, dau.,age 17, b. NJ; Ella, dau., age 14, b. NJ;
Austin, son, age 10, b. NY; Elizabeth, dau., age 7, b. NJ;
Eveline White, age 24, other, single, age 24, b. NY, servant,
parents b. England
--(?)1910 Census, p.71B, Wayne Twp., Passaic Co.: Augusta
B. Smith, boarder, age 25 single, b. PA, parents b. PA,
school teacher; at res. of William B. and Loretta Ryerson.

- - - - -

Smith, Jacob*   b.
(gmnj)   d,
wife, Sophia*   b.
(gmnj)   d.
daughter, CATHERINE   b.
(gmnj)   d. August 22, 1775

*"Here lies ye Body of Catherine, Daughter of Jacob and
Sophie Smith
who Died August 22, 1775 aged 7 months and 14 days"*

Notes:
--(?)Jacob Smith served New Jersey State Militia (*New
Jersey in 1793* by,James S. Norton, p. 151)
--CHILDREN of Jacob Smith and Sophia .....:
Catherine   b. abt. 1775; d. August 22, 1775

- - - - -

| Smith, JOHN | b. 1826 England |
| (gmnj) | d. 1905 |

"Father"

wife, ANN (Stagg)	b. 1830 (June 10,1830)
(gmnj)(npfh)	d. 1912
	(bur. November 21, 1912)

"Mother"

daughter, HANNAH M.	b. 1859
(gmnj)	d. 1880
daughter, EMILY G.	b. 1873
(gmnj)	d. 1891

Notes:

--Ann Stagg was born Shipdham, Norfolk, England, daughter of Uriah Stagg q.v. and Mary Gunton.

--1860 Census: #393 Caldwell/Cedar Grove: John Smith, age 35, farmer, b. England; Ann, age 29, b. England; James, age 8, b. England; Mary Ann, age 6, b. England; Hannah M. age 1 month, b. NY;Also Uriah Stagg, age 50, laborer, b. England. (Between Barney Belding and Robert Hawthorne.)

--1880 Census:p.417A, #330 Caldwell/Cedar Grove.John Smith, age 54, b. England;Ann, wife, age 50, b. England;William, son, age 19, b. NJ; Hannah M., dau., age 21, b. NY;Elizabeth, dau., age 18, b. NJ;Agnes, dau., age 12, b. NJ;Maria, dau., age 9, b. NJ;Emily, dau., age 6, b. NJ;Uriah Stagg, father-in-law, age 70, b. England, gardener.

--1900 Census: #1, Verona/Cedar Grove: John Smith age 74, retired gardener; Ann, age 69, b. England; Agnes, age 32, single; adj. to William Smith, age 29

--1910 Census: #163, Cedar Grove: Ann Smith, age 79, widow, b. England; Agnes, age 39, single. Adj. to William E. Smith and James Smith.

--CHILDREN of John Smith and Ann Stagg:

James   b. abt 1852; m. Ellen A. _____

--1900 Census #12, Cedar Grove: James Smith, b. England, gardener; Ellen A. wife John J.; Annie; Ellen A.; Edward A.;William b.; Jane; Lillian; Elizabeth; Josephine; 3 hired men

--1910 Census #165, Cedar Grove; James Smith, age 58, b. England, gardener, own business; Ellen A., age 52, b. NY;

--1920 Census #82, Cedar Grove: James Smith, age 67, b. England, retired; Ellen, age 61, b. NY, father b. Scotland, mother b. NY

Mary Ann   b. abt 1854

Hannah M.   b. 1859; d. 1880

William E.   b. abt. 1861; m. Sarah Davenport

--1900 Census #2, Verona: William Smith, age 29, b. NJ, parents b. England, gardener; Sarah, age ?; James B. age 12; William E., age 9; Howard, age 2

--1910 Census, #164 Cedar Grove: William E. Smith, age 49, gardener, own business; James D., age 22, labor, gardener; William E. age 18, labor, gardener; Howard, age 12; Mary Bennett, sister-in-law, age 35, single, housekeeper; 2 garden laborers

--1920 Census: #71, Cedar Grove: William Smith, age 59, retired, b. NJ, parents b. England; Sarah, age 53, b. England; Helen Davenport, age 75, widow, mother-in-law, b. England; adj. to William C. Smith, Jr. and James Smith.

Elizabeth   b. abt. 1862

Agnes   b. abt 1868

Maria   b. abt. 1871

Emily G.   b. 1873; d. 1891

- - - - -

Smith, PAULINE   b.
(lfrc)(Lot #16)   d.

Notes:
--Pauline Smith purchased Lot #16 in 1871.
--(?)1880 Census, p.14C, Newark, NJ: George Smith, age 24,
b. NJ, Bu... Maker, parents b. Germany; Pauline, wife, age
21, b. Wisconsin, parents b. Germany

- - - - -

Smith, Thomas*   b.
                           d.
wife, ELIZA   b. (Abt. 1833)
(gmnj)   d. July 23, 1878

"Aged 45 yrs."

Notes:
--(?)1870 Census, p.337A, 2Wd Paterson: Thomas Smith,
age 37, b. England, moulder at iron factory; Elizabeth, age
34, b. England; 4 children
--(?)1880 Census, p.181B. Little Falls, NJ: Thomas Smith,
widower, age 51, b. England, works in carpet factory; Lydia,
dau., age 18, b. England, works in carpet factory; Sydney,
son,age 14, b. England, works in carpet factory; Emma, dau.,
age 5, b. NJ

- - - - -

Smith, W. M.(H)   b. (abt. 1851)
(Vreeland Project)   d. Februay 2, 1922
(gmnj)

wife, ELIZA (Vreeland) b. December 25, 1858
         d. August 1, 1894
daughter, EDITH   b. July 20, 1882
(gmnj)   d. September 4, 1884

Notes:

--Daughter, Edith, on same stone as Hester E. Vreeland,wife of John Henry Vreeland (q.v.)

--(?)William Smith was b. in Rhode Island; d. February 2, 1922. He m. Eliza C. Vreeland April 20, 1876.

--(?)Or, is this William Monroe Smith?

--(?)1870 Census, p.741A, Wayne Twp., Passaic Co.: William Smith, age 19, b. Rhode Island, no occup. listed; at res. of James? Stuart?, age 50

--1880 Census, p.188C, Little Falls, NJ: William Smith, age 30, b. NJ(?), brick mason, parents b. NJ; Eliza, age 21, b. NJ, parents b. NJ; Annie, age 3, b. NJ; Wilber Vreeland, other, single, age 5, b. NJ, parents b. NJ; James Washington, other, single, age 11, black, parents b. VA, servant (same page as John and Rachel Vreeland,q.v.)

--CHILDREN of William Smith and Eliza Vreeland:

Annie   b. September 8, 1876; d. January 1, 1955
Edith   b. July 20, 1882; d. September 4, 1884
Bessie   b. abt. January 12, 1885; d. abt.Oct.20.1960
Jennie Mae b. September 7, 1887; d. February 16, 1980

- - - - -

Smith, WILLIAM b.
(lfrc)(Lot #17) d.

Notes:

--William Smith purchased Lot. #17 in 1871.

--(?)m. Margaret Sanderson,dau. of George and Ann Sanderson (1860 Census, #453,Caldwell)

--(??)1870 Census, p.203B, Acquackanonk: Wm. C. Smith, age 30, farmer, b. Ireland; Margaret, age 27, b. Ireland; Merutt? E., age 2, b. NJ; John T., age 11 months

--(?)1870 Census #549,p.137A, Caldwell: William A. Smith, age 32, brushmaker, b. Canada; Margaret(Sanderson?), age 21, b. Ireland; Alice, age 1, b. NJ; Ann Reveret,(q.v.) age 24, works brush factory, b. Ireland; Mary R. age 3, b. NJ

--(?)1880 Census #273 Caldwell: Margaret Smith, widow, age 29, b. Ireland, making brushes; Alice, dau., age 11, father b. Canada, mother b. Ireland; William, son, age 9; Susan, dau., age 7; Annie, dau., age 5; Reveret, Ann, sister, widow, age 34, b. Ireland, works in cotton mill; Mary Reveret, niece, age 13, b. NJ

--(?)1910 Census #90 Cedar Grove: Margaret Smith, age 64, widow, b. Ireland, sewing mops; Alice A., age 41, single; Susan B. age 37, single; Annie A., age 35, dressmaking at store; Ann J. Reveret(q.v.), sister, age 65, widow, b. Ireland, sewing mops.

--(?)1920 Census #51, Cedar Grove: Anna J. Reverett, age 85,widow; Alice Smith, niece, age 50 single; Anna L. Smith, niece, age 44 single

- - - - -

SPEER

Speer, Margaret
m. William G. Jacobus(q.v.)

- - - - -

SPEIGHT

Speight, WILLIAM	b. July 16, 1816
(gmnj)	d. September 17, 1896
wife, HANNAH	b. January 1, 1830
(gmnj)	d. June 8, 1883

son, WILLIAM	b. February 8, 1856
(gmnj)	d. January 29, 1878
daughter, GRACE	b. October 21, 1848
(gmnj)	d. September 15, 1887
son, ALEXANDER	b. March 27, 1870
(gmnj)	d. April 21, 1894

Notes:

--1860 Census, p.96, Wallkill, Orange Co., NY: William Speight, age 43, b. England, woolen manufacturer; Anna, age 38, b. England; Grance, age 10, b. NY; John, age 8, b. NY; Richard age 7, b. NY; Mary J., age 4, b. NY; William age 3, b. NY; Emma, age 1, b. NY

--1870 Census, p.246B, Little Falls: William Speight, age 56, works cotton mill, b. England; Anna, age 40, b. England; ....., daughter, age 20, b. NY; John, age 18, b. NY; Richard, age 16, b. NY; Mary J. age 14, b. NY; Emma, age 12, b. NY; William age 10, b. NY; Harriet, age 8, b. NY; Anna age 6, b. NY; Samuel, age 3, b. NY; Alexander age 4 months b. NJ

--1880 Census: p.184D, Little Falls, Passaic Co., NJ: William Shaight(sic.), age 66, b. England, works in carpet factory; Hannah, wife, age 51, b. England; Richard, son, age 26, b. NY, works in carpet factory; Emma, dau., age 22, b. NY, works in carpet factory; Harriet, daughter, age 18, b. NY, works in carpet factory; Hannah, dau., age 16, b. NY, at home; Samuel, son, age 13, b. NY, works in carpet factory; Alexander, son, age 10, b. NJ, at school.

-- This family probably worked at the Beattie Carpet Factory which was located at the former site of a grist mill at Little Falls. The factory was later converted to condominiums.

--CHILDREN of William Speight and Hannah ...:

Grace	b. October 21, 1848; d. September 15, 1887
John	b. abt. 1852
	--1880 Census, p.181A, John "Straight" age 28, b. NY, parents b. England, works at carpet factory; Mary Ann, wife, age 29, b. England; Auther Wadsworth, age 7, b. NY, at school,

parents b. England; William Wadsworth, age 4, b. England, parents b. England; Charles Wadsworth, age 4, b. England, parents b. England; Annie Stanley, age 8 months, b. NJ, parents b. NJ

Richard b. abt. 1854; m. Sarah A. .....

--1900 Census, p.83, Little Falls: Richard Speight, b. May 1848, NY, parents b. England; m. 17 yrs; Sarah A., b. August 1844, England, 12 born 10 living; Hanah b. July 1883; Richard b. Aug. 1885; grace E. b. Dec 1887; Arthur b. Feb. 1890; Henry Hackett, stepson b. Oct. 1875

--1910 Census, p.200B, Little Falls Twp: Richard Speight, age 58, m. 29 yrs (2nd marriage); Sarah, wife, 4 born 4 living; Anna, age 27; Grace, age 22; Arthur age 20; John Hackett, stepson, age 40, m. 19 yrs; Alfred Hackett, stepgrandson, age 13

--1920 Census, p.115B, Little Falls: Richard Speight, age 70 weaver at carpet mill; b. NY, parents b. England; Sarah, age 73, b. England; Arthur age 30; John E. Cocker, age 31, son-in-law, Grace E. Cocker, dau., age 32

--1930 Census, p.280B, Little Falls: Richard Speight, age 76, b. NY; Sarah, age 82, b. England

Mary J. b. abt. 1855

William b. February 8, 1856; d. January 29, 1878

Emma b. abt 1858

--1900 Census, p.80A, Little Falls: Emma Speight, sister-in-law, b. February 1860, age 40, single, at Stainton (q.v.) residence

Harriet b. 1862

Hannah b. abt 1864

Anna b. February 1867; m. Philip Stainton(q.v.)

--1900 Census, p.80 & 80A, Little Falls:
Philip Stainton, b. Nov. 1863, carpet weaver,
b. NY; Anna, b. Feb. 1867, wife, b. NY, 5
born 4 living; Philip b. 1889; William b. Aug.
1890; John, b. Oct. 1892; Earnest b. March
1895; Roy Masker, nephew, b. March 1885,
cotton dyers helper; Emma Speight, (q.v.)
sister-in-law, b. Feb. 1860, age 40, single, b.
NY, works carpet mill

Samuel   b. abt. 1868
--1910 Census: p.203A, Little Falls Twp;
Samuel Speight, brother, age 41, single;
at res. of Anna Stainton, widow, age 47
--1920 Census, p.120B, Little Falls: Hannah
Stainton, b. NY, age 64 widow; Philip E. son,
age 30, b. NJ; John E. son,age 26, b. NJ;
Samuel Speight, age 52, single, boarder, b.
NY

Alexander b. March 27, 1870; d. April 21, 1894
Jennie(?)   b. abt. 1855; possible daughter, m. George
Willever; had son, Louis Willever (q.v.)

- - - - -

SPENCE

Spence, JOHN   b. (November 16, 1796)
(gmnj)   d. April 4, 1874

"Aged 77.4.18"

wife, Euphemia** (McVicar) b. (1802-1811)
         d. (aft. 1880)
son, JOHN   b. 1834 (March 3, 1834)
(gmnj)   d. February 3, 1848

"Aged 13 yrs. & 11 mos."

Notes:

--Son, John Spence was baptised September 7, 1834, Campbelltown, Argyll, Scotland, son of John Spence and Euphemia McVicar.

--1850 Census, p.360A, #408, Acquackanonk, Passaic Co., NJ: John Spence, age 50, quarryman, b. Scotland; Euphemia, age 48; Charles, age 14; Euphemia, age 10

--1860 Census, p.1030, Acquackanonk: John Spence, labor; Euphemia, age 58; Euphemia, age 19, seamstress

--1870 Census, p.242B, Little Falls: John Spence, age 73, b. Scotland, stone cutter; Euphemia, age 69, b. Scotland

--1880 Census, p.186D, Little Falls, NJ: "Phemea" Spence, widow, age 79, b. Scotland; Ellen Simms, other, single, age 70, b. Ireland; George Bieder, other, married, age 60, b. England, laborer

--CHILDREN of John Spence and Euphemia McVicar:

John	b. March 3, 1834, Scotland; d. Feb. 3, 1848
Charles	b. abt. 1836
Euphemia	b. abt 1840

- - - - -

STAFFORD
(Strafford)

Stafford, THOMAS   b.
(npfh)   d. January 27, 1911

Notes:

--(?)1910 Census, p.212A, 11 Wd.Paterson: Agustine J. Stafford, age 38, m. 8 yr, b. PA, parents b. Ireland; .....wife, age 37, 0 born 0 living; Nelly? Moore, sister-in-law, age 39, single, b. NJ, silk winder

- - - - -

STAGER

Stager, Cornelius*	b.
	d.
wife, Mary*	b.
	d.
daughter, ELIZABETH	b.
(cghs)	d. November 8, 1840

Notes:

--See "Stayer" burial record.

--(?)Cornelius Stager m. Molly Gilman, December 15, 1810, Essex County.

--1830 Census: p.280, Acquackanonk

--1840 Census, p.101A, Acquackanonk

--1850 Census,p.356A, #347, Acquackanonk, NJ: Cornelius Stager, age 59, blacksmith; Mary, age 58;Abraham Reynolds, age 9

--1860 Census: #531 Acquackanonk, Passaic Co., NJ: Cornelius Stager, age 70, blacksmith; Mary, age 68; James age 28, carpenter; Mary, age 20; Walter, age 1; Cornelius, age 8??

--1870 Census, #252, Caldwell, NJ:adj. to Thomas Stager

--(?)1870 Census #388, Caldwell: Cornelius Stager, age 66, b. NJ, farmer; Effie M. age 39; James H., age 16, farm labor; William B., age 13; George F. age 10; Sarah E., age 8; Amelia, age 5; Charles H., age 9 months;adj. to John VanRiper and Charles Bach(q.v.)

--1880 Census , p.405A, Caldwell: Cornelius Stager, age 42, b. NJ, milkman; Catharine, wife, age 30, b. NJ

- - - - -

STAGG

Stagg, URIAH	b. 1809 (November 29,1808)
(gmnj)	d. 1898
(In Smith family plot)	

"Grandfather"

wife, ...	b.
	d.

daughter, ANN	b.
m. John Smith (q.v.)	d.

Notes:
--See:Uriah Stagg was b. November 29, 1808, Shipdham, Norfolk, England, son of James Stagg and Jane Rivett.
--1870 Census, p.322B, Bayonne, Hudson Co.NJ: Uriah Stagg, age 60, labor, b. England; boarder at res. of Thomas Boys?, age 25?, b. England
--1880 Census: p. 417A,#330, Caldwell/Cedar Grove: Uriah Stagg, father-in-law, widower, age 70, b. England, gardener, parents b. England; at res. of John and Ann Smith (q.v.) (his daughter)
--CHILDREN of Uriah Stagg and ......:
Ann   b. abt.

- - - - -

STAINTON

Stainton, Thomas**	b. (abt. 1830)
	d. (bef. 1900)
wife, SARAH	b. (Abt. 1831) Wales
(npfh)	d. March 1913
	(bur. March 7, 1913)

Notes:

--1880 Census, p.186D, Little Falls, NJ: Thomas "Stanton",
age 50, b. England, laborer; Sarah, wife, age 50 b. N. Wales;
Thomas, son, age 23, b. England, works carpet factory; John
E., son, age 20, b. NY, works carpet factory; Philip E., son,
age 17, b. NY, works carpet factory; Sarah E., dau., age 15,
b. NJ, works carpet factory; Mary W., dau., age 14, b. NY,
works carpet factory; Moses E. son, age 10, b. NJ, works
carpet factory; Ida J. Kifkirt, other, single, age 19, b. NJ,
parents b. NJ, works carpet factory

--1900 Census: #27, Verona/Cedar Grove: Sarah Stainton, b.
Wales; (Adj. to Sarah Schoonmaker, widow of Daniel
Schoonmaker,q.v.)

--1910 Census, p.192b, Little Falls Twp: Thomas Stainton, b.
England, age 53, m. 29 yrs, weaver at carpet mill; Mary,
wife, age 47,b. England, 4 born, 3 living; Thomas, age 22, b.
NJ, labor at carpet mill; John, age 15, b. NJ, labor at carpet
mill; Sarah, mother, age 80, b. England, widow, 9 born, 3
living

--CHILDREN of Thomas Stainton and Sarah .....:

Thomas E.   b. January 1857

        --1900 Census, p.78A, Littel Falls: Thomas E.
        Stainton, b. Jan 1857, b. Wales, carpet
        weaver; Mary, b. November 1862, NY,
        parents Ireland; Mary b. July 1881, NJ
        Thomas b. Oct. 1887; John b. June 1893
        --1910 Census, p.192b, Little Falls Twp:
        Thomas Stainton, b. England, age 53, m. 29
        yrs, weaver at carpet mill; Mary, wife, age
        47,b. England, 4 born, 3 living; Thomas, age
        22, b. NJ, labor at carpet mill; John, age 15, b.
        NJ, labor at carpet mill; Sarah, mother, age
        80, b. England, widow, 9 born, 3 living
        --1920 Census, p.173A, Totowa, Passai Co:
        Mary A. Stainton, widow, age 57, b. NY;

John E. son, age 26, single, b. NJ, pipe fitter, hotel work

John E.   b. June 1860

--1900 Census, p.76, Little Falls: John E. Stainton, b. June 1860, carpet weaver, b. NJ; Reanie?, wife, b. NJ, Setp. 1860, m. 18 yrs. 0 born 0 living; Susie Nolan, cousin, b. June 1881, age 18, b. NJ, single

--1910 Census, p.208B, Little Falls: John E. Stainton, boarder, age 50, single, carpet weaver, b. NY; at res. of Everett Weaver

Philip E.   b. November 1863

--1900 Census, p.80 & 80A, Little Falls: Philip Stainton, b. Nov. 1863, carpet weaver, b. NY; Anna, b. Feb. 1867, wife, b. NY, 5 born 4 living; Philip b. 1889; William b. Aug. 1890; John, b. Oct. 1892; Earnest b. March 1895; Roy Masker, nephew, b. March 1885, cotton dyers helper; Emma Speight, (q.v.) sister-in-law, b. Feb. 1860, age 40, single, b. NY, works carpet mill

Sarah E.   b. abt. 1865

Mary W.   b. abt. 1866

Moses E.   b. abt. 1870

- - - - -

STAPERT

Stapert, Siebrigje
m. Klaas K. Fijlstra (q.v.)

- - - - -

STAYER

(This is may be a transcription error for "Stager" q.v.)

Stayer, Cornelius*	b.
(gmnj)	d.
wife, Mary*	b.
	d.
daughter, ELIZABETH	b. (September 15, 1815)
(gmnj)	d. November 10, 1840

"Aged 25.1.25"

Notes:
--(?)Daughter Sarah, m. William Story (q.v.)

- - - - -

STOR

Stor, Isaac* Rev.	b. (October 28, 1805)
	d.
wife, ANN (Doremus)	b. (August 1, 1806)
(gmnj)	d. April 11, 1848

"Aged 41 yrs. & 11 mos."
"who fell a sacrifice to the violence of fire on the fatal night of April 11, 1848"

son, JACOB	b. (March 6, 1831)
(gmnj)	d. April 11, 1848

"Aged 17 yrs. & 5 dys."

son, WESLEY	b. (June 24, 1843)
(gmnj)	d. April 11, 1848

"Aged 4.9.20"

son, PETER WITTEN   b. (March 6, 1831)
(gmnj)   d. April 11, 1848

"Aged 17 mos."

Notes:
--Isaac Stor was b. October 28, 1805, Bergen, New Jersey.
--Rev. Isaac Stor m. Ann Brooks Doremus May 8, 1828,
(Paterson Intelligencier)
--Ann Brooks Doremus was bapt. January 4, 1807, Ref.
Dutch Church, Stone House Plains, NJ, daughter of Peter T.
Doremus and Catherine (nee) Doremus
--Ann died in a house fire with three of her children: Jacob,
Wesley and Peter.
--Isaac and Ann "lived in a small frame house near her
father's, on the Newark and Pompton Turnpike, at Cedar
Grove, near the new Congregational Church. Mr. Stor was a
local Methodist preacher, who also taught school. She d. 11
April 1848, and is bur. in the Doremus cemetery at Cedar
Grove. The fire is supposed to have originated from an
overheating of the oven. Mr. Stor afterwards m. a second
time, and removed to the vicinity of Pine Brook, Morris
County, New Jersey." (Eberhart, pp.175,176)
--(?)Isaac "Stur" of Manchester, Passaic County, NJ, m. Oct.
17, 1859, Paterson Dutch Church, Sophia Hopper of Small
Lots.
--CHILDREN of Isaac Stor and Ann Brooks Doremus:
Sarah Catherine   b. March 12, 1829, m. December 4,
    1851,Francis D. Moore
    --1880 Census, p.167B, Newark, NJ:
    Frances D. "Moor", age 51, b.
    NJ,builder; Sarah C. wife, age 51, b.
    NJ; 4 children; 4 boarders
Jacob   b. March 6, 1831, d. April 11, 1848
Jemima   b. April 26, 1833, m. #1 Henry W.
    Baldwin;

m. #2 Charles R. Hopson;(?)widower
of Mary E. May

--1860 Census, p.793, 9 Wd Newark:
Henry W. Baldwin, age 29, 'hard
work'; Jamima, age 27; Anna E. age
5; Henrietta W., age 2; Elizabeth
Baldwin,a ge 49, widow; Mary
McGocklin, age 30, b. Ireland

--1870 Census, p.295A, Newark:
Jemima Baldwin, age 37; Anna, age
15; Henrietta, age 12; Katy, age 6;
Cyrus, age 9

--1870 Census, p.319A, 2Wd Paterson:
Charles R. Hopson, age 38, harness
maker, b. PA; Samuel R. age 18,
carpenter; Wm. A., age 16, clerk in
cigar store; Andrew M. age 15,
bookkeeper; Charles W. age 13;
Edward, age 1; William, age 72, b.
NY; Sophia Lewis, age 42, b. PA

--1880 Census, p.141B, Paterson,NJ:
Chas. Hopson, age 49, b.PA,
harness maker; Mina, wife, age 48, b.
NJ; 4 children; 1 cook

--1900 Census, p.225A, 3Wd Paterson:
Charles Hopson, b. April 1832, PA,
age 68, harness maker;Jemima, b.
April 1832, NJ, age 68; William A.,
son, b. June 1853, widower, b. NJ,
harness maker

Wesley P.	b. September 23, 1837, d. 1843
Wesley	b. June 25, 1843, d. April 11, 1848
Peter Witten	b. May 8, 1846, d. April 11, 1848

- - - - -

STORY
(STOREY)

Story, William*	b. (abt. 1802)
	d. (aft. 1860)
1st wife, SARAH (Stager)	b. (abt. 1812)
	d. (aft. 1860)

'Sacred to the memory of
Sarah Story
Daughter of Cornelius
and Mary Stager'

daughter, HARRIET	b. (Abt. 1840)
(gmnj)	d. August 18, 1868

"Aged 28 yrs."

Notes:

--William Storey m.#1, July 19, 1828, Sarah Stager.

--1830 Census, Acquackanonk: William Story

--1840 Census, p.103A,Acquackanonk: William Storey

--1850 Census, #537, Acquacknonk, NJ: William Storey,age 49, wool spinner, b. Washington, D.C.; Sarah, age 38, b. NJ; William, age 18, boatman, b. NJ; Harriet, age 10, b. NJ; George Jackson, age 28, b. England, hair merchant

--1860 Census, p.1022, Acquackanonk: Henry Story, carpet weaver, age 31; Mary, age 38;Theodore, age 7; Isabelle age 5; Lorenzo age 2; William age 58, farm labor

--1860 Census: p.1027,#533, Acquackanonk, Passaic Co: Sarah Story, age 69, William, age 34, farm labor; Harriet, age 19

--CHILDREN of William Storey and Sarah Stager:

William	b. abt. 1826;
	--1870 Census, p.247B, Little Falls: William Story, age 38, laborer; Anna, age 38; William,

age 15, farm labor; Munson, age 13; John, age 9; Sarah age 7; Mary, age 5; Harriet age 2 "Philene" age 4? months
--1880 Census, p.197B, Manchester, NJ: William Story, age 52, b. NJ,parents b. NJ; farm laborer; Martha, age 36, wife, b. NJ, parents b. NJ; Pauldean, son, age 12; Wallace, son, age 7

Henry   b. abt. 1829 (possible child);m. Mary .....
--1850 Census, p.361A, #425, Acquackanonk, NJ; Henry Storey, age 21, carpet weaver,b.NJ; Mary A., age 28, b. Ireland; Mary E, age 1;
--1860 Census, p.1022, Acquackanonk: Henry Story, carpet weaver, age 31; Mary, age 38; Theodore, age 7; Isabelle age 5; Lorenzo age 2; William age 58, farm labor

Harriet   b. abt. 1840; d. August 18, 1868

- - - - -

STRAFFORD
(Stafford)

Strafford, THOMAS   b.
(npfh)   d. January 1911
    (bur. January 27, 1911)

Notes:
--not found

- - - - -

SUPENOR

Supenor, CORNELIUS   b. (Abt. 1809)
(gmnj)   d. August 16, 1889
(Will #23380G)

"In 80th yr."

wife, MARY (Post)   b. (December 1815)
(gmnj)   d. February 21 1904

"In 89th yr."

Notes:
--He was son of Christopher Supenor and Mary 'Polly'
Simonson; (bur. Old Burying Ground, Presbyterian Church,
Caldwell)
--Cornelius Supenor m. October 15, 1834, Caldwell
Presbyterian Church, Mary Post.
--Mary Post was daughter of Mjr. Francis R. Post,q.v. and
Elenor 'Leah' Doremus.
--1840 Census: #275,p.331, Caldwell: Christopher and Mary.
No children. (Adj. to Abraham and Christopher Supenor)
--1850 Census: #119, Caldwell/Cedar Grove: Cornelius
Supenor, age 39; farmer; Mary, age 34; John H. Courter, age
13 (Adj. to Christopher Supenor, age 87
--1860 Census: #422, Caldwell/Cedar Grove: Cornelius
Supenor, age 49, farmer; Mary, age 44; Leah (Doremus)
Post, age 73; Ellen (Post) Personett, sister-in-law, widow of
John S. Personett; Mjr. Francis R. Post, age 74, carpenter,
father-in-law; Leah (Doremus) Post,age 73, mother-in-law.
Charles Jacobus, age 14; Cyrus W. Price/Pier, age 24,
wheelwright
--1870 Census #500 Caldwell: Francis R. Post, age 83, no
occupation; Mary Supenor, age 54; Cornelius Supenor, age
59, farmer, real estate $2000; Cleveland Courter, age 10;
James Doremus, age 40 no occupation

--1880 Census: p.417A,#324, Caldwell/Cedar Grove:
Cornelius Supenor, age 70, farmer; Mary, wife, age 64, b.
NJ. James Doremus,(q.v.) single, age 52, no occupation;
Henry A. Jacobus, single, age 71, labor. (Adj. to John and
Mary Courter)
--1900 Census: #55 Verona/Cedar Grove: Mary Supenor,
widow. Boarder with George B. Oughletree family. She had
"0 children born and 0 children living".

- - - - -

TAGGART

Taggart, ...   b.
       d. (bef. 1900)

wife, SUSAN   b. (March 1844?)
(npfh)   d. January 1915
       (bur. January 11, 1915)

Notes:
--(?)1859 Paterson City Directory:Murray & Taggert,
grocers, 69 John St.; William Taggart, 69 John St.; Matilda,
widow of James E. Taggart, 71 Ellison St.; Joseph R.
Taggart, clerk, boards at 41 Ward St.; Catharine, widow of
Peter, 41 Ward Street
--(?)1860 Census, #620 East Ward, Paterson: Matilda
Taggart, age 30, b. NJ; Robert M. Taggart, age 13; lived
with Mary A. Morrow, age 50
--(?)1880 Census, p.121A, Paterson, NJ: Peter Taggart, age
16, b. NJ, parents b. NJ; at res. of Charles and Mary Spice.
--1900 Census, p.81, Little Falls:Emma VanWinkle, b. Oct.
1831, age 68, single; Mary, step-mother, b. July 1834; Susan
Tagart, sister, b. March 1844, widow
--1910 Census, p.202B, Little Falls Twp., NJ: Emma
VanWinkle (q.v.), age 78, single; Susan Taggart, sister, age
72, widow, 0 born 0 living

- - - - -

THATCHER

Thatcher, JOHN J.	b. (November 16, 1834)
(lfrc)(Lot#8)	d. (after 1926)
wife, Sophia** (Granger?)	b. (abt. 1834)
	d. (bef. 1900 Census)

Notes:

--John Thatcher purchased Lot #8 in 1871.

--John James Thatcher was b. Kingston, Ulster Co., New York, son of John Thatcher and Mary Ann Wheatland. Their marriage is recorded at Basingstroke, Hampshire, England.

--John's brother, Caleb G. Thatcher m. Little Falls, 1863, Leah E. Jacobus; In 1880, Caleb was a farmer at Readington, Hunterdon County, NJ.

--"A very popular grove of cedars, on the property now in possession of J. J. Thatcher, used to attact much attention, and Cedar Grove thus came to displace the old name(Peckmantown)."(*History of Essex County, p.847*)

--1850 Census, p.195B, Orange Twp: John Thatcher, age 43, farmer b. England; Mary Ann age 44, b. England; Mary Ann, age 44, b. England; Charles A. age 16, labor, b. NY; John J. age 15, b. NY; Caleb G. age 13, b. NY; Mary Ann, age 11, b. NJ; Phebe J. age 9, b. NJ

--1860 Census: #417 Caldwell/Cedar Grove: John Thatcher, age 26, punchmaker, b. NY; Sophia A.,age 26, b. NY; Washington, age 2, b. NJ; Frank H. age 1, b. NJ; Also, Caleb G. Thatcher, (brother) age 23, hatter, b. NY (Adj. to John J. Courter)

--1870 Census:p.136A, #534 Caldwell/Cedar Grove: John Thatcher, age 35, tool manufacturer; Sophia A.,age 34; Washington, age 12; Frank H., age 10; John G., age 8; Norman H., age 6; Wallace W., age 3; Mary H. Granger, age 60

--1880 Census: p.414D,#274 Caldwell/Cedar Grove: John Thatcher, age 45, b. NY, manufacturer of bronze powder, parents b. England; Sophia A. wife, age 46, b. NY, parents b. England; Wallace W., son, age 13, b. NJ; Florence M., dau., age 7, b. NJ; Mary A. Granger, mother-in-law, age 70, widow, b. England

--1880 Census, p.532A, East Orange, NJ. John Thatcher, age 73, b. England, farm laborer retired; Mary A. wife, age 75, b. England (Parents of John J. Thatcher)

--1900 Census:p.249, #40 Verona/Cedar Grove: John Thatcher, age 65, widower, farmer, b. NY,parents, b. England

--1910 Census: #106 Cedar Grove: John Thatcher, age 75, widower

--1920 Census: #57 Cedar Grove: John Thatcher, age 85, widower

--CHILDREN of John J. Thatcher and Sophia (Granger?):

Washington	b. abt 1858
Frank H.	b. abt 1859
	--1880 Census, p.44C, Montclair: Frank Thatcher, age 20, b. NJ, clerk in grocery store; Anthony Duffy, age 22, b. NJ, clerk in grocery store
John G.	b. abt 1862
	--1880 Census, p.511D, E. Orange: John G. Thatcher, nepher, age 19, b. NJ, apprentice to son; at res. of Charles A. Thatcher, age 47, upholsterer
Norman H.	b. abt 1864
	--1880 Census, p.409A, Caldwell: Norman Thatcher, other, age 17, b. NJ; occupation'household'; at res. of Geroge W. Dorr, age 42
	--1900 Census, East Orange: Wallace W. Thatcher, b. July 1866; Kathie A., b. Sept. 1864, England; Ernest A. b. July 1890; Love A. b. Jan. 1893

--1910 Census, p.3B, 5Wd.Orange: Norman H. Thatcher, age 46, m.22 yrs,builder; Hannah, age 46; Jennie, age 20; Myrtle, age 18

Wallace W.   b. abt 1867
Florence M.   b. abt. 1873??

--Excerpts from an interview with John Thatcher, *Caldwell Progress*, abt. 1926:

"...John J. Thatcher, former proprietor of the old VanOrden mill, and the house he lives in is the old Personett homestead on Pompton Avenue, built in 1782 by John Personett, a French Huguenot, and from this same quarry, so tradition has it, the stone used in the building of Trinity Church in New York also came.The house is the oldest one in Cedar Grove and it is condiered quite a coincidence that the oldest man and the oldest house should be passing their winter years together.

"...Mr. Thatcher was born in New York ninety-two years ago last November 6th and soon after his birth, his parents moved to East Orange, where Mr. Thatcher grew to manhood.
In 1860, Mr. Thatcher moved to Cedar Grove and with his brother, Caleb, erected the house now known as the old Price house, at present owned by the county. The house is still standing on a little rise just off of Grove Avenue. Part of the land was at one time farmed by Mr. Thatcher.

"...he bought the old mill on Little Falls Road from Demas Harrison of Caldwell and began making shoemakers punches...Mr. Thatcher gave up the business.He then bought a farm of several acres extending on both sides of Pompton Turnpike and also purchased the house in which he now resides. The land was farmed by him for some time but he

later sold all that section west of the turnpike. "He retired from active work shortly after his wife died a few years ago.

"Mr. Thatcher...judge of elections in the old Caldwell Township for two years and also in old Verona Township for ten years.

"... remembers Bloomfield and Pompton Avenues as turnpikes with toll gates at various places, one being at the Newark line, another at the Mountain House in Montclair, and the other one at Singac on the Pompton Turnpike.

- - - - -

TOMASSE

Tomasse, FRANK   b.
(npfh)   d. October 1913
    (bur. October 16, 1913)

Notes:
--(?)1910 Census, p.33A, 4th Ward, Paterson: Michael Gidyn?, age 30 b. Italy; Jennie, wife, age 25, b. Italy; Rose Floris, mother, age 43, widow; Frank Tomaso, brother, age 18, apprentice barber; Vido Benseva, cousin, age 30, m. 3 yrs.

- - - - -

TRUBECK

Trubeck, Mrs. Phillip*   b.
(lfrc)   d. June/July 1918
    bur. July 2, 1918

Notes:

- - - - -

UNKNOWN

_____, _____
(gmnj)
(wooden marker)

b. 1869
d. November 11, 1895

- - - - -

VANDERLAY

Vanderlay, JOHN
(npfh)

b. (September 1847)
d. April 1918
(bur. April 30, 1918)

Wife, BERTHA
(npfh)

b. (December 1849)
d. July, 1922
(bur. July 19, 1922)

Notes:
--1900 Census, p.90, Little Falls, NJ: John Vanderlay, b.
September 1847, Holland, m. 29 years, day labor; Bertha, b.
December 1849, Holland, 5 born 2 living; Katie/Gertie?, b.
February 1887, works carpet mill.
--1910 Census, p.224A, Little Falls Twp: John Vanderlay,
age 62, m. 39 yrs, b. Holland, labor-odd jobs; Bertha, age 60,
b. Holland, 5 born 2 living; Joseph Mosher, son-in-law, b.
NJ, parents b. NJ, age 24, m. 8 yrs, RR Trainman; Katie
Mosher, daughter, b. Holland, m. 8 yrs. age 23
--1920 Census, p.140A, Little Falls: Joseph J. Mosher, age
38, b. NJ, floorman at factory; Gertrude, age 32, b. Holland;
Bertha Vanderlay, mother-in-law, widow, age 70, b. Holland
--CHILDREN of John Vanderlay and Bertha .....:
Gertrude   b. February 1887; m. Joseph Mosher
4 other children.

- - - - -

VANDER MEIJ

Vander Meij, HARMON   b.
(gmnj)   d. (no dates)

Notes:
--This was on the same 'wooden marker' as Cornelius Hager,
q.v.
--(?)1900 Census, p.86, Little Falls: Michael Vandermay, b.
January 1870, Holland, carpet weaver; Emma, b. April 1870
Holland; Maggie, niece b. September 1890, NJ (adj. to
Annie Hager; see Cornelius P. Hager)
--(?)1900 Census, p.79A, Little Falls: Edson Vandermay, b.
April 1865, Holland, carpet weaver; Nellie, b. December
1865, Holland; Herman(Harman), b. March 1889, NJ;
Acke?, dau., b. July 1891; Jennie, dau., b. April 1894
--(?)1900 Census, p.101, Little Falls: George Vandermay, b.
September 1861, Holland, carpet weaver; Julia b. April
1862, Holland; Jennie, b. February 1885, NJ;
Herman(Harman) b. December 1891, NJ; 8 other children
--(?)1920 Census, p.138B, Little Falls: George VanDerMei,
age 58, wet wash; Julia, age 57; Herman,a ge 28; Sadie, age
23; Sam, age 22; Barney, abe 19

- - - - -

VAN DER MEULEN

Van Der Meulen, GERRITJE
(gmnj)   b. April 10, 1891
                       d. December 30, 1891

Notes:
--(?)1880 Census, p.355D, Paterson, NJ: Abram Vermeulen,
age 52, b. Holland, Justice of the Peace; Jane, wife, age 38,
b. Holland; David, son, age 10, b. NJ, works silk mill; John,

son, age 16, b. NJ, tobacco stripper; Tunis, son,age 13, b. NJ, works silk mill; Minnie, dau., age 14, silk weaver; Elizabeth, age 7, b. NJ; Mattie, dau., age 6; Isaac, son, age 5; Abram, son, age 3; Martin, age 2; Samuel, age 1; William, son, age 2 months.

--1900 Census, p.77, John Vandermeullen, b. May 1861, m. 15 yrs. b. Holland; Pauline, b. April 1865; 3 born 3 living, b. Belgium; Eva, b. May 1885, NJ; Mary b. Sept. 1886, nj; Harry, b. Aug. 1897; John Shooge, father-in-law, b. March 1836, widower, b. Belgium

--1910 Census, p.204B, Little Falls Twp: Andrew Vandermeulen, age 30, m. 5 yrs, b. Holland, carpet weaver; Emma, wife, age 32, 0 born-0 living.

--(?)1910 Census, p.205B, Little Falls Twp: John Vandermuhlen, b. Holland, age 47, b. 25 yrs, weaver at carpet mill; Pauline, age 45, 6 born, 4 living, b. Belgium; Garry, age 12, b. NJ; Frank, age 9, b. NJ; Garry, father, age 84, widower, b. Holland

--(?)1920 Census, p.123B, Little Falls: John Vandermeulen, age 56, weaver, b. Holland, Pauline, age 53;Garry, age 22; Frank, age 17

--(?)1920 Census, p.123B, Little Falls: Frank VanDerMeulen, age 41, single, shoemaker; Barney father, age 67; Eve, mother age 66

--(?)1920 Census, p. 133A, Little Falls: Andrew Vandermeulen, b. Holland, laborer, age 48; Ann, age 42; Elsie, age 8, b. NJ

--(?)1930 Census, p. 257A, John Vandermeulen, age 67, b. Holland, retired; Pauline, age 64, b. Belgium;(Adj. to Frank Vandermeulen, age 28, b. NJ, truck chauffeur; Virginia, b. NJ; Mollie C. Bateman, aunt

--(?)1930 Census, p.242A,Singac, Little Falls: Garrey Vandermeulen, merchant, age 32; Jennie, age 29

--(?)1930 Census, p.258A, Singac: Barney? Vandermeulen, age 78, b. Holland, retired; Fabin, wife, age 67, b. Holland; Frank, son, age 51, single, b. Holland

- - - - -

VAN GIESEN

Van Giesen, REYNEAR	b. August 6, 1799
(gmnj)	d. May 18, 1888
wife, Sophia** (Jacobus)	b. (Abt. 1799-1804)
Will #18352G,1874)	d. (Abt. 1874)

Notes:
--(?)NJ Will of Rynear VanGieson, #21149G, 1883
--(?)NJ Will of Sophia VanGieson, #18352G, 1874
--He m. February 8,1823, at Caldwell, Sophia/Sarah
Jacobus, daughter of Derick Jacobus of Peckman's River.
She was b. abt 1799 and d. before 1880.
--1830 Census: #344, Caldwell: (Adj. to Francis R. Post)
--1850 Census: #421, Caldwell: Rynear VanGiesen, age 50,
farmer, real estate $3000; Sophia (Jacobus), age 50. Adj. to
John J. Courter and Thomas VanNess.
--1860 Census: #424 Caldwell/Cedar Grove. Reynear
VanGiesen, age 56; Sophia age 56 (Near Cornelius Supenor)
--1870 Census #494, Caldwell: Ryner VanGiesen, age 66,
farmer, real estate $7,000; Sophia, wife; at res. of Ann
Sanderson,age 50, housekeeper
--1880 Census:p.413 B, #252 Caldwell: Rynier VanGiesen,
age 83, widower, farmer; Sarah M.Nimtoreye (Mintonyea),
widow, age 39, b. NJ, housekeeper, Alice M. Nimtoreye, age
16; Frederick Harrison, single, mlatto, age 23, b. CT, farm
labor

- - - - -

VAN GILDEN

Van Gilden, JACOB	b.
(npfh)	d. June 1915
	(bur. June 28, 1915)

Notes:
--(?)1910 Census, p.199A, Little Falls: Charles Goar?, age 54, b. Holland, grading labor; Ida, age 44, b. Holland; Samuel, age 27, single, b. Holland, labor at carpet mill; Jacob Young, step son,age 22, b. Holland, ironer at shirt factory; Jacob "VanGelder", uncle, age 67, widower, b. Holland

- - - - -

VAN NESS

Van Ness, ELIAS	b. May 13, 1824
(gmnj)	d. January 3, 1893
wife, MARY E. (Marley)	b. October 15, 1839
(gmnj)(npfh)	d. May 18, 1911
	(bur. May 22, 1911)

daughter, MAGGIE
(m. James Madden,q.v.)

Notes:
--Elias VanNess was son of Henry VanNess and Hester Francisco
--Elias VanNess was a farmer at Little Falls, 1871-74. (Boyd)
--1850 Census: #98 Caldwell/Cedar Grove: Mary with her parents. Patrick and Ruth Marley.(q.v.)
--1860 Census: #419 Caldwell/Cedar Grove, Mary with her parents.
--(?)1860 Census: p.1031, Acquackanonk, Passaic Co.Elias VanNess, age 33, merchant
--1870 Census: p.243A, Little Falls: Elias VanNess, age 46, retail grocer; Mary E. age 30; Margaret age 10; Cyrus, age 7
--1880 Census:. p.184C, Little Falls, NJ: Elias VanNess, age 56, b. NJ, store keeper; Mary, wife, age 38, b. Ireland; Maggie, daughter age 18; Cyrus, son, age 16, clerk in store;

Mary Gilmore, single, age 46, b. Ireland; Thomas Peer, single, age 18, b. NJ, servant.
--1900 Census, p.79, Little Falls: Mary E. VanNess, b. October 1844, widow; Margaret E., b. 1887
--1910 Census, p.201B., Little Falls Twp: Marie VanNess, age 68, widow, 2 born, 0 living; b. Ireland
--CHILDREN of Elias VanNess and Mary E. Marley: Margaret'Maggie'

	b. May 30,1860;d. Feb. 22, 1887; m. James M. Madden(q.v.)
Cyrus	b. abt. September 1862 m. Louisa M. Steinmetz, dau. of George Steinmetz; child George VanNess b. June 1894

--1920 Census, p.137B, Little Falls: Marrie Steinmits, age 78, widow, b. Germany; Louise M. VanNess, age 49, widow, age 49, b. NY; Elsie B. Steinmits, age 35, single, b. NY
--1930 Census, p.287B, Singac,Little Falls: Louise M. VanNess, age 61, widow, b. NY; George J. son, age 35, single, b. NJ, statistician,brokerage office; Elsie Steinmetz, sister, age 45, single, b. NY

- - - - -

Van Ness, William E.*	b.
	d.
wife, LYDIA (Yorks)	b. (Abt. 1806)
(gmnj)	d. August 25, 1889

"Aged 83"

Notes:
--(On Linus Crane stone)

--The record lists her as Lydia Varmer. This is probably a transcription error.

--(?)William may be son of Henry H. VanNess.

--1840 Census, p.103A, Acquackanonk: Wm. E. VanNess

--1850 Census p.75, #125 Caldwell: Henry H. VanNess, age 66, farmer, real estate $8000; Margaret, age 64

--1850 Census:p.75, #126, Caldwell/Cedar Grove: William VanNess, age 45, farmer, real estate $3000;Lydia, age 44; Peter, age 25; Margaret VanAllen, age 23; Henrietta, age 3.; adj. to Henry H VanNess and his wife, Margaret.

--1860 Census: #347 Caldwell: William E. VanNess, age 55, farmer; Lydia, age 54, Henry, age 12; adj. to William P. VanNess age 35; and, Henry H. VanNess age 77

--1870 Census #262, Caldwell: William E. VanNess, age 64, real estate $7,000; Lydia, age 63; adj. to Peter VanNess

--1880 Census: p.431B, Dist. 2, Caldwell, NJ: William E. VanNess, age 75, b. NJ, farmer; Lydia, wife, age 74, b. NJ; Fred Beider, age 12, works on farm, b. Germany

--CHILDREN of William E. VanNess and Lydia Yorks:

William   b. abt 1825

             --1850 Census p. 76,#128, Caldwell: William VanNess,age 25, farmer; real estate $1000; Sarah VanNess, age 63

             --1860 Census, #348, Caldwell William P. VanNess, age 35 lumber dealer; Jane, age 27, John, age 8, Maria, age 6; William age 1

Peter   b. abt. 1825

             --1850 Census, p.76, #126 Caldwell: William E. VanNess, age45, farmer; Lydia, age 44; Peter, age 25, farmer

             --1870 Census #263, Caldwell: Peter VanNess, age 44; Jane E., age 38; John, age 17; Maria, age 15; William, age 11, Maggie, age 8; L. Catherine, age 5;adj. to William and Lydia VanNess

             --1880 Census, p.431B, Caldwell: Peter VanNess, age 54, dealer in timber; S.J. wife,

age 39, b. NY;Leah C., dau., age 14, b. NJ;
William, son, age 21; Theresa, dau-in-law,
age 20, b. NY, father b. England, mother b.
NY

Henry(?)   b. abt. 1848 (son of William P. VanNess?)
--(?)1880 Census, p.425B, Dist.2,Caldwell:
Hamilton Walling, age 59, b. NJ, farmer;
Elisabeth, wife, age 57, b. at sea, father b.
Scotland, mother b. NY; Hamilton, son, age
32, b. NY, farmer; Margaret E. VanNess,
dau., age 29, b. NY; Henry L. VanNess,
son-in-law, age 30, b. NJ, salesman; Lizzie
Nichols, granddau., age 7, b. NY; James
Wheeler, other, age 21, b. England, laborer

- - - - -

Van Ness, WILLIAM H.	b. (October 1842)
(lfrc)(Lot. #20)	d. (aft. 1930 Census)
wife, Corintha* (Yorks)	b. (June 1845)
	d.(aft. 1920 Census)

Notes:
--William H. VanNess purchased Lot #20 in 1871.
--William Henry VanNess, b. October 31, 1841;d. January
29, 1933; son of Isaac Evert VanNess and Catherine
Bone.(see William M. Morrell)
--William Henry VanNess m. Corintha Jane Yorks (q.v.),
December 31, 1863
--1870 Census, p.240B. Little Falls: William VanNess, age
29, laborer; Corintha, age 25
--1880 Census, p.188C, Little Falls, NJ: William VanNess,
age 39, b. NJ, felt manufacture; Cornethe, wife, age 35, b.
NJ, father b. NJ, mother b. CT; Emma, dau., age 8, b. NJ

--1900 Census, p.101 Little Falls Twp: William H. VanNess
b. October 1842, NJ, landlord; Corintha b. June 1845, NJ
(near Vandermay family,q.v. and Daniel family,q.v.)
--1910 Census: p.194b, Little Falls Twp: W. H. VanNess,
farmer, b. NJ, age 68, m. 48 yrs; Corintha, wife, age 64, 2
born, 1 living; b. NJ, father b. NJ, mother b. CT; Emma
Breakey, age 39, m. 11 yrs, dau., 5 born 4 living; John
Breakey, son-in-law, age 39, b. NY, 'house bldr'?; William
Breakey, age 5; Elsie Breakey, age 3; Raymond Breakey, age
2; Gladys Breakey, age 10 months.
--1920 Census, p.138B, Little Falls: William VanNess, age
78; Corinta J., age 74; Wm. R. Brakey, grandson, age 14
--1930 Census, p.274B, Little Falls:John A. Breakey, age 59,
b. NY, concrete contractor; Emma M. age 58, b. NJ; William
R. age 25; J. Raymond, age 23, truck driver; Genevieve, age
19; William H. VanNess, age 88, widower, father-in-law
--CHILDREN of William Henry VanNess and Corintha Jane
Yorks:
Emma Morrell VanNess
   b. 1876; m. John Andrews Breakey
   --1880 Census, p.361C, Paterson: Jennie
   Breakey, age 43, b. NY, widow; John, son,
   age 10, b. NY, father b. CT, mother b. NY; 4
   other children; Andrew Breakey, other, age
   52, b. NY, butcher
   --1900 Census, p. 79, Little Falls: John
   Breakey, b. February 1870,NY, baker;
   Emma, b. August 1887
   --1910 Census: p.194b, Little Falls Twp: W.
   H. VanNess, farmer, b. NJ, age 68, m. 48 yrs;
   Corintha, wife, age 64, 2 born, 1 living; b. NJ,
   father b. NJ, mother b. CT; Emma Breakey,
   age 39, m. 11 yrs, dau., 5 born 4 living; John
   Breakey, son-in-law, age 39, b. NY, 'house
   bldr'?; William Breakey, age 5; Elsie
   Breakey, age 3; Raymond Breakey, age 2;
   Gladys Breakey, age 10 months.

--1920 Census, p.138B, Little Falls: John A. Brakey, age 49, b. NY, contractor; Emma M. age 48; Elsie J. age 13; John R. age 12; Gladis age 10; Jennie age 9

--1930 Census, p.274B, Little Falls:John A. Breakey, age 59, b. NY, concrete contractor; Emma M. age 58, b. NJ; William R. age 25; J. Raymond, age 23, truck driver; Genevieve, age 19; William H. VanNess, age 88, widower, father-in-law

- - - - -

VAN RIPER

Van Riper, JOHN   b. (January 5, 1818)
(gmnj)   d. August 30, 1855

'Age 37.7.25"

Notes:
--Next to Peter Van Riper stone (his father?)
--(?)John B. VanRiper m. Gertrude VanHouten; they had a daughter Helen Maria, b. Dec. 7, 1846, bapt. at Acquackanonk; Helen m. Henry G. Vreeland, 1868 at Acquackanonk.
--(?)1850 Census,p. 347B, #232, Acquackanonk, NJ: John B. VanRiper, age 36, farmer, real estate $4000; Gertrude, age 34; Philip H., age 10; Margaret, age 7; Adrian age 5; Helen M. age 3; Catherine J., age 6 months; John Duane? age 31, labor, b. Ireland; Julia Duane? age 21, labor, b. Ireland
--(?)1860 Census, p.969, Acquackanonk: Adrian VanRiper, age 59, farmer; Margaret age 43; Catherine, age 15; John, age 12; Mary, age 9; Philip age 6; Emma age 2 (This record is included due to the similarity of names)
--(?)1860 Census, p.1010 Acquackanonk: Philip VanRiper, age 40; Rachel, age 39; Catherine age 16; Abram, age 14

- - - - -

Van Riper, PETER	b. (August 25, 1766)
(gmnj)	d. March 11, 1849

"Aged 82.6.17"

wife, LYDIA (Riker)	b.
(gmnj)	d. June 31(?), 1849

"Aged 80.4.16"

Notes:
--Peter VanRiper m. Lydia Riker, June 19, 1797, Essex Co.
--"The estate of Cornelis Spier (1729-1827) which included land on the Peckamin River was to be divided between Peter VanRiper and Peter VanRiper, Jr. Apparently Cornelis had no surviving children." (Cornelis m. #1, prob. Seytie Jacobusse; m. #2 Hannah Stimets.)(*The Early Spier Family*, GMNJ, Volume 55)
--?1830 Census: p.376, Acquackanonk, Passaic County, NJ

- - - - -

VAN STRATTEN

Van Stratten, MARTIN	b.
(npfh)	d. March 1907
	(bur. March 11, 1907)

Notes:
--1900 Census, p.79, Little Falls: Martin VanStratten, b. Sept. 18--, Holland, widower, contractor; Annie, b. July 1882; Julia, b. Dec. 1885; John b. Dec. 1888;
--(?)1910 Census: p.193B, Little Falls Twp: John Van Stratten, b. NJ, parents b. Holland, age 21, single,

brother-in-law; at res. of William 'Laboussiere'?age 27, m. 2 yrs., b. Mass., parents b. Mass; Julia, wife, b. NJ, parents b. Holland, 0 born 0 living

--(?)1910 Census, p.211B, Little Falls Twp: Annie VanStratton, maid, age 27, single; at res. of Michael A. Wray

- - - - -

VAN WINKLE

Van Winkle, EMMA   b. (October 1831)
(npfh)   d. May 1912
     (bur. Mary 15, 1912)

Notes:

--1850 Census,p.362A, #438, Acquackanonk, NJ: Charles VanWinkle, age 48, physician, real estate $1000; Hannah, age 42; Mack, age 23; Mary, age 21; Emma, age 19; Susan, age 16; Thomas, age 13

--1860 Census, p.1032, Acquqackanonk: Charles VanWinkle age 58, physician; Mary Frence age 28; Emma Van Winkle, age 25; Susan age 22; Thomas age 20

--1870 Census: p.243A, Little Falls, NJ: Charles VanWinkle, age 58, physician; daughters:Mary, age 35; Margaret, age 40; Emma, age 36; Susan age 34

--1880 Census: p.185A, Little Falls, NJ: Emma VanWinkle, single, age 43, seamstress, b. NJ; Susan VanWinkle, single, age 39, b. NJ; Charles Jeralemon, single, age 32, b. NJ, servant.

--1900 Census, p.81, Little Falls:Emma VanWinkle, b. Oct. 1831, age 68, single; Mary, step-mother, b. July 1834; Susan Tagart, sister, b. March 1844, widow

--1910 Census, p.202B, Little Falls, NJ; Emma VanWinkle, age 78, single; Susan Taggart (q.v.), sister, age 72, widow, 0 born 0 living

- - - - -

VAN ZILE

Van Zile, Granden S.(?)*	b.
(gmnj)	d.
wife, Caroline* (Vreeland)	b.
	d.
son, JOHN A.	b. (January 24, 1834)
(gmnj)	d. August 4, 1835

"Aged 1.6.11"

Notes:
--"Grandine VanZile m. August 6, 1828, at Paterson, Catherine Vreeland, daughter of John A. Vreeland of Little Falls" *(Paterson Intelligencier)*

- - - - -

Vanzile, PETER	b.
(npfh)	d. November 1907
	(bur. November 30, 1907)

Notes:
--(?)Peter Nelson VanZyle, b. January 31, 1855, son of Elizabeth Doremus and her husband, Nelson VanZyle. Peter Nelson VanZyle m. Sarah Sindle.
--(?)Nelson VanZyle and Elizabeth Doremus had a daughter Malvina VanZyle who was b. October 6, 1860 and married a William H. Storey.
--(?)1870 Census, p.272A, 1Wd Paterson: Peter Vanzile, age 27, brick mason; Hester A., age 28

- - - - -

VARMER
(This is may be   a transcription error for Van Ness.)

Varmer, William E.*	b.
	d.
wife, Lydia (Yorks)	b. (Abt. 1806)
(gmnj)	d. August 25, 1889

"Aged 83 yrs."

Notes:
--Lydia Yorks m. William E. VanNess, q.v.
--Same stone as Linus Crane

- - - - -

VREELAND

Vreeland, AARON	b. (July 1836)
(ougheltree)	d. (abt. 1920-22)

Notes:
--Aaron Vreeland was son of Jacob Vreeland and Lydia
VanRiper; brother of Amzi Vreeland (q.v.)
--1850 Census: Caldwell: Jacob Vreeland, age 47, farmer?,
Real estate $2000; Lydia (VanRiper) age 39; Henry age 16,
farmer; Aaron, age 14; Mary Ellen age 12; Sarah, age 7;
Letty Ann, age 5; Aletta(?), age 3; Amzi age 10 months.
--1860 Census #457 Caldwell: Jacob Vreeland, age 58,
farmer, real estate $2000; Lydia, age 48, Henry, age 26,
carpenter; Aaron, age 23, carpenter; Mary E., age 21; Sarah
C. age 19; Letta A., age 15; Electa J., age 113; Amzi, age 11;
John J., age 7; John H. Jacobus, age 19, labor
--1870 Census #501 Caldwell: Jacob Vreeland, age 66,
farmer, $2000; Lydia, age 58; Aaron, age 38, carpenter;
Amzi D., age 20; John, age 18, carpenter apprentice

--1880 Census: p. 416D, Caldwell,NJ: Jacob Vreeland, age 77, b. NJ; Lydia, wife, age 69;Aaron Vreeland, son, age 43, single, carpenter; John Brower, single, age 18, b. NJ, laborer.
--1900 Census, p.265, 1 Wd, Bloomfield: Aaron Vreeland, b. July 1836, age 63, single, carpenter; boarder

- - - - -

Vreeland, AMMIE (Amzi)
(ougheltree)   b. (abt. 1849)
                      d. (abt. 1920-22)

Notes:
--This is probably Amzi Vreeland, b. abt. 1849, son of Jacob Vreeland and Lydia VanRiper; brother of Aaron Vreeland (q.v.).
--1850 Census #121 Caldwell: Jacob Vreeland, age 47, real estate $2000; Lydia, age 39; Henry, age 16, farmer; Aaron, age 14; Mary Ellen, age 12; Sarah, age 7; Letty Ann, age 5; Aletta, age 3; Amzi, age 10 months;
--1860 Census #457, Caldwell: Jacob Vreeland, age 58, farmer; Lydia, age 48; Henry, age 26, carpenter; Aaron,age 23, carpenter; Mary E., age 21; Sarah C., age 19; Letta A., age 15; Electa J., age 13; Amzi, age 11; John J. age 7; John H. Jacobus, age 19, labor
--1870 Census #501, Caldwell: Jacob Vreeland age 66, farmer $2000; Lydia, age 58; Aaron, age 38, carpenter; Amzi D., age 20; John, age 18, carpenter apprentice
--1880 Census, #312, Caldwell: Amzi Vreeland, age 29, carpenter; Annie, wife, age 30, b. Wales; Wilbur B., son, age 2; adj. to Jacob and Lydia Vreeland
--CHILDREN of Amzi D. Vreeland and Annie _____:
Wilber B.   b. abt 1878
Amzi?
Chester?

- - - - -

Vreeland, ELIAS E.   b. (December 22, 1750)
(gmnj)   d. March 29. 1828

"Aged 77.3.7"

Notes:
--NJ Will of Elias E. Vreeland, #12017G, 1828
--(?)Elias E. Vreeland m. Joanna Crane, dau. of Ezekiel
Crane and Abigail Baldwin
--Son of Elias Claesse Vreeland and Cathlyntje Smith.
--1780 Census: p.091, Acquackanonk
--1793 Census: Essex Co., NJ
--1830 Census: p.373 or 377 or 408: Acquackanonk, Passaic
Co., NJ
--1840 Census: #267 Caldwell Twp: widow? (Adj. to Isaac I.
Jacobus)
--(?)1860 Census, p.1024, Little Falls, Acquackanonk Twp:
Elias Vreeland, age 81; Thomas, age 35; Abram age 49;
Mary, age 45
--(?)1870 Census, p.254B, Newfoundland, Manchester Twp.,
Passaic Co.:Elias E. Vreeland, age 59, farmer, real estate
$12,000; Ann, age 59; Elias Jr. age 27, farmer;
Artilla?(dau.-in-law?), age 21; Anna, age 4

- - - - -

Vreeland, JOHN   b.
(ougheltree)   d. (abt. 1920-22?)

Notes:
--John Vreeland, b. May 11, 1852; son of Jacob Vreeland
and Lydia VanRiper; brother of Amzi Vreeland (q.v.) and
Aaron Vreeland (q.v.)
--m. Anna A. Jacobus
--"Garret's (Jacobus) daughter, Anna, married John J.
Vreeland." (Boardman, p.15)

--"John J. Vreeland, both before and after, the death of his wife, lived in a house he had built on his wife's land.(inherited from Garret Jacobus who had inherited from Isaac I. Jacobus) Vreeland is said to have made a will leaving all his property to churches in Verona...no will could be found after his death, and his nearest relatives, all living out of (Cedar Grove)...inherited his property under the law and later partitioned it in chancery court." (Boardman, p.19)
--(?)1880 Census, p. 22C. Montclair, NJ: John Vreeland, age 30, b. NJ; Anna, wife, age 30, b. NJ
--(?)1910 Census, p.16B,#80, Cedar Grove: John J. Vreeland, age 57, carpenter; Anna A., age 59

- - - - -

Vreeland, John Elias*   b. (September 20, 1816)
(gmnj)   d. (September 22, 1896)
wife, RACHEL A.(Lutkins/Luttgens)
(gmnj)   b.. September 12, 1816
                        d. March 5, 1885

Notes:
--John Elias Vreeland was b. September 20,1816; d. September 22, 1896; son of Elias Vreeland and Sarah Sigler
--He m. Rachel Lutkins/Luttgens.
--?1840 Census, p.49A,Acquackanonk: John Vreeland
--1850 Census. p. 356B, #361, Acquackanonk, NJ: John Vreeland, age 31, wheelwright; Rachel A., age 32; Eliza A., age 15; Jemima, age 10; Elias, age 5; John H. age 2
--1860 Census: #475, Acquackanonk Passaic Co., NJ: John Vreeland, age 40, wheelwright; Rachel, age 42; Elias, age 15; John, age 12; Ellen, age 9 and Eliza age 1; Lewis Cook, age 7
--1870 Census: p.236D, Little Falls: John E. Vreeland, age 48; Rachel A. age 50; John H. age 21, carpenter; Ellen, age 19; Eliza, age 12; Ann Cook, age 16

--1880 Census: p.188C, Little Falls, NJ: John Vreeland, age 65, b. NJ, carpenter; Rachel, wife, age 65, b. NJ; John, son, married, age 31; Hester, 'other'(dau.-in-law) married, age 26, b. NJ

--CHILDREN of John Vreeland and Rachel A. Lutkins:

Eliza A.   b. abt 1835

Jemima   b. abt 1840

Elias   b. September 9, 1845; d. aft. 1880
     m. Margaret Sims
     --1870 Census, p.290A, Montclair Twp: Elias
     Vreeland, age 25, carpenter; Margaret, age
     24; Jennie, age 1
     --1880 Census, p.156C, Orange, NJ: Elias
     Vreeland, age 33, b. NJ, carpenter; Margaret,
     age 32, b. NJ, parents b. Scotland; Jennie,
     dau., age 11, b. NJ
     --1900 Census, p.247, 3Wd Orange: Elias
     Vreeland, b. Setpember 1846, carpenter;
     Margaret, b. Nov. 1847 NJ, parents b.
     Scotland; Bessie Smith, niece, b. January
     1874

John H.(q.v.) b. July 22, 1849; d. November 30, 1915
     m. #1 Hester E. VanNess; b. September
     20, 1853;d. April 9, 1887
     m. #2, Julia VanKirk
     --Hester was b. September 10,1853; d.
     April 9. 1887
     --1850 Census, #361, Acquackanonk, NJ:
     John Vreeland(q.v.), age 31, wheelwright;
     Rachel A., age 32; Eliza A., age 15; Jemima,
     age 10; Elias, age 5; John H., age 2
     --1880 Census, p.188C, Little Falls: John
     Vreeland, age 65, carpenter; Rachel, wife, age
     65; John Vreeland, son, age 31, b. NJ,
     carpenter; Hester, other (dau-in-law), age 26,
     b. NJ

--1920 Census, p.138B, Little Falls: Julia "Verland", age 54, widow; Clarance, son, age 19, carpenter

Ellen   b. May 9, 1851; d. October 19. 1929
m. Albert W. Jacobus
--1880 Census, p.415A, Caldwell, NJ: Hetty M. Jacobus, widow, age 50, b. NY, parents b. NJ; Albert W., son, age 24, b. NJ, grocery store; Ella L. dau-in-law, age 27, b. NJ; Ella O. Jacobus, age 22, b. NJ; Carrie E., dau.,age 18; Charles G., age 6; Cornelius R. Jacobus, grandson, age 9 months, b. NJ

Elizabeth C.   b. December 25, 1858; d. August 1, 1894
m. April 20,1876, William Smith (q.v.)

- - - - -

Vreeland, John Henry*   b. (July 22, 1849)
(gmnj)   d. (November 30, 1915)
1st wife, HESTER E.(VanNess)
    b. September 20. 1853
(gmnj)   d. April 9, 1887
2nd wife, Julia*(VanKirk)   b. (September 28, 1865)
    d. (February 23, 1939)

Notes:
--same stone as Edith Smith and Rachel A., wife of John E. Vreeland
--John Vreeland was son of John Vreeland (q.v.) and Rachel Luttgens.
--John E. Vreeland m. #1, Hester E. VanNess;
--John E. Vreeland m. #2, Julia VanKirk
--John E. Vreeland was a farmer at Peckman River at Little Falls, 1871-74.(Boyd)
--1880 Census: p.188C, Little Falls, NJ: John Vreeland, age 65, b. NJ, carpenter; Rachel, wife, age 65, b. NJ; John

Vreeland, son, age 31, b. NJ, carpenter; Hester Vreeland, age 26, b. NJ.

--1880 Census, p.149B, Sparta, Sussex Co., NJ: Julia VanKirk age 15, b. NJ, parents b. NJ; James VanKirk, age 13, b. NJ, farm labor; at res. of William G. and Ella Hopkins.

--1910 Census, p.194B, Little Falls: John Vreeland, age 60, m.18 yrs, carpenter at carpet mill; Julia, age 44, 2 born 2 living; Vincent age 17, office boy; Clarence, age 10

--CHILDREN of John H. Vreeland and Hester E. VanNess:

Wilber H.	b. February 14, 1876
	m. Hattie Zellif
	--1880 Census, p.188C, Little Falls: Wilber Vreeland, age 5, b. NJ. parents b. NJ; at res. of William and Eliza Smith,(w.v.) next door to John and Rachel Vreeland and Hester Vreeland
	--1910 Census, p.197B, Little Falls: Wilbur Vreeland, age 36, b. NJ, plumber; Hattie, age 38, 0 born 0 living, b. NJ
	--1920 Census, p.119A, Little Falls: Wilbur H. Vreeland, age 44, plumbing contractor; Hattie, age 47

--CHILDREN of John H. Vreeland and Julia VanKirk:

Vincent H.	b. January 10, 1893
	m. Jessie Elizabeth Alyea (1891-1945)
	--1920 Census, p.119B, Little Falls: Vincent H. Vreeland, age 26, plumber; Jessie, age 28; Howard A., age 2
Clarence F.	b. April 9, 1900; d. December 3, 1946

- - - - -

Vreeland, John H.*   b.
(lfrc)(Lot #10)   d.

Notes:
--John H. Vreeland purchased Lot #10 in 1882.
--(?)John H. Vreeland(q.v.) m. Rachel A. Lutkins?
--(?)1910 Census:p.145B, #109 Verona: John H. Vreeland, age 55, m. 34 yrs; Nellie, age 52; Roswell R. age 33; Amy, age 24; Lealand, age 24

- - - - -

Vreeland, JOHN J.	b. (July 27, 1779)
(gmnj)	d. November 1, 1854

"Aged 75.3.5"

wife, ELEANOR (Brower)	b. February 18, 1799(1779?)
(gmnj)	d. February 23, 1842

Notes:
--NJ Estate Inventory, #14636G
--John "Vreland" m. "Lenah Brewer", 1802, Newark Twp.
--"The farm of John J. Vreeland, on the north side of Cedar Street, was divided among his children, and the parcel running up from the turnpike between Cedar Street and the brook more than half way to Ridge Road was allotted to Jacob Vreeland."(Boardman, p.9)
--?1830 Census: #248 Caldwell
--?1840 Census: #269, Caldwell/Cedar Grove: (between Isaac I. Jacobus and Rachel (Brower) Doremus, widow of Cornelius.)
--1850 Census: #70 Caldwell/Cedar Grove: John J. Vreeland, age 73, farmer, Real estate value $5000; Sally, age 42; Richard, age 32, farmer; Sarah Jane age 26; Ellen A. VanRiper, age 11, b. NY(?)
--CHILDREN of John J. Vreeland and Elenor Brower:
Sally   b. abt. 1808
Richard   b. abt. 1818

--(?)1880 Census, p.276C, Cayuta, Schuyler Co., NY: Richard Vreeland, age 62, b. NJ, parents b. NJ, laborer; Mary J., wife, age 56, b. NJ, parents b. NJ

Sarah Jane   b. abt. 1824

- - - - -

WALTON

Walton, JOSEPH	b. (July 1860)
(npfh)	d. July 1922
	(bur. July 14, 1922)
wife, MARY	b. (January 1867)
(npfh)	d. September 1913
	(bur. September 19, 1913)

Notes:
--(parents?)1880 Census, p.206D, Manchester, NJ: John Walton, age 53, b. England, silk weaver; Martha, wife, age 53, b. England
--1900 Census, p.78, Little Falls; Joseph Walton, b.NJ, parents b. England, b. July 1860, m. 10 yrs, carpet weaver; Mary S., b. Jan. 1867, b. NY, parents b. England, 4 born 3 living; Joseph F. b. July 1891, Pennsylvania; Paul A., b. July 1894, NJ; Elizabeth M. b. Dec. 1898, b. NJ
--1920 Census, p.122B, Little Falls: Joseph F. Walton, age 59, widower, b. NJ, parents b. England; carpet weaver; Paul A. age 25; Bessie M. age 21; Leo A. age 14;Earl, age 11
--(2nd wife?)1930 Census, p.262B, Little Falls: Ella F. Walton, age 77, widow, b. NY; Lillie M. Beckwith, stepdau., age 63, widow, b. NY
--(?)1930 Census, p.258A, Singac, Little Falls Twp: Louis Hockenberg, age 27, b. NY; Bessie, age 31, b. NJ; Leo Walton, bro-in-law, age 25; Earl Walton, bro-in-law, age 22

- - - - -

Walton, MARY   b.
(npfh)   d. October 1917
                            (bur. October 3, 1917)

Notes:
--(?)1850 Census, p.347B, Acquackanonk Twp: Carlyle
Walton, age 35, moulder, b. NJ; Mary age 32, b. NJ; carlyle,
age 4, b. NY; Mary E. age 1, b. NY
--(?)1880 Census, p.256D, Paterson, NJ: Richard Walden,
age 24, b. NJ, cigar maker; Mary, wife, age 22, b. NJ
--(?)1880 Census, p.488B, East Orange, NJ: David S.
Walton, age 38, b. NH,painting & paper sale room; Mary W.
wife, age 34, b. MA, father b. MA, mother b. RI; David S.
Walton, son,a ge 7, b. WI; Edith, dau., age 3, b. NJ; Harrold,
son, age 6 months, b. NJ; Jessie Shaw, father
(father-in-law?)age 64, b. MA, no business, father b. MA,
mother b. RI; Harriet A. Shaw, mother (mother-in-law), age
61, b. RI, at home, parents b. RI; Mary McMahan, single,
age 20, b. PA, servant, parents b. Ireland
--(?)1880 Census, p.18C, Newark: Benjamin Walton, age 30,
b. PA, upholsterer, parents b. PA; Mary, wife, age 30, b. PA,
parents b. PA; Mary E., dau., age 3, b. PA; Franklin, son, age
1, b. NJ
--(?)1910 Census, p.204A, Little Falls, NJ: Joseph F. Walton,
age 49, m. 20 yrs., b. NJ, parents b. England; Mary, age 43, 8
born 5 living, b. NY, parents b. England; J. Victor? age 18;
Paul A. age 15, b. PA; Bessie M. age 11 b. NJ; George A.
age 5; Earle F. age 2; Mary A., mother, age 80, widow, b.
England, 7 born 4 living

- - - - -

WANNAMAKER

Wannamaker, LAURENCE
(npfh)   b.
                                d. May 1907
                                (bur. May 20, 1907)

Notes:
--See *Wannemacher Families of New York and New Jersey,* p.147, Jean G. Rigler, Honolulu, HI, 1984. (re: descendants of Joh. Dietrich Wannemacher and Joh. Pieter Wannemacher who arrived in New York in 1710. After 1712 they moved to the 'Hackensack, N.J. camp'.
--(?)1880 Census, p.537A, Brooklyn, Kings Co., NY: Lawrence Wanamaker, age 28, b. NJ, father b. NY, mother b. NY, blacksmith; Matilda, wife, age 30, b. NY, parents b. NY; Frank, son, age 4, b. NY
--(?)1880 Census p.183A, Little Falls: Henry Wanamaker, age 33, b. NJ, parents b. New York, laborer; Lavina, wife, age 30, b. PA, father b. PA, mother b. NJ; George, son, age 8, b. NJ; Sarah, dau., age 5; Jerry, age 3
--(?)1880 Census, p.138C, Paterson: Josia Wanamaker, age 39, b. NJ, parents b. NY, stone mason; Julia, wife, age 36, b. NY; Elija, son, age 14, b. NJ
--(?)1880 Census, p.183A, Little Falls, NJ: Henry Wanamaker, age 33, b. NJ, laborer, parents b. NY; Lavina, wife, age 30, b. PA, father b. PA, mother b. NY; George, son, age 8, b. NJ; Sarah, dau., age 5; Jerry, (male), age 3
--(?)1910 Census, p.193A, Little Falls Twp: Jerry Wannamaker, boarder, age 32, single, driver, b. NJ, father b. NY, mother b. PA

- - - - -

WARDE

| Warde, Martha* | b. |
| (lfrc)(Lot. #39) | d. |

Notes:

--Martha Warde purchased Lot #39 in 1871. (Perhaps, for her father?)

--(?)1860 Census: #405, Caldwell Twp.,/Cedar Grove: Jonathan B. Ward, age 29, brush manufacturer, b. NY: Martha (Dean), age 22, b. NJ; Sarah M. age 1; 3 boarders

--(?)1870 Census #535, Caldwell: Jonathan B. Ward, age 38, brush maker, personal $3000, real estate $3000; Martha , age 32, b. NY; Sarah M; Zophar W., age 9; Mary E., age 7; Carrie L, age 5; John B., age 3; William Dean, age 63, b. NY

--(?)1880 Census, #270, Caldwell: Jonathan B. Ward, age 49, brush manufacturer; Martha, wife, age 42, b. NY, father b. CT, mother b. Wal?; 6 children, 1 son-in-law; 4 boarders

- - - - -

WELLS

Wells, Abby Jane
m. Cornelius G. Yorks(q.v.)

- - - - -

Wells, George C.*	b. (December 28, 1816)
	d. (September 13, 1875)
	bur. (Mattituck, LI, New York
(2nd?)wife, MARIETTA P. (Post?) Wells	
	b. (abt. 1836)
(gmnj)	d. November 26, 1887

In her 51st year

son, ELMER E. b. (abt. 1863)
(gmnj) d. April 13, 1880 (?)

"In his 28th year" (?)

Notes:
--Marietta/Mary was married 1st to James M. Courter. The three children were by this marriage. Perhaps they were "adopted" by George C. Wells? They may or may not have changed their names from Courter to Wells.
--The dates transcribed for Elmer E. Wells seem to be in error. In the 1880 Census which was dated June 10, 1880, Elmer is clearly listed as age 17.
--George C. Wells was son of Benjamin Wells and Patience Dingee.
--(?)1860 Census, p.253, 9Wd, New York City: George C. Wells, age 44, agent; Hester, age 41; Elisabeth, age 18
--1860 Census, p.271, 20Wd. New York City: James M. Courter, age 25, porter, b. NJ; Mary(Marietta), age 23, b. NJ; Eva, age 2, b. NY; Edgar, age 4 months, b. NY; Adelia Personett, age 15, b. NJ; Ellen (nee Post)Personette, age 47, nurse, b. NJ
--1870 Census, p.94A, 18 Wd, New York City: George C. Wells, age 53, b. NY, restaurant; Marietta P., age 33, b. NJ; Eva Courter, age 11, b. NJ; Elmer Courter, age 7, b. NJ;5 other persons
--1880 Census, p.630A, Manhattan, New York City: Marietta P. Wells, age 40, b. NJ, boarding house keeper, parents b. NJ; Eva P., dau., age 21, b. NY, parents b. NJ: Edgar C., son,age 19, b. NY, bookkeeper; Elmer E., son, age 17, b. NY, clerk in store; George T. "Lougan"(Lorigan q.v.); widower, age 35, b. Ireland, editor; Nellie "Lougan", age 9, b. NY, parents b. Ireland; 2 servants
--CHILDREN of James M. Courter and Marietta P. (Post?):
Eva P. b. May 1858; m. George T. Lorigan(q.v.)
    --1900 Census, p.258A, Manhattan Boro:

George Lorigan, b. Ireland, Feb. 1842,
journalist; Eva P., b. May 1858 NY, parents b.
NJ; Nellie E. dau., b. November 1871

| Edgar C. | b. abt. 1861 |
| Elmer E. | b. abt. 1863; (d. April 13, 1890) |

- - - - -

WETTER

Wetter, Elizabeth
m. Charles Bach (q.v.)

- - - - -

WHITE

| White, JOHN W. | b. (Abt. 1789) |
| (gmnj) | d. April 9, 1841 |

"Aged 52 yrs."

Notes:

--(?)1860 Census: p.970 Acquackanonk, Passaic Co.:John
White age 36, b. Germany; Elizabeth age 36; Conrad, age 7;
Eliza age 9; Anna age 6; Mary age 1, b. NJ; Anna, age 1, b.
NJ. (all except Mary and Anna were b. Germany)

- - - - -

WIDENSOBLIE

Widensoblie, August*	b. (abt. 1878)
	d. (aft. 1930)
1st wife, MARY	b. (abt. 1872)
(npfh)	d. November 1916
	(bur. November 26, 1916)

Notes:
--1910 Census, p.50B, 4 Wd Paterson: August Widensoblie, age 32, b. Germany, machinist, m. 6 yrs; Mary Widensoblie, age 38, 0 b 0 living, b. Spain; lodgers at res. of Walter B. Morecroft.
--(?)1930 Census, p.244B-245A, Singac, Little Falls: August Wildensablicon(?), age 52, b. Germany, machinist; Sarah, age 42, b. NJ

- - - - -

WILLEVER

Willever, LOUIS	b. September 13, 1887
(gmnj)	d. July 9, 1889

Notes:
--On stone of William Speight. Perhaps he is a son of George Willever and his wife, Jennie (Mary J.) (nee Speight,q.v.)
--1880 Census p.182D, Little Falls: George Willever, age 27, b. NY, parents b. England, works in carpet factory; Jennie, wife, age 24, b. NY, parents b. England; Charles, son, age 9 months, b. NJ
--1900 Census, p.84A, Little Falls: George Willever, b. April 1853, m. 20 yrs, b. NJ, parents b. NJ, mason; Mary J. b. July 1855, 6 born 4 living; Charles b. August 1879; Saddie b. 1886; Mable b. June 1891; Hazel b. Sept. 1898

--1910 Census: p.202A, Little Falls Twp: George Willever, age 57, m. 32 yrs, mason, b. NJ, parents b. NJ; Mary J., age 54, wife, 6 born, 4 living, b. NY, parents b. England; Charles, age 31, labor at carpet mill; Sadie,dau., age 24; Mable, age 18, sorter at carpet mill; Hazel, age 16, dau., sorter at carpet mill

--1920 Census, p.116A, Little Falls: George Willever, age 65, b. NJ, laborer; Mary J. age 64, b. NY, parents b. England; Sadie, dau., age 33, single; Mabel, age 28, single

--1930 Census, p.263B,Little Falls: George Willever, age 73, widower, odd jobs at water works; Sadie E. age 43, single, Mabel, age 38, single

- - - - -

WILLIAMS

Williams, G. W. (George W.
(gmnj)   b.
                                d.

"Co. H., 39th Regt. N.J. Inf. Vol" (Pvt.)

Notes:
--(?)G. W. Williams is probably the son,b. abt. 1844, of Zabina Williams (q.v.)

--George W. Williams served in the Civil War; Private, 39th Regt. Infantry, NJ Volunteers, Co. H; enlisted September 14, 1864; discharged June 27, 1865.

--George W. Williams resided at Verona.

--(?)1880 Census #174, Caldwell: George W. Williams, age 34, carpenter; Pauline K., wife, age 37; Phebe E., dau., age 7; Frank, son, age 6; Herbert, son, age 4

--CHILDREN of George W. Williams and Pauline K.....)

Phebe E.	b. abt. 1873
Frank	b. abt 1874
Herbert	b. abt. 1876

--(?)Herbert A. Williams, b. 1875;d.1940
bur. Prospect Hill Cemetery, Caldwell

- - - - -

Williams, Zabina*	b. (abt. 1814)
(gmnj)	d. (bef. 1880?)
wife, Phebe* (Stager)	b. (abt. 1819)
	d. (bef. 1880?)
son, CHARLES H.	b. (December 20, 1831)
(gmnj)	d. October 23, 1864

"Aged 22.10.3"

Notes:
--Zabina Williams was b. 1814, son of Zadok Williams, Jr.
and Mary Corby.
--(?)Phebe may have been daughter of Cornelius Stager(q.v.)
--?1830 Census, Orange Twp: Zebina Williams
--1840 Census, Orange Twp: Zebina Williams
--1850 Census,p.357A, #363, Acquackanonk, Passaic Co.,
NJ: Zabina Williams, age 32, shoemaker; Phebe, age 31;
Cornelius age 13; Charles, age 10; George, age 6
--1860 Census:p.113B, #429 Caldwell:Zabina Williams, age
46, shoemaker: Phebe, age 41; Charles, age 18; George, age
15.
--1870 Census #402,p.128A, Caldwell: Zabina Williams, age
55, farm labor; Phebe, age 51; Geroge, age 25, farm labor;
Walter A. Stager, age 10, attending school
--CHILDREN of Zabina Williams and Phebe Stager:
Cornelius   b. abt 1837
                --1880 Census, p.408C, Caldwell: Cornelius
                Williams, age 43, b. NJ, carpenter; Rachael,
                wife, age 42, b. NJ, parents b. England;
                Charles A. son, age 18; Clara A. dau., age 16;
                Nettie I., dau, age 11
Charles H.   b. abt 1842, d. October 23, 1864

George   b. abt 1845

- - - - -

WINTER

Winter, BARBARA   b. February 15, 1846
(gmnj)   d. October 22, 1897

Notes:
--(?)1880 Census, p.224B, Ghent, Columbia, New York:
Fredrick Winters, age 34, b. Germany, farmer; Barbara wife,
age 33, b. Germany; Elizabeth, dau.,age 8, b. NY; Fredrick,
son, age 7, b. NY; Barbara, dau., age 3, b. NY
--(?)1920 Census, p.123A, Little Falls: Anna Winters, age 65,
widow, b. Holland, nurse

- - - - -

YORKS

Yorks, CORNELIUS G.   b. December 7, 1812
(gmnj)   d. July 6, 1888
wife, ABBY JANE (Wells)   b. July 22, 1825
(gmnj)   d. August 11, 1878
son, ELIAS MILTON   b. April 4, 1843
(gmnj)   d. August 24, 1850
son, FRANKLIN   b. November 15, 1849
(gmnj)   d. September 12, 1850

Notes:
--Cornelius was son of Garret Yorks and Elsje Doremus.
--Cornelius m. October 9, 1841, Morris Co., Abigail Jane
Wells.
--Cornelius G. Yorks was a farmer at Peckman River, Little
Falls.
--1830 Census: #225, Caldwell

--1840 Census, p.102A,Acquackanonk:Cornelius Yorks
--1850 Census, p.357B, #371, Acquackanonk, Passaic Co.,
NJ: Cornelius Yorks, age 37, carpenter; Abby J.; Corintha J.
age 5; Anna A., age 3; Elsey, age 71;Elias M. age 7;
Franklin, age 1 month; Charles P. Kiesler, age 13
--1860 Census: p.1021, #481, Acquackanonk: Cornelius
York, age 48, farmer; Abigail, age 35; Corintha age 15, Ann
age 13; Emma age 9;Margaret age 5;William, age 3;
Frederick age 1.
--1870 Census:p.236, #52 Little Falls: Cornelius Yorks, age
56, farmer, Abby Jane, age 41; Elsie (Doremus) Yorks, age
91, (widow of Garret Yorks); Milton age 13; Frederick age
11; Margaret age 15; Minnie age 6; Elsie Jenks, age 91
--1880 Census: p.187A, Little Falls, Passaic Co., NJ:
Cornelius Yorks, age 67, b. NJ, farmer; Maggie, single, age
25, b. NJ; Minnie, single, age 16; Eddie, age 10
--CHILDREN of Cornelius G. Yorks and Abigail Jane Wells:
Elias Milton   b. April 4, 1843; d. August 4, 1850
Corintha Jane b. abt 1845;m. William H. VanNess(q.v.)
Anna A.   b. abt 1847
Franklin   b. November 15, 1849; d. September 12, 1850
Margaret   b. abt. 1855
                 --(?)1870 Census, p.610A, 7Wd Paterson:
                 Margaret Yorks, age 18, works silk mill, b.
                 NJ; at res. of Thomas and Catherine Blakely.
William   b. abt. 1857 (Milton?)
Frederick   b. abt. 1859
Emma   b. October 1861
                 --1880 Census, p.193C, Paterson, NJ: Emma
                 L. Yorks, single, age 27, b. NJ, father b. NJ,
                 mother b. Connecticut, lives in family;at res.
                 of William H. and Mary I. Blauvelt
                 --1900 Census, p.241, 3Wd,Paterson: Wm. H.
                 Blauvelt, b. April 1836, widower, coal dealer;
                 Erastus, son, b. Oct. 1867; Wm. H.,son b. Feb.
                 1870; Herbert A., b. Nov. 1876; Emma L.

Yorks, b. October 1861, housekeeper; Minnie
Yorks b. May 1868, boarder

Minnie   b. May 1868
--1900 Census, p.241, 3Wd,Paterson: Wm. H.
Blauvelt, b. April 1836, widower, coal dealer;
Erastus, son, b. Oct. 1867; Wm. H.,son b. Feb.
1870; Herbert A., b. Nov. 1876; Emma L.
Yorks, b. October 1861, housekeeper; Minnie
Yorks b. May 1868, boarder

Eddie   b. abt. 1870

- - - - -

Yorks, D.*   b.
(lfrc)(Lot. #12)   d.
--D. Yorks purchased Lot #12 in 1871.

Notes:

- - - - -

Yorks, GARRET   b. July 16, 1777
(gmnj)   d. April 4, 1847
wife, ELSY (Doremus)   b. September 18, 1779
(gmnj)   d. January 15, 1875
daughter, Lydia
m.William VanNess,(q.v.)

Notes:
--(See Wm. E. Varmer and Wm. E. VanNess)
--Garret Yorks birthdate is sometimes recorded as April 16,
1777, Paterson.
--Garret Yorks m. December 22, 1799, Caldwell
Presbyterian Church, Elsje Doremus, daughter of Egbert
Doremus and Geesje Jacobus
--Elsje received $30 in her father's NJ will #11044G, 1817).
Her brother Cornelius received the Egbert Doremus dwelling

house and "all lands (53 acres) adjoining the Cedar Grove
Cotton Manufacturing Co." Her sister, Elenor, wife of
Francis R. Post,(q.v.),also inherited $30.

--The Yorks family is descended from the immigrant, Paulis
Jurckxem, who came to the Kingston area of New York in
1642 from Texel in the Netherlands. The family moved from
New York to New Jersey and some back to the Haverstraw
and Phillipsburgh areas of New York. Many Yorks family
members are buied at the Old Dutch Church at Sleepy
Hollow.

--1840 Census, p.101A,Acquackanonk: Garret Yorks
--1870 Census: #52, Little Falls; Elsie Yorks, age 91, widow.
At res. of son, Cornelius Yorks, q.v.

--CHILDREN of Garret Yorks and Elsje Doremus:
Cornelius(q.v.) m. Abby Jane Wells
Lydia   m. William VanNess, q.v.
Margaret   m. Linus Crane, q.v.

- - - - -

Yorks, Margeret
m. Linas Crane (q.v.)

- - - - -

Yorks, MILTON   b. February 23, 1857
(gmnj)   d. February 18, 1874

Notes:
--Same as William Yorks, son of Cornelius G. Yorks????

- - - - -

YOUNG

Young, JOHN   b.(Abt. 1833)
(gmnj)   d. February 10, 1891

"Aged 58 yrs."
"Co. D., 71st Regt. N.J.Vol."

Notes:
--(?)1860 Census, p.1029, Acquackanonk: John Young, age
20, b. NJ,farm labor; Eliza, age 24; Henry, age 2
--(?)1870 Census, p.386A, 3Wd Paterson: John Young, age
38, laborer, b. Holland; Cornelia, age 35, b. Holland; Harriet,
age 3, b. NJ; Cornelius age 1, b. NJ
--(?)1880 Census, p.211A, Paterson: John Young, 47, b.
England, works in silk mill; Elizabeth, wife, age 45, b.
England

- - - - -

Young, Moses*   b.
(lfrc)(Lot #25)   d.

Notes:
--Moses Young purchased Lot #25 in 1871.
--(?)1840 Census, p.102A, Acquackanonk: Moses Young
--(?)1860 Census:p.1037, #610, Acquackanonk, Passaic Co.;
Moses Young, age 50, farmer; Mary, age 47; Elizabeth, age
17; Isaac, age 13; Hester, age 9; Richard, age 9
--(?)1870 Census, p.237A, Little Falls: Moses Young, age 62,
farmer; Mary age 60; Elizabeth age 7; 'unnamed' age 3
months; Richard age 19, farm labor; Isaac, age 22, farm
labor; John Wright, age 40, farm labor

- - - - -

ZELLE

Zelle, BELINDA   b. August 6, 1887 (?)
(gmnj)   d. July 27, 1890
(wooden marker)

Notes:
--(?)1900 Census, p.88, Little Falls: William Zelle, b.
Holland, carpet weaver, b. 1863, m. 13 yrs; Cornelia, b.
Holland Oct. 1866, 6 born 3 living; Edgar b. Dec. 1892,NJ:
Peter, b. Sept. 1895, NJ; Jeanette b. October 1899 NJ

- - - - -

SOURCES

boyd   *Boyd's Directory for the City of Paterson*
1871-1872; 1873-1874

cghs   Cedar Grove Historical Society

gmnj   *The Genealogical Magazine of New Jersey*
Vol. II;

lfrc   Records of Little Falls Reformed Church

ougheltree   Personal Records of Mrs. George B.
Ougheltree
(abt. 1920-22)

npfh   Records of Norman A. Parker Funeral Home
Main Street, Little Falls, New Jersey 07424

Boardman,Samuel Ward, Jr.,
From Then to Now---A History of Cedar Grove, Verona-Cedar Grove Times, Verona, N.J.

Eberhart, Edith W.,
The Doremus Family in America, Gateway Press, Baltimore, 1990

Gilmore, Jean Fairchild
"Early Fairchilds in America"
Gateway Press Inc., Baltimore, 1991

Jacobus, F. Leslie,
Early Cedar Grove, Cedar Grove Historical Society, 1976

Lockward, Lynn G.,

A Puritan Heritage
1955

Erwin-McGuire, Barbara
The Vreeland Genealogy Project
RootsWeb.com

Williams, Lyle K.,
The Williams Families of New Jersey,
Fort Worth, Texas, 1998

Williams, Robert
The Other Side of the White Rock; The
Early History of Verona, NJ from
1700 to 1907
Verona, New Jersey, c 1989

www.ingramcontent.com/pod-product-compliance
Lightning Source LLC
Chambersburg PA
CBHW070611270326
41926CB00013B/2506